Abriendo Puertas, Cerrando Heridas (Opening Doors, Closing Wounds)

Latinas/os Finding Work–Life Balance in Academia

Abriendo Puertas, Cerrando Heridas (Opening Doors, Closing Wounds)

Latinas/os Finding Work–Life Balance in Academia

edited by

Frank Hernandez

The University of Texas of the Permian Basin

Elizabeth Murakami

Texas A&M University–San Antonio

Gloria Rodriguez

University of California–Davis

INFORMATION AGE PUBLISHING, INC.
Charlotte, NC • www.infoagepub.com

Library of Congress Cataloging-in-Publication Data

A CIP record for this book is available from the Library of Congress
http://www.loc.gov

ISBN: 978-1-68123-064-1 (Paperback)
978-1-68123-065-8 (Hardcover)
978-1-68123-066-5 (ebook)

Copyright © 2015 Information Age Publishing Inc.

All rights reserved. No part of this publication may be reproduced, stored in a retrieval system, or transmitted, in any form or by any means, electronic, mechanical, photocopying, microfilming, recording or otherwise, without written permission from the publisher.

Printed in the United States of America

CONTENTS

PART I

PERSONAL IDENTITY AND IDEOLOGIES

PART III

BUILDING PEDAGOGY AND ACADEMIC/SOCIAL CAPITAL FOR LATINA/O STUDENTS

FOREWORD

Gerardo Lopez

The title of this book was, in all likelihood, loosely borrowed from the title track of Gloria Estefan's 1995 Grammy Award winning album, *Abriendo Puertas.* Estefan's sixth studio album quickly rose to #1 on the U.S. Billboard Tropical/Salsa Album chart, peaked at #2 on the U.S. Billboard Top Latin Album chart, and reached the Top 100 Albums on various international music charts in its release year.[1] The title track of this hugely successful album pays homage to the spirit and celebration of New Year's Eve through its refrain, *abriendo puertas/cerrando heridas*—which beckons listeners to let go of the past in order to embrace the future.

Much like the Robert Burns classic, *Auld Lang Syne,* Estefan's song solicits listeners to recall the acquaintances and memories of the past, both the good and the bad. Although Estefan's track is unmistakably Latin with a decidedly vallenato twist, both songs are equally introspective and anticipative: they both embody the hopes, dreams, and expectations of the New Year as well as trials, tribulations, and wounds of years past. As the lyrics of Estefan's track declare:

Abriendo Puertas, Cerrando Heridas (Opening Doors, Closing Wounds), pages ix–xii
Copyright © 2015 by Information Age Publishing
All rights of reproduction in any form reserved.

Y vamos abriendo puertas,	Let us open doors,
y vamos cerrando heridas.	and let us close wounds.
Porque en el año que llega	Because in the coming year
vamos a vivir la vida.	we are going to live life (to the fullest).
Y vamos abriendo puertas,	Let us open doors,
y vamos cerrando heridas.	and let us close wounds.
Pasito a paso en la senda	Step by step on the path,
vamos a hallar la salida.[2]	we will find a way out.{\poem}

To hammer this point home, Estefan employs contrasting metaphors throughout her song—night/day, rain/calm, despair/hope, and so on—to communicate that things usually get better after a tumultuous past. In the same vein, Estefan reminds listeners, "No existen barreras para ti/Si te propones serás feliz, muy feliz!" ("Barriers do not exist for you /If you set your mind to it, you will be happy, very happy!"). The larger significance of the song is that the past should never be a barrier for the future. In short, *Abriendo Puertas* is an expression of faith, hope, and rebirth; a clarion call for individuals—and perhaps Latinas/os specifically—to keep hope alive, to keep persevering, and to keep opening doors in the face of life's most difficult challenges.

It is quite appropriate, therefore, that the editors for this book chose this particular title for the current collection of work/life balance *testimonios*. Indeed, the anecdotes, stories, and narratives reflected in this book, by both emerging and veteran Latina/o scholars, serve to reflect on the past while providing concrete *consejos*[3] to future generations of Latina/o professors and critical friends who care about the future of Latinas/os in academe.

Interestingly, the majority of the voices reflected in this book are from young assistant professors and/or emerging scholars, most of whom have recently transitioned from graduate student life into the professorate. Their individual and collective experiences provide unique insights into the daily world of junior faculty: the challenges of publishing, the politics of identity, and the importance of maintaining an authentic voice within an academic system that is often foreign, hostile, unwelcoming, and cold. Negotiating this new space often engenders putting on new *máscaras* or masks—as new roles, demands, and expectations are silently acknowledged, yet never openly discussed.[4] This book provides a much-needed window into this process of "fitting in" to the academy, especially the dynamic of balancing personal and familial obligations, roles, and identities that often conflict with or rub up against institutional demands. We learn that for these young scholars, the future often seems contentious or uncertain. Yet, as their stories suggest, most of them will persevere fully knowing that they must keep that door open for future generations of Latina/o scholars. This persistence is the essence of *abriendo puertas.*

In the same vein, the *testimonios* of the veteran scholars provide a more nuanced take on the work–life balance issue, fully recognizing that our culture, language, and traditions are significant sources of strength that can often mitigate the daily demands and pressure of academe. In addition, these senior colleagues are quick to remind readers that Latina/o faculty also have a unique responsibility: namely, to use our privilege for lifting up our communities, to support and mentor each other throughout the tenure and promotion pipeline, and to ensure that the doors of academe remain open for others. This, too, is the essence of *abriendo puertas*.

Indeed, we "open doors" for others because someone, at some point in the past, opened a door for us. When I began my faculty career a mere 15 years ago, there were only five other Latina/o educational leadership faculty members in Research 1 universities who regularly attended the annual professional conference of the University Council for Educational Administration (UCEA): Flora Ida Ortiz, Maria Luisa González, Pedro Reyes, Reynaldo Contreras, and Leonard Valverde. These five professors looked out for me, pushed my academic thinking, and encouraged me to continually push the field forward. My "radical" ideas (though somewhat mainstream by today's standards) were not generally accepted in the field back then. Yet my senior *colegas* always encouraged me to hone my language of critique, carve my own theoretical and epistemological spaces, and make the field my own by re-territorializing the discourse on school–community relations.

As a graduate student, I often felt that I didn't "belong" in the field of educational leadership. I was an outsider with no previous principal experience, I was too young for anyone to take me seriously, and I always felt that my own scholarship was never good enough. Yet these five professors constantly encouraged me, gave me *consejos*, and convinced me that what I brought to the academic table was not only worthy, but critically important. That message of validation was particularly significant. More importantly, hearing that message from my senior Latina/o mentors was especially significant. There is no doubt that their wisdom and advice embodied the true meaning of *abriendo puertas*.

As Latinas/os, our pain is our strength and our strength is transformative. Together, and in solidarity with our allies, we can, and will, find new ways to keep those doors open for future generations of Latina/o professors and scholars. Without a doubt, as we work to transform our spaces of work, we will also fundamentally transform our world at the same time. There is an incredible amount of work to do, but it all begins with a first step. The *testimonios* in this collection are a key part of that first step in the transformational process. Pasito a paso/Step by step down the path, we will find our way. ¡'Pa 'lante y con fé!

NOTES

1. http://www.billboard.com/artist/302943/Gloria+Estefan/chart?f=330
2. Estefan, G. (1995). Abriendo Puertas. From the album *Abriendo Puertas* (Emilio Estefan Jr., Producer). Miami, FL: Crescent Moon Studios.
3. *Consejos* are cultural understandings of knowledge, wisdom, sage advice, and life-lessons, typically passed on from one generation to another.
4. This does not imply that all identities are silently accepted. Certainly, many roles, expectations, and identities are often resisted, transformed, modified, accommodated, and even discarded altogether.

INTRODUCTION

ABRIENDO PUERTAS, CERRANDO HERIDAS

Opening Doors, Closing Wounds

Frank Hernandez and Elizabeth Murakami

HOW THIS WORK CAME TO BE

Once or twice a year, during national or regional conferences, Latina/o professors are able to come together to exchange and test conceptual ideas, showcase their scholarship, plan collaborative projects, or review work for awards or publications. Opportunities to meet are not only paramount in terms of developing scholarship—they are equally important in providing opportunities to dialogue about finding work–life balance as academics. In fact, Marshall and her colleagues recognized the importance of these dialogues during one of the national conferences we attend, the University Council of Educational Administration (UCEA). Joanne Marshall began bringing together professors who would agree to share their work–life experiences. Those included filled-up sessions, with shared "tears, laughter, applause, hugs, and thick emotions," as Theoharis (2012, p. xxxi) described. A sense of shared support and solidarity occurred during this session, on a

Abriendo Puertas, Cerrando Heridas (Opening Doors, Closing Wounds), pages xiii–xxvi
Copyright © 2015 by Information Age Publishing
All rights of reproduction in any form reserved.

commonly rushed life of teaching, researching, serving the institution, and balancing family, children, and life struggles.

At the same national conference, while we reported on our research in the National Latino Leadership Project (NLLP), a group of us organized a similar session related to the experiences of Latinas/os in the academy. These too were filled with emotional accounts, bringing to light deep conversations and *testimonios* about issues particular to Latinas/os seeking work-life balance. For example, many of these scholars were first-generation doctoral degree graduates, and first in the family to achieve positions in higher education. These scholars talked about their struggles, their gratitude for their families' support, and their responsibility to give back to their community, including Latina/o students. Maria E. Torres-Guzman explicitly writes about these struggles as she navigates her journey through higher education (1993). As an assistant professor she reached a point where she made conscious decisions to create balance between her work and her life outside of work. As she states, "I sought to balance my personal and professional lives by separating them. In other words, I gave to Caesar what was Caesar's and to God what was hers" (p. 55). This balancing act also involved managing the multiple demands placed on her as a Latina faculty member. Torres-Guzman released some of the demands, kept other demands, and began to integrate her community and professional projects and make writing a priority. For Latinos, balancing one's person is complicated and must be examined.

These sessions (mentioned in the above paragraph) richly illustrated the importance of work–life balance. In the first book in the Work–Life Balance series (Marshall et al., 2012), the authors collected experiences and stories from a diverse pool of faculty in educational leadership trying to find balance in academia. In the introduction, Marshall reflected on how people attend sessions, present papers, and meet colleagues during conferences, with little meaningful time to share their struggles and stories.

As Latina/o scholars, we can attest that during the past decade (since we joined academia as neophyte professors), we have witnessed Latinas/os face a genuine struggle to establish ourselves in academia. Flora Ida Ortiz, distinguished professor of institutional leadership and policy studies, for example, candidly spoke to some of us before retiring. She reflected that during her early career, she was one of only two Latinas at a national convention. She felt ignored and invisible throughout these years since she started in 1972, in a field that is arguably still heavily White-male dominated.

Since we began in academia, we learned, through joys and sorrows, that even though Latina/o professors have been represented in higher education and colleges of education, little is known about their experiences. They are also less represented in mentoring and leadership positions such as the national organizations to which Dr. Ortiz referred. For example, only two Latinos have been elected president of one of the national organizations in educational leadership since 1956. A Latino professor was the 33rd president-elect after 28 White males and 4 White females, followed by a Latina professor, who was the 41st president-elect, after 9 White women and 31 males. As recent as during this decade, some of us were also part of the first petition to establish a Latina/o research special interest group (SIG) in two national organizations focused on education and educational leadership respectively. Dr. Ortiz was finally recognized for her contributions to the field, 33 years later in 2005, receiving the Roald F. Campbell Lifetime Achievement Award. Undeniably, the representation and contributions of Latina/o scholars in the field of education is scarce and restricted to a very few individuals who choose to persist in this profession.

LATINO FACULTY DEMOGRAPHICS

Opportunities to relate among Latina/o scholars in higher education are rare. This fact can be attributed to the low representation of Latina/o scholars operating in full-time college and university faculty. In 2009, for example, Latinas/os represented only 4% of all full-time college and university faculty in degree-granting institutions of higher education, while 79% were White (Delgado-Romero, Flores, Gloria, Arredondo, & Castellanos, 2003; U.S. Department of Education, National Center for Education Statistics, 2011; Ponjuan, 2011). Most Latino faculty work at public institutions of higher education. For instance, in 2005, 38% of Latinos faculty were employed at public four-year institutions, 33% were at public two-year institutions, and 26% were employed at private four-year institutions (Santiago, 2008). Among all full-time faculty, Latinas were most concentrated in foreign languages (8%), education (3%), and psychology (3%). Latinos were concentrated most in political science (5%) and economics (5%). A smaller percentage of Latinas/os can be found in colleges of education, the field in which we serve.

Interestingly, even though the representation of Latino scholars is small, Latinos in general have become a representative group in the U.S. According to the Pew Hispanic Trust (2011), the Latino population grew 43% from 2000 to 2010, now comprising 16% of the total U.S. population. The Pew Hispanic Trust (2011) also has reported that Latinos "account for most of the nation's growth—56 percent from 2000 to 2010" (p. 1). Equally important, Latinos account for 23% of children under the age of 17 (Pew, 2011) and "will continue to compose larger and larger portions of the preschool, school-age, college-age, and general populations" (Chapa & De La Rosa, 2004, p. 136). Despite these growing numbers, Latinos continue to be underrepresented among those preparing these students. This fact represents a concern of larger proportions.

LATINA/O FACULTY: WHAT WE KNOW

Several issues of concern can be raised when we see these numbers: First, the majority of full-time faculty in colleges and universities are White (Alger, 2000), not necessarily meeting the needs of Latina/o students; second, despite efforts to improve college access for minority groups, including Latinos, college students continue to lack role models; lastly, Latina/o college students are less likely to encounter Latina/o faculty with which to share similar experiences and provide academic and cultural capital. Two of the aforementioned statements, are also true for Latina/o faculty: Latina/o faculty will not encounter many role models or mentors; and Latina/o faculty are less likely to meet other Latina/o faculty with whom to share similar experiences. As Ponjuan (2011) recognized, recruiting and retaining Latina/o faculty members is the missing piece in generating Latina/o student success. Nonetheless, colleges fail to retain and promote the few Latinas/os entering academia.

Even after recruitment efforts, Latino faculty are still in the periphery of higher education in general and colleges of education specifically. Critical and important work is still needed, from the policy arena to the recruitment efforts of Latinos in higher education, in order for Latinos to move from being an anomaly to core members of higher education institutions. The literature suggests that for the last 25 years there have been concerns regarding the recruitment, retention, promotion, and support for entering administrative work of Latinos working in institutions of higher education. Literature exists that examines the selection, promotion, and tenure process and the importance of retention for Latino faculty (Ibarra, 2003; Padilla, 2003) and challenges related to Latino faculty success in higher education (Delgado-Bernal, 2002; Delgado-Romero et al., 2003; Reyes & Halcon, 1996). Despite this literature, Latino faculty continue to work disproportionally in community colleges, Hispanic-serving institutions, and foreign language departments (Delgado-Romero, Manlove, Manlove, & Hernandez, 2007). These same authors also report that Latino faculty have lower tenure rates than their White counterparts and also report that Latinos earn tenure at higher rates than their Latina colleagues.

Despite these growing numbers, Latinos continue to be under-represented at all levels of higher education. Only 11.4% obtain a bachelor's degree (Delgado-Romero et al., 2003) and 5% earn a doctorate (National Science Foundation, 2007). Latinos comprise about 3.6% of tenure-track professors and only 2.7% of full and associate professors. In terms of tenure rates, only 64% of Latino faculty attain tenure, as compared to 73% overall and 75% among White faculty (Delgado-Romero et al., 2007). This also suggests that "there is little opportunity to increase the proportion of Latino full professors in the near future" (Chapa, 2006, p. 244). In the face of these challenges, Latino faculty, scattered across the country and often working in isolation from each other, must find ways to develop their own networks, support structures, and spaces where they can share their wisdom, strategize, and forge alliances to ensure collective success. Like Holling and Rodriguez's (2006) work, this manuscript is "concerned with lessening the costs and tolls exacted from [Latino faculty] on our journeys and of devising ways not only to exist but also to live within the academy" (p. 51).

WHY IS THIS WORK IMPORTANT

As mentioned earlier, this volume in the work–life series centers on the experiences of Latina/o faculty as underrepresented in higher education. Samano (2007) used *testimonios* to explore the diversity-related work experiences of faculty of color in predominantly White community colleges. He similarly included questions related to achieving a sense of balance between personal and professional lives. The lack of Latino faculty in educational leadership programs specifically (masters, certification and doctoral) and in education generally is evidence of the "leaky" pipeline into academia but is also a testament to the inability of Latino scholars to access the structures, policies, positions, and power bases needed to empower communities of color at all levels of education. Gonzalez (2007) describes the Latino community as one that "is extremely underpowered and has low representation in the academy" (p. 161). We would argue that the Latino community is underpowered *because* of the low representation in academia. The future of many Latino communities depends on our ability, as Latino faculty, to invent and/or reinvent our roles, our networks, our institutions in ways that promote change and improvement throughout the P–20 educational system and beyond.

LATINO RACIAL IDENTITY DEVELOPMENT

Individuals raised in the United States and in other Western countries are often aware of racial identity from an early age, whether fully consciously or semiconsciously, and are bombarded with racial depictions of different groups that are often embedded with stereotypes and misinformation about particular racial groups.

Latinos in the United States have also had a long history with racial categories and have not easily fit either the labels that have been developed for them (Chicanos, Hispanics, Latinos, and Illegals) or the boxes they have been required to check (Latino and White; Latino and non-White; Hispanic). As the growing population of Latinos increases, a properly complex understanding of their racial identity development is critical to families, schools, business organizations, and institutions of higher education across the country. Family, religion, values, education, and language often influence Latino racial identity (Hernandez, 2005). Racial identity also impacts the commitment that Latinos have toward their community as well as how they balance their lives between work and family. Ferdman and Gallegos (2001) explore the topic of racial identity development and Latinos in the United States and propose a framework for looking at Latino racial identity.

Ferdman and Gallegos argue that their model captures the intricate nature of Latino identity development and state that "the difficulty in understanding Latinos is caused primarily by attempts to impose models from other racial groups onto Latinos" (2001, p. 48), models that generally do not address the array of identities that Latinos display. To this end, any model that is intended to facilitate an understanding of Latino racial identity development must take into account the complexities of these Latino identities. Ferdman and Gallegos (2001) argue that Latinos' varied historical experiences of the social construction of race "make it difficult to describe the racial identity of Latinos in conventional ways" (p. 42).

The model proposed by Ferdman and Gallegos (2001) is not a stage-development theoretical model but a systematic conceptualization illuminating patterns and orientations found within Latino identity. According to the authors, this model identifies several dimensions—individuals' identities as Latinos, individuals' perceptions of identity, how Latinos identify themselves, how Latinos as a group are perceived, how Latinos perceive Whites, and how race fits into the equation—as the most important dimensions in any rigorous understanding of Latinos' orientation. Rather than restating the literature on Latino racial identity, this introduction will briefly provide an overview of the orientations proposed by Ferdman and Gallegos (2001).

The first orientation in the model is called *Latino-integrated,* and individuals in this orientation can deal with the complexity of their Latino identity and are closely connected to their national origin and other social identities, such as gender, profession, and class. *Subgroup identified* Latinos are closely connected to their identity within the subgroup and not to the broader Latino community. For example, one might identify oneself as Puerto Rican and not Latino on the basis of this model. The next orientation is *Latino as "Other"*; that is, individuals who are not connected to their specific Latino background, including history and culture, and who identify themselves as a person of color without identifying themselves as members of a Latino subgroup. The orientation of *undifferentiated* describes Latinos who have closed lenses and "prefer to identify themselves and others as 'just people' often claiming to be color-blind and promoting this orientation to others of all groups" (Ferdman & Gallegos, 2001, p. 53). Individuals in this orientation are not aware of differences and adhere to the dominant values and norms of society. The final orientation is called *White-identified,* which describes Latinos who see themselves racially as White and consider themselves superior to people of color. These individuals value Whiteness over all other systems of values, assimilate to mainstream society, and are disconnected from Latino culture.

It's important to note that racial identity is generally described as "one's identification with a particular racial group" (Reynolds & Baluch, 2001) and has historically included elements associated with ancestry, ethnicity, physical appearance, early socialization, and personal experiences (Wijeyesinghe, 2001). Other scholars have asserted that racial identity is also defined as one's racial category—for instance Black and White—and is often referenced as a collective identity based on individual perceptions that one belongs to a specific racial group (e.g., Helms, 1995).

Racial identity development constitutes the processes or experiences that, over time, contribute to an individual's identification with a racial group and the cultural aspects of that racial group and is usually described by models using typologies (Cross, Parham, & Helms, 1991; Helms, 1990; Parham & Williams, 1993) or a linear path characterized by stages in racial identity development (Cross, 1991; Helms, 1995). For example, Helms (1984, 1990, 1993, 1995) proposed that White racial identity development is based on the attitudes, behaviors, and feelings that White people have developed as a result of their being raised to embrace and to perpetuate White racist attitudes. Finally, racial identity development experiences in higher education impact Latino faculty in a diverse ways. Racial identity will also be used as a filter as Latinos reflect on their work–life balance.

TESTIMONIOS OF LATINA/O FACULTY IN COLLEGES OF EDUCATION

We focus on faculty in colleges of education, since many of these Latinas/os carry the important mission to prepare new teachers and research new pedagogies that have the power of improving and transforming education. Ponjuan (2011) and others posit that students of color, especially in predominantly White institutions (PWIs), are more prone to persisting toward degree completion when they have faculty of color as role models (Viernes, Gonzales, & Wood, 2008). In many instances, Latina/o faculty are treated the same way White teachers once treated children of color (McLaren,

1987; Sleeter, 1995). They are perceived as different, with obscure agendas, and too focused on service (Quijada, Ek, Alanis, & Murakami-Ramalho, 2011; Ponjuan, 2011; Turner, Gonzales, & Wood, 2008). It is important, however, to examine the truth behind these perceptions. There is a reason why Latinas/or are more heavily represented in the humanities, and why they focus on service and community issues.

Bernal and Villalpando (2002) revealed two main reasons why a higher concentration of Latinos and other faculty of color can be found in the areas of humanities, social sciences, and also education: One reason is related to the common practice in K–12 tracking, of placing Latinos is vocational tracks instead of science-based or related fields. The authors assert, "Few students of color have an opportunity to benefit from adequate resources and academic support to pursue interests in these fields, and are consequently ineligible for graduate programs and for jobs in the academic profession" (p. 172). Those who became academics have experienced some of these practices, including attacks to forms of qualitative and participatory research (Denzin, 2003).

The second reason Latinas/os are in the humanities, and especially in education, relates to having a sense of purpose and responsibility towards the community. In relation to supporting the community, Latina/o faculty often support students who experienced similar struggles and often generate research inquiry about these issues of social justice (Ek et al., 2009). Delgado-Bernal and Villalpando's (2002) study shows that even though social justice theories have been expanded and recognized by many scholars, it is slower in its practice when it comes to promotion and tenure of academics of color. In their study, Delgado-Bernal and Villalpando provide evidence of how an understanding of culturally relevant research among Latinas/os may hinder their promotion and tenure processes when evaluated by Whites. Delgado-Bernal and Villalpando (2002) remind us that because of the imbalance in the majority-minority representation of faculty, Latinas/os are often reviewed by a majority of White faculty. These faculty may still draw from Eurocentric knowledge in their practices, based on their own upbringing and experiences. In addition, there is a "scientific tradition" still followed in higher education, which has been historically created by White males. Such tradition did not consider context and community as relevant in research.

So, Delgado Bernal and Villalpando (2002) show in their research that when evaluating scholars who focus on social justice, White faculty's evaluation of research that reveals "the educational needs of an underserved and disenfranchised racial/ethnic community" (p. 177) may be biased toward what they may consider valid and scientific, based on what they consider tradition of research. As a result, Latinas/os' research agendas may be perceived as biased, or lacking academic rigor. Latina/o faculty, in turn, will advocate in their research about the link between scientific research and the promotion of social justice within communities, with a mission to improve the lives of those underserved. It shows that they have experienced similar struggles and that they are advocating for transforming the field.

It is important to current and upcoming scholars to discern research and evaluation of research on the same basis. For example, scientific literature that attempted to equalize education in the 1990s contained discussions of a lack of understanding of how to better serve K–12 and college students of color. While this paradigmatic approach or vantage point reveals that this research is aimed at informing those unfamiliar with the experiences of students of color, it also reminds us that most of the educators in this country are Whites, living in White-dominated spheres.

Excellent scholars such as Ladson-Billings (1995), Sleeter, 1992, 1995, 2002), Omi and Winant (1986), and Wellman (1977), in fact, indicated the importance of addressing race, ethnicity, and power among educators. When reflecting on K–12 White teachers, for example, Sleeter (1995) said: "I fear the consequences of a rising tide of historical amnesia, as White teachers enter increasingly diverse classrooms with little or no cognizance of the legacy of racism in the U.S. Maintaining space to teach White teachers about racism is a very important political project for teacher educators" (p. 44). Many of the university/college faculty serving college students of color were once K–12 teachers and bear the responsibility of preparing the next generation of teachers. As for those becoming faculty, it would be naïve to think that an understanding of race and social inequity paradigms has changed once anyone transfers from K–12 to higher education. As a result, Eurocentric-focused faculty, evaluating a new wave of scholars of color, may similarly be limited in their knowledge about the nature and contribution of communities of color.

It is our hope that scholars of color are increasingly recognized for their culturally relevant pedagogies and research/theory building—a revolutionary praxis, as McLaren (1997) once proposed as involving a rejection of discourses that once excluded and marginalized peoples—to one that informs about how to prepare a larger representation of Latinos and students of color in the country.

METHODOLOGY: AUTOBIOGRAPHICAL TESTIMONIOS

Following the format of the work–life balance book series, this volume guides chapter authors to use autoethnographical *testimonios* in its methodological approach. When employing Latina/o epistemology, we expand the autoethnographical design as a way to collect *testimonios* (Cervantes-Soon, 2012; Delgado-Bernal & Villalpando, 2002; Samano, 2007). Cervantes-Soon

(2012) posits that *testimonios* are counter-narratives that provide confessions and *consejos* (advice). The author reminds us of the role of a critical school in promoting a situated, and sociopolitical discourse. Cervantes-Soon (2012) highlights the value of *testimonios* as a way to provide educational institutions and individuals with organic healing, critical consciousness, and agency in dystopic times by cultivating the use of testimonios as a way to center and legitimize knowledge. Denzin (2003), in turn, defined this type of research as performance autoethnography—a tool of liberation and a way of being moral and political in the world. He asserted that "in the discursive spaces of performativity there is no distance between the performance and the politics that the performance enacts. The two are intertwined, each nourishing the other, opposite sides of the same coin, one and the same thing" (p. 259).

LATINA/O CRITICAL RACE THEORY

The tradition of autoethnography, as Theoharis (2012) highlights in this series, provides the opportunity to open the experience of academics so that it can be studied in a critical and reflective manner. The value of reflection, and telling stories within a sociocultural context, also aligns with Cole and Knowles' (2001) approach, which allows for the situated positionality of self in relation to "broader sociocultural elements, issues, and constructs" (p. 16). In the case of Latinas/os, critical race theory (CRT) further defines the theoretical framework for this volume. Denzin, in fact, recognized that "critical race scholars use performative, storytelling autoethnographic methods to uncover the ways in which racism operates in daily life" (p. 271). CRT testimonios or CRT storytelling as Delgado-Bernal and Villalpando (2002) defined it, is a method which often reveals dominant Eurocentric epistemologies through interactions that include "both the stock story from a majoritarian perspective and a counterstory from a non-majoritarian perspective" (p. 172). Perez-Huber (2009) argues that in Latino critical race theory (LATCRIT) research, *testimonios* provide a strategic approach in the study of Latinas/os.

While framing the focus of struggles between work and life balance for Latinas/o faculty in education, we connected our goals with Denzin's (2003) reminder of the timeliness and relevance of this work. The author speaks of a current disconnect between the public and private spheres in contemporary U.S. society. He asserts that "the pursuit of private satisfaction and the consumption of consumer goods become ends as well as goals for the good life. Human tragedies fall by the way-side" (p. 261). Similarly, Marshall talked about the lack of emphasis in the private life in the profession: "As professionals, we tend not to talk about our personal lives, unless there is a crisis that intrudes upon and keeps us from our professional responsibilities" (p. xv). These authors highlight how the personal and public are deeply intertwined. Denzin (2003) further invites us to provoke our critical imagination to address this divide—a radically democratic, pedagogical, and interventionist approach to insert ourselves in the world, "provoking conflict, curiosity, criticism, and reflection" (p. 261). Latina/o *testimonios* within performance autoethnography, then, become a way of "acting on the world in order to change it" (Denzin, 2003, p. 262), especially recognizing that the practice of democratic freedom from race, class, or gender oppression is only developed through conditions of permanent struggles. What we know is that Latinos in the academy have been impacted by injustices and as Padilla and Chavez so eloquently argue, these individuals have been "made to question their own humanity in the everyday experience of academic life... [and have] instinctively reoriented themselves" (1993, p. 3). This volume is about how Latino professors in education have reoriented themselves as they attempt to balance their work and life within the added pressures of being Latino in the academy.

GUIDING QUESTIONS

The purpose of this volume is to share the experiences of Latina/o scholars in education, as they provide *testimonios* of spaces that foster the survival and ability to succeed and thrive in academia. Borrowing from Verdugo (2005) and Holling and Rodriguez (2006).

This volume will address three guiding questions:

- What are the existing structures that isolate/discriminate against Latino faculty?
- How can Latino faculty disrupt these to achieve work–life balance?
- Based on their experiences, what are the transformative ideologies regarding Latino faculty seeking work–life balance?

The chapters' authors, invited to offer their autoethnographical *testimonios,* become instruments of what Spender (1984) situated in "the effects of a particular stage of civilization upon a civilized individual" (p. ix). The chapter authors reflect on "an extreme external situation through his [or her] own extremity" (Spender, 1984, p. ix), or as Denzin (2003) highlights in Spencer's text, they become diagnosis—not just of themselves, but of a phase in history through their collective stories—a universal singular. The authors in this volume reflect how the process of *abrir puertas* (opening doors) in academia takes courage and risks, sometimes involving a process of healing wounds (*cerrar heridas*). In *Abriendo Puertas, Cerrando Heridas,* we consider the emotional and physical costs in seeking work–life balance related to barriers encountered by Latinas/os. This volume will also inform us of the lessons learned by these scholars—lessons that we hope will translate into transformative resistance and purposeful new ideologies for Latinas/os in academia.

REFERENCES

Alger, R. J. (2000). How to recruit and promote minority faculty: Start by playing fair. *Black Issues in Higher Education, 17*(20), 160.

Bernal, D. D., & Villalpando, O. (2002). An apartheid of knowledge in academia: The struggle over the" legitimate" knowledge of faculty of color. *Equity &Excellence in Education, 35*(2), 169–180.

Cervantes-Soon, C. G. (2012). Testimonios of life and learning in the borderlands: Subaltern Juarez girls speak. *Equity and Excellence in Education, 45*(3), 373–391. DOI: 10.1080/10665684.2012.698182

Chapa, J. (2006). Preparing a future professoriate to successfully teach California's and the nation's Latino and African American students. In P. Gandara, C. Horn, & G. Orfield (Eds.), *Expanding opportunities in higher education* (pp. 243–264). Albany: State University of New York Press.

Chapa, J. & De La Rosa, B. (2004). Latino population growth, socioeconomic and demographic characteristics, and implications for educational attainment. *Education and Urban Society, 36*(2), 130–149.

Cole A. L., & Knowles J. G. (2001). *Lives in context: The art of life history research.* New York, NY: Altamira.

Cross, W. E. (1991). *Shades of Black: Diversity in African American identity.* Philadelphia, PA: Temple University Press.

Cross, W. E., Parham, T. A., & Helms, J. (1991). The stages of Black identity development: Nigrescence models. In R. L. Jones (Ed.), *Black psychology* (3rd ed., pp. 319–338). Berkeley, CA: Cobb & Henry.

Delgado-Romero, E. A., Flores, L., Gloria, A., Arredondo, P., & Castellanos, J. (2003). Developmental career challenges for Latino and Latina psychology faculty. In L. Jones & J. Castellanos (Eds.), *The majority in the minority: Retaining Latina/o faculty, administrators, and students in the 21st century* (pp. 257–283). Sterling, VA: Stylus Books.

Delgado-Romero, E. A., Manlove, A. N., Manlove, J. D., & Hernandez, C. A. (2007). Controversial issues in the recruitment and retention of Latino/a faculty. *Journal of Hispanic Higher Education, 6*(1), 34–51.

Denzin, N. K. (2003). Performing [auto] ethnography politically. *The Review of Education, Pedagogy, and Cultural Studies, 25*(3), 257–278.

Ferdman, B. M., & Gallegos, P. I. (2001). Racial identity development and Latinos in the United States. In C. L. Wijeyesinghe & B. W. Jackson III (Eds.), *New perspectives on racial identity development: A theoretical and practical anthology* (pp. 32–66). Albany: State University of New York Press.

Gonzalez, C. (2007). Building sustainable power Latino scholars and academic leadership positions at U.S. institutions of higher learning. *Journal of Hispanic Higher Education, 6*(2), 157–162.

Helms, J. E. (1984). Toward a theoretical explanation of the effects of race on counseling: A Black and White model. *The Counseling Psychologist, 13*, 695–710.

Helms, J. E. (1990). Toward a model of White racial identity develoment. In J. E. Helms (Ed.), *Black and White racial identity: Theory, research, and practice* (pp. 49–66). Westport, CT: Greenwood Press.

Helms, J. E. (1993). I also said, "White racial identity influences white researchers." *The Counseling Pshchologist, 21*(2), 240–243.

Helms, J. E. (1995). An update of Helms' White and people of color racial identity models. In J. G. Ponterotto, M. J. Casas, L. A. Suzuki, & C. M. Alexander (Eds.), *Handbook of multicultural counseling* (pp. 181–198). Thousand Oaks, Ca: Sage Publications.

Hernandez, F. (2005) The racial identity development of selected Latino school principals and its relation to their leadership practice. [Unpublished Doctoral Dissertation] The University of Wisconsin-Madison.

Holling, M. A., & Rodriguez, A. (2006). Negotiating our way through the gates of academe. *Journal of Latinos and Education, 5*(1), 49–64.

Ibarra, R. A. (2003). Latino/a faculty and the tenure process in cultural context. In L. Jones & J. Castellanos (Eds.), *The Majority in the minority: Retaining Latina/o faculty, administrators, and students in the 21st century.* Sterling, VA: Stylus Books

Ladson-Billings G. (1995). Toward a theory of culturally relevant pedagogy. *American Educational Research Journal, 32*, 465–491.

Marshall, J. M., Brooks, J. S., Brown, K. M., Bussey, L. H., Fusarelli, B., Gooden, M. A., . . . & Theoharis, G. (2012). *Juggling flaming chainsaws: Academics in educational leadership try to balance work and family.* Charlotte, NC: Information Age.

McLaren, P. (1997). *Revolutionary multiculturalism: Pedagogies of dissent for the new millennium.* Boulder CO: Westview.

National Science Foundation. (2007). *Survey of earned doctorates.* Retrieved from www.nsf.gov/statistics/doctorates

Omi, M. & Winant, H. (1986). *Racial formation in the United States: From the 1960s to the 1980s.* New York, NY: Routledge and Kegan Paul

Padilla, R. V. (2003). Barriers to accessing the professoriate. In L. Jones & J. Castellanos (Eds.), *The majority in the minority: Retaining Latina/o faculty, administrators, and students in the 21st century* (pp. 179–204). Sterling, VA: Stylus Books

Padilla, R., & Chavez, R. C. (1995). *The leaning ivory tower: Latino professors in American universities.* Albany: State University of New York Press.

Parham, T. A., & Williams, P. T. (1993). The relationship of demographic and background factors to racial identity attitudes. *Journal of Black Psychology, 19*(1), 7–24.

Pew Hispanic Trust. (2011). Census 2010: 50 million Latinos—Hispanics account for more than half of nation's growth in past decade. Retrieved from www.pewhispanic.org

Perez-Huber, L. (2009). Disrupting apartheid of knowledge: Testimonio as methodology in Latina/o critical race research in education. *International Journal of Qualitative Studies in Education, 22*(6), 639–654. DOI: 10.1080/09518390903333863

Ponjuan, L. (2011). Recruiting and retaining Latino faculty members: The missing piece to Latino student success. *Thought & Action, 99.*

Quijada, P., Ek, L., Alanís, I., & Murakami Ramalho, E. (2011). Transformative resistance as agency: Chicanas/Latinas re(creating) academic spaces. *Journal of the Professoriate, 5*(1), 70–98.

Reyes, M. L. & Halcon, J.J. (1988). Racism in academia: The old wolf revisited. *Harvard Educational Review, 58*(3), 229–314.

Reynolds, A., & Baluch, S. (2001). Racial identity theories in counseling: A literature review and evaluation. In C. L. Wijeyesinghe & B. W. Jackson (Eds.), *New perspectives on racial identity development: A theoretical and practical anthology* (pp. 153–181). Albany: State University of New York Press.

Samano, M. L. (2007). Respecting one's abilities or (post) colonial tokenism? Narrative testimonios of faculty of color working in predominantly White community colleges. [Unpublished Doctoral Dissertation] Oregon State University Electronic Theses and Dissertations Collection. Retrieved March 26, 2015.

Santiago, D. A. (2008). The Condition of Latinos in Education: 2008 Factbook. *Excelencia in Education* (NJ1).

Scheurich, J. J. (Ed.). (2002). *Anti-racist scholarship: An advocacy.* Albany: State University of New York Press.

Sleeter, C. (1995). Teaching Whites about racism. In R. J. Martin (Ed.), *Practicing what we teach: Confronting diversity in teacher education* (pp. 117–130). Albany: State University of New York Press.

Spender, S. (1984). Introduction. In M. Lowry (Ed.), *Under the volcano* (pp. vii–xxii). New York, NY: New American Library. (Original work published 1947)

Theoharis, G. (2012). A note on methodology: Autoethnography and other reflections. In J. M. Marshall, J. S. Brooks, K. M. Brown, L. H. Bussey, B. C. Fusarelli, M. A. Gooden, C. A. Lugg, L. Reed, & G. Theoharis (Eds.), *Juggling flaming chain saws: Academics in educational leadership try to balance work and family* (pp. xxxi–lii). Charlotte, NC: Information Age Publishing.

Torres-Guzman, M. E. (1995). Surviving the journey. In R. V. Padilla, R. C. Chavez (Eds.), *The leaning ivory tower: Latino professors in American universities* (pp. 53–65). Albany: State University of New York Press.

Turner Sotello Viernes, C., Gonzalez J. C., & Wood, J. L. (2008). Faculty of color in academe: What 20 years of literature tells us. *Journal of Diversity in Higher Education, 1*(3), 139–168.

U.S. Department of Education, National Center for Education Statistics. (2011). *Digest of Education Statistics, 2010* (NCES 2011-015), Chapter 3. Retrieved from http://nces.ed.gov/fastfacts/display.asp?id=61

Verdugo, R. R. (1995). Racial stratification and the use of Hispanic faculty as role models: Theory, policy, and practice. *Journal of Higher Education, 66*(6), 669–685.

Wellman, D. (1977). *Portrait of White racism.* New York, NY: Cambridge University Press.

Wijeyesinghe, C. L. (2001). Racial identity in multiracial people: An alternative paradigm. In C. L. Wijeyesinghe & B. W. Jackson (Eds.), *New perspectives on racial identity development: A theoretical and practical anthology* (pp. 129–152). Albany: State University of New York Press.

ACKNOWLEDGMENTS

I would like to acknowledge and thank the Latino Special Interest Group of the UCEA. Those meetings gave birth to this book. A very special "thank you" to Elizabeth and Gloria, two wise Latinas, for their hard work and dedication to this collection of testimonios. A tremendous gratitude is owed to Jon McPhetres for managing this project and taking great care of the stories and understanding why this book was so important to so many of us. Thank you mom for your love and for helping me understand what "hard work" is. Thank you Steven for the countless hours of reading over my work and supporting me for the last 23 years. I am forever grateful for you, your love, and your wisdom.

—Frank Hernandez, PhD

This book came to fruition because of Latina and Latino mentors like Flora Ida Ortiz, Maria Luisa Gonzalez, Pedro Reyes, Ellen Clark, Bob Milk, Berta Perez, Ray Padilla, Ruben Martinez, and Gerardo Lopez, among others who are most influential in academia—and who have been a large part of my academic growth since back in graduate school. They understood and nurtured my cultural identifiers and my *Latin American* roots. They were the ones who showed me that passion and purpose go together in the development of research. They shared their wisdom, expertise and experiences—of being trailblazers in the field of education. Since then, with dear colleagues like Frank, and Gloria, and contributors of this book, I developed a broader understanding of life in academia, and the value of generating

Abriendo Puertas, Cerrando Heridas (Opening Doors, Closing Wounds), pages xxvii–xxviii
Copyright © 2015 by Information Age Publishing
All rights of reproduction in any form reserved.

safe spaces—where testimonios strengthen us as professionals. Colegas—a todos les dedico esta obra—mis respetos y mis saludos!

—Elizabeth Murakami PhD

I wish to acknowledge the wonderful support offered by co-editors Frank Hernandez and Betty Murakami, as the timing of this volume came at a time of challenge for my family and me. I also deeply appreciate our authors' entrusting of their testimonios to us, as this is always an act of courage and love for the broader endeavor of creating safe and welcoming spaces within the realm of academia for each other and those in the next generation.

—Gloria Rodriguez PhD

PART I

PERSONAL IDENTITY AND IDEOLOGIES

CHAPTER 1

"WHY DID HE THINK I WAS THE CUSTODIAN OR THE MAINTENANCE PERSON?"

The Challenges of Balancing Love, Life, and Work

Frank Hernandez

In our lives, there are events that either help us to stay balanced and focused or throw us off balance, challenge our focus, and make us question ourselves. These questions challenge the core of who we are and often saturate us with doubt. Many of these challenging events are brought on by others; some we create for ourselves. What follow are two stories about challenges in my own life. The first story relates how I, as a high school student, tried to balance my view of myself as attending college with the views held by my counselor, who could not imagine it. The other story is about my first day on the job as a professor, a day that I remember like yesterday. In some ways, these are my confessions, the sides of stories most often told by others, not by us.

This book represents an opportunity for Latinos to tell their own stories. Critical race theory (CRT) posits that oppressed groups, specifically those

Abriendo Puertas, Cerrando Heridas (Opening Doors, Closing Wounds), pages 3–10
Copyright © 2015 by Information Age Publishing
All rights of reproduction in any form reserved.

that have been marginalized and silenced historically, can tell their own story because they are possessors of knowledge. Theorists like Solorzano and Yasso (2002) have coined the term "counterstories" and defined it as an account of events that conflicts with accounts told from a dominant social perspective. Counterstories challenge a dominant discourse, a process that, in this case, concerns deconstructing the existing structures that isolate or discriminate against Latino students and faculty. Montoya (1998) argued that "personal narratives... are more than stories" in that they "invent, reform and refashion personal and collective identity" (p. 37). My retelling of my own stories from a Latino perspective is, in many ways, an effort to work against the dominant ideologies that so often identify Latino students and professors as one monolithic group.

MY EARLY YEARS

As a high school student, I rarely imagined myself as a person who would hold a PhD title. In fact, my main goal was to graduate from high school. The truth is that many of us who had been growing up in the Elmer Scott Housing Projects—or as we called them, "the projects"—never achieved this goal. What I recall most about living in the projects was that temperatures were always hot, fighting was an everyday occurrence, and a candy truck would stop by our block every day, including twice a day during the summer at regular intervals. The fighting was also predictable; it was always the Mexicans versus the Blacks. Sometimes there would be twenty of us and twenty of them throwing rocks, sticks, and anything else we could find at each other. Other times it was my mom hurling profane invectives at another mom for something either we had done to this other family's child or the other way around. And then there was the occasional fist fight between my Tia (my maternal aunt) and grown Black women. This fighting almost invariably resulted in the disputants' rolling around in the dirt and tearing at each other's clothes with such efficiency that I and other kids could see exposed bras or indeed the flesh underneath.

When I was seven years old we moved from Dallas, Texas to Wichita, Kansas, a distance of six hours by vehicle north, straight up Interstate 35. We were one of the first Mexican families in our new community. We lived in what essentially was a military community. It had been developed during the Korean War to house defense workers and their families. When our family moved there, the community was recovering from a cutback in production at the large airplane plant in the area. The resulting turmoil prompted some families to move out of the community while a few others, like my own family, moved in. It was there that I learned, from my parents, that English would be the language of choice at home as well as in school and that a good command of the English language and a high school diploma would be all that I would need to secure a good job, a good car, a nice house, and the like.

We lived in Wichita, Kansas for the next twenty years. It was there that I graduated from high school. Shortly before graduation, my fellow seniors and I were impatiently attending our final round of classes, all the while waiting to be called over the loud speaker for our individualized senior meeting with the school counselor. I had witnessed many of my friends being called to Mr. Garrison's office and I knew that his conversations with them had concerned college. And even though I had participated in the Upward Bound program (a federally funded educational program for low-income students who are first-generation college attendees), it had been the only context in which I had ever discussed my possible future enrollment in a higher-education institution. So, yes, I was a bit surprised when my name was called to the counselor's office and I saw brochures on his desk for both the marines and the army. I knew then he was going to talk with me not about college but about service in the armed forces, and I was right.

After high school graduation, I did not know what I was doing; I was lost. I moved from job to job, attempted to take college courses but ended up failing them, and never felt stable. After two years, I finally landed a job at a meat packing company where I knew the manager, who had played volleyball with me at the local YMCA. When I told my mom about the job, she jumped with joy. This was what she meant about obtaining the American Dream. I had found a good job through which I could afford a good car, a nice home, and the like.

The job entailed that I work in a huge, cold, loud factory filled with sides of beef. I would stand on a metal box with one big conveyer belt running in front of me and two smaller conveyer belts running on either side of me. As pieces of meat passed by on the large belt, it was my job to identify which types of cut of meat they were and to place them, accordingly, on the smaller belt to my left or my right. I wore a hardhat, earplugs, and a heavy glove on my right hand. Between my middle and ring finger I had a sharp hook, similar to a pirate, which I would use to grab the different cuts of meat. From my workstation, I was able to see the entire warehouse, which was a mass of conveyer belts where, for the most part, Mexican men with sharp knives would carve pieces of meat from big slabs of meat working their way down a belt. Occasionally, the men would tap their knives on the stainless steel counter, creating a din capable of penetrating my earplugs.

I was privy to a rumor that the workers were planning a walk out because of working conditions. The idea terrified me because I had no idea what I should do if some of the men around me were to start walking off the job. I suppose I would have walked off with them. However, my reaction to a walk off was never tested, as I lasted there for only one week and one day. At the end of that time, I walked into the manager's office and he looked at me and said, "Hey Frankie." There was a short pause and then he said, "You can't do it, can you?" I said, "I can't and I am so sorry." I remember that walk to my car, a 1983 Chevy Chevette that I had purchased from my sister and brother-in-law. It dawned on me that I needed to get my ass to college.

REFOCUSING MY PRIORITIES

After stints at several more jobs, I enrolled in a small liberal arts Friends (Quaker) college, located two hours west of where I was living, where I would be studying Bible Theology and Education. However, early conversations that I had there with my advisor and other college administrators seemed very much like the one I had had with Mr. Garrison, my high school senior counselor who had highly encouraged me to join the military. It wasn't so much the content of the conversation as the underlying theme: I would not do well in higher education and I would need lots of support. For example, one instructor with whom I spoke reminded me that if I found college to be too difficult, I could always take a semester off and come back later. I hadn't even started yet and I was getting the "this may not work out for you" lecture. The general negativity threw me off balance, and, as a result, I began to question my own skills. Perhaps my counselor was right. I didn't have the skills I needed for college and the military was my best bet.

I did just fine as an undergraduate, and I graduated with honors, earning the highest academic-achievement honors that the college awarded. After graduation I moved back to the same Wichita community where I had once lived and began my career as a classroom teacher. Soon after that I moved further north (Minnesota), completed a master's degree, and decided that I would earn a PhD before turning forty.

I applied to several PhD programs at schools that had received high rankings from a national journal esteemed for its assessments of graduate schools of education and education programs. I had to be conscious of where I would attend graduate school since I would be commuting. After much deliberation with my family, I decided to accept an offer from the University of Wisconsin–Madison, the program closest to home. I never doubted that I had made the right decision: this program had the highest ranking in its category, awarded me a three-year fellowship including a monthly stipend, and was only a four-hour drive from my family. My three years of study went by very fast. It is interesting to note that, although very few Latino students were attending graduate school in my department, I was able to develop friendships with Latino students from other departments.

I learned many lessons in graduate school that I use today in my leadership role as a dean of education. However, I recall my academic advisor at

Wisconsin doing her best to educate me on the ins and outs of the life of a professor. She connected me to senior scholars of color so that I could develop a network after leaving graduate school. She knew that I would need a support system for the challenges that I might encounter as I began my first professorship. She taught me how to work the conference scene and to manage the meet-and-greet.

Having finished my coursework at Wisconsin by the spring of 2005, I concentrated mostly on my dissertation. At the same time, I searched for potential jobs as a professor, eventually applying for a faculty position at a research university in the Midwest. Yes, I applied for only one position: I was limited as to where I could work because my family was based in the Twin Cities of Minnesota, limiting me to a radius not farther than the four-hour-long commutes I had been undertaking for the last three years from St. Paul to Madison. Being with my family was always a priority for me, so I predictably found it difficult to be away from my partner and our son and all of our friends that we had made over the previous ten years of our relationship (this past fall 2014, we celebrated our 22nd anniversary).

As I searched for faculty positions, my family and I agreed to the stipulation that I would not apply for a faculty position longer than a three-hour drive from our home. Three years of balancing my graduate studies in one city with my family in another had been extremely trying at times, but we felt that a three-hour commute was manageable. And so I applied to a land-grant university that was exactly three hours south of the city where my family and I lived. I was interviewed and hired. Having landed this position, I now focused my energies on completing my dissertation.

ENTERING THE PROFESSORSHIP

I was very deliberate in my packing as I transitioned from full-time graduate student to full-time professor. I looked at this transition as an opportunity to downsize what I had collected during graduate school. After three years, I was surprised that I had collected so much stuff. Consequently, I packed three types of boxes: boxes that would go back home where my family lived, boxes that would come with me to my new office, and boxes that would go straight to the dump. I recall the excitement that I felt as I began to pack all the books that I had collected in my three years of graduate school.

As the summer was ending, I anticipated moving into my new office. I had a pretty good idea of its location and contemplated where I would hang pictures, set up my computer and printer, and place my books. Some offices in the building were located directly off the main hallway itself; others were located in suites. Mine was in a suite where I needed to pass through one door and room before I could access my office. Because it was located on the west side of the second floor of the building, I decided to use temporary parking instead of parking across the street in the lot, which would have made carrying boxes into my office a bit more stressful because of the distance. I typically carried one box at a time. During my third trip up the stairs and into the long hallway, another faculty member, whose office was not in a suite, interrupted me and said, "Please be sure to push my garbage can all the way underneath the desk the next time you clean the office."

I paused for about a half-second, which felt like an eternity, and not knowing what to say at that moment, I replied "Okay" to the other professor, and hurried to my office suite. I sat at my desk in disbelief at what had just happened. I could feel my face heat up and my heart start to race. The occurrence confused me and prompted me to make sense of it. I started asking myself questions: "Why did he think I was the custodian or the maintenance person? Was it the jeans and black t-shirt I was wearing? Was this the custodian outfit and I didn't know it? Should I have dressed up a bit more—perhaps wear slacks and a dress shirt?" I immediately presented myself with an answer to the last question: "That would have been silly, to move into my new office wearing dressy clothes." But questions kept nagging me: "Didn't the professor even momentarily consider the possibility that I have a PhD just as he does? Couldn't he have suspected that the box was filled not with trash but academic materials or office keepsakes?"

The experience left me feeling baffled and isolated. And it added a needless complication to what was already looming ahead as a very delicate balancing act in which I would strive to distribute my efforts thoughtfully and proportionately to research, teaching, administrative tasks, myself in one city, and my family in another. All I could think about was this single brief encounter: How should I address this issue with the professor? Go back and explain to him that I'm faculty and ask him what it was about me that gave them the impression I was the janitor? I also wondered, was the professor new and did not know that I was a new hire too? All kinds of possibilities were floating around in my head. This is not how I envisioned the start of my first day as a professor. In the end, I decided that I would walk the long way out of the building, get in my car, and move it to the lot. As a way to avoid the professor in question and to avoid causing him embarrassment, I carried each box the long way in the hope that our paths would not cross again that day. I also found myself trying to be as quiet as possible so that neither he nor anyone else for that matter would hear me. By day's end, my confusion had doubled as I'd begun asking myself rather pointedly: Whom was I trying to protect in this situation and why was I afraid to make the other professor uncomfortable?

THE IMPORTANCE OF THE COUNTERSTORIES AND TESTIMONIALS

The experiences that I have shared in this chapter have helped me strike a balance between cultivating myself and achieving my goals—two tasks that are not always necessarily in line with each other. Of course, these two experiences were not the only ones to keep me off balance: We all experience many painful events that wound us, that stay with us through the years, and that often—though not always—remain unobserved by others.

As attested to by many of my colleagues who have written chapters for this book, challenges in the groves of academe can be overwhelming. Whether trying to earn tenure and promotion or to land an administrative job, many faculty members with a Latino background continue to find themselves isolated from and challenged by students, staff, and other faculty. The chapters in this section of the book are both inspiring and heart wrenching. Readers of these chapters observe a weaving together of theoretical constructs with personal experiences and learn that Latino faculty continue to struggle with tenure and promotion issues, particularly while seeking to reconcile home and family with career expectations.

Some authors here discuss students' resistance to issues arising from faculty members' race and ethnicity: student perceptions and assumptions are capable of erecting barriers between students and Latino faculty, in turn impeding faculty development and promotion. Other authors in this section discuss how they navigated isolating and discriminatory structures by relying on friendships with fellow Latinos. Some authors describe unreasonable work expectations that include large teaching loads, few resources, and little collegiality. These same authors note how, by openly affirming their own identity, they overcame such structural obstacles. Many of the authors focus on individual resiliency as a way to be resourceful and even to thrive in the presence of hardship. Others speak about family resiliency as the foundation for a successful academic career. Still others talk about community resiliency and how they—being the only Latino professor in their department or program—have drawn strength from the Latino community outside the given school or college. All of these stories are "counterstories" that should be told and heard—testimonials that matter to the storytellers individually, to colleagues currently serving in the field, and to people who will come to this work in the future. It is these stories that have the power to improve and transform education.

REFERENCES

Montoya, E. M. (1998). Law and language(s). In R. Delgado & J. Stefancic (Eds.), *The Latino condition: A critical reader* (pp. 37–43). Albany: State University of New York Press.

Solorzano, D. G., & Yosso, T. J. (2002). Critical race methodology: Counter-story-telling as an analytical framework for education research. *Qualitative Inquiry, 8*(1), 23–44.

CHAPTER 2

MAESTRITA

Sandra Rodriguez-Arroyo

Sometimes I have a hard time believing that I am a teacher educator. Through many ups and downs, I learned that it was not an easy journey to pursue a higher education degree as a Puerto Rican first-generation student. Nowadays, I remember this journey as I try to motivate myself to continue the tenure track process. As the only Latina faculty in the College of Education of a predominantly White institution (PWI) in the Midwest I have felt isolated, frustrated, and overwhelmed with the research, teaching, and service responsibilities that I have been asked to balance as part of my tenure requirements. Nonetheless, I know that I am in the right place as my students make me feel appreciated, ask me for hugs, and give me the energy to continue what I started in 2011. Through this chapter I share my testimonio as a counter-narrative, confession, and consejo for new Latina faculty, who as I am, are surviving in academia and striving to find a sense of belonging where there is no one who looks like you (Cervantes-Soon, 2012).

Abriendo Puertas, Cerrando Heridas (Opening Doors, Closing Wounds), pages 11–19
Copyright © 2015 by Information Age Publishing
All rights of reproduction in any form reserved.

TESTIMONIOS AS COUNTER-NARRATIVES OF LATINA WOMEN IN ACADEMIA

Scholars have recognized the importance of sharing our testimonios as a "springboard for theorizing about latinidades in the academy, in our communities, and in our lives" (Latina Feminist Group, 2001, p. 2). When as Latina scholars we share our testimonios we recognize how at "every step" in our academic journeys our "professional, personal, and communal identities have come together. At times they clash, create much dissonance, and cause emotional pain" (Delgado Bernal, 2008, pp. 135–136). It is in this process of sharing our testimonios that we grow as a community of scholars and gain the strength not only to continue our journeys, but also to not lose our Latina identity in the tenure process. Cervantes-Soon (2012) emphasizes that

> Testimonios as a pedagogical practice fosters humanizing knowledge stemming from students' and teachers' own narratives of survival and resistance, and promotes theory that offers both a language of critique and a language of hope through the reclamation, transformation, and emancipation of their own lives and communities. (p. 387)

My testimonio is not unique, but is MY testimonio, which is my own counterstory and consejo for those who want to enter this professional path. Through sharing my story, I know that I am not alone; as Latinas we have each other and our cultural roots to ground our mission to become a stronger presence in academia.

MY JOURNEY INTO ACADEMIA: FROM TEACHER TO TEACHER EDUCATOR

Sandra, ven acá. Esta es mi maestrita.
(Sandra, come over here. This is my little teacher.)

My first memory of considering an education career was when I was a little girl and my father called me his "maestrita" (little teacher). I will never forget the conviction that my dad used every time to introduce me to his friends. Most times, I dragged my feet to where my dad was talking to his friends and felt ashamed that he was calling me maestrita AGAIN. In contrast, I was told at school that I had to become a doctor, because I was an "A" student, and smart students should not become teachers. According to some teachers and school counselors, teaching was for those who did not have any other options. Therefore, I decided that I was going to become a psychologist, because they were doctors. Still, my dad would not let it go, and even when I kept denying I was his maestrita, he never stopped.

In high school something happened that made me think that I could actually become a teacher. One day after class I had a talk with my eleventh grade history teacher, Mrs. Torres, during which I shared how for career day I had shadowed the social worker at the school and I was not sure that I wanted to be a psychologist anymore. I did not want to sit all day inside an office listening to other people's problems. Mrs. Torres then told me that she was a teacher because she knew that she could also be anything else she had considered becoming while growing up. In one day, she could be a psychologist, a nurse, and a performer. Moreover, my teacher also knew that she could not be everything for her students, but she tried to be there for them when they needed her. That was it! My bad view of teaching changed, and I recognized that my dad was right; I did like teaching and until this day I am his *maestrita.*

When I entered college and started taking education and English classes, I was convinced that I made the right decision. I combined two things that I loved: English and teaching. I enjoyed the discussions and knowledge about theories of learning and teaching and dreamed of becoming the best English teacher my students ever had; I wanted students to love English as much as I did. After finishing my teacher education program, I taught for a year and a half year in my hometown, and that was enough to know that to teach English in Puerto Rico, teachers have to understand Puerto Rican history and politics. If teachers do not take time to do this, they will be as I was: unable to understand why English is a combination of fear, hate, and love for Puerto Rican people. As somebody who had learned to love English early in life through bilingual education programs in Boston, I had a hard time understanding why the language was received with such mixed feelings. I did not know that if I wanted to change the image of English I had to be aware of our historical/political circumstances, plus make language learning more relevant to the students' lives, something closer to them. If I could teach English again in Puerto Rico, I would let my students use English language words that express their culture, their history to others, especially to our colonizer. I was not a happy English teacher in Puerto Rico; therefore, when a friend gave me an application to apply to graduate school at Penn State, I did not think it twice and sent it. This is how I started my master's degree in bilingual/multicultural education. I applied to this graduate program because I thought it could be exciting to study a profession that had been part of my education. Although I hate to admit it, I was looking for an escape from what I believed was my failure as a teacher; I knew I was a first-year teacher who could not survive in the schools. I packed some belongings and on a very cold winter afternoon, I arrived in State College, Pennsylvania. This was a tough decision in my life, because I knew I was neither Sandra, the daughter or student, nor Miss Rodríguez, the English teacher; now I was Sandra Rodriguez (without the accent on Rodríguez), and I was a graduate student. At the beginning of my graduate school experience I dreamed of becoming an English professor back in Puerto Rico, but my goal changed when I met and took classes with Dr. Lourdes Diaz-Soto. Her commitment to bilingual education brought back memories of my time as a bilingual education student back in the 1980s in Boston. After finishing my master's degree, I received a doctoral fellowship and decided to continue working towards my doctorate.

It was a long emotional journey that took a toll on my health and tested my commitment every step of the way, but one through which I became a teacher educator. I still remember my doctoral graduation and I saw the proud look on my parents' faces: Their *maestrita* was now a "*doctorcita*" (little doctor). I was told that my dad cried when he heard my name being called as Dr. Sandra Rodriguez-Arroyo. When I asked my dad if he had cried, he did not deny it. He looked at me and said that he was proud to have a daughter with a doctorate, when he was not even able to graduate from high school. I knew this was an important step and I have to keep making him proud.

GIGI AND MENTORSHIP

Throughout my life I have recognized the importance of mentorship. Reyes and Ríos (2005) reaffirm that "for me, service to the broader community and mentoring are inseparable from my professional role as an educator" (p. 384). The first mentor I had at my institution was Dr. Evangelina "Gigi" Brignoni.

I met Gigi when I interviewed for my faculty position on February 2011. I was informed that the doctors had found that Gigi's cancer was back and worse. What started about six years ago as breast cancer made a comeback as bone cancer. The chemo treatment was not working and she later told me her doctors had instructed her to get ready and coordinate her funeral arrangements. Even under these circumstances, Gigi managed to meet me for my interview and let me know she that she needed help. The bilingual and ESL teacher education programs were growing and she could not handle the task by herself. When I finished my job talk, she went into the elevator with me and very firmly took my hand, look me straight in the eyes, and gave me an order: "TAKE THE JOB." Gigi even sent me a message in Spanish a little bit afterwards that made me feel that I did fine during my job interview:

Querida Sandra:

Para mí, fue un gran placer conocerte. Me encantó tu entusiasmo, tu humor, tu humildad, y tu energía. Lo que haces en Penn State es lo que necesitamos en esta Universidad. Lo que sabes, es lo que necesitamos en bilingüe, e (inglés como segunda idioma) ESL. Para mí, fue un martes maravilloso aprender de tí.

Abrazos,

Gigi o como mi abuela escribía—Yiyi

Dear Sandra,

For me, it was a great pleasure to meet you. I really liked your enthusiasm, your humor, your humility, and your energy. What you do at Penn State is what we need at this university. What you know is what we need in bilingual and (English as a Second Language) ESL. For me, it was a wonderful Tuesday to learn about you.

Hugs,

Gigi or like my grandmother wrote it—Yiyi

Thus, when I received the job offer I heard the order in her voice, and I accepted it. When I came to search for an apartment in May 2011, Gigi looked a lot better. The doctors had found another chemo treatment that was working. She met with me and told me that I was "her Christmas gift." Gigi kept in touch all throughout the summer and made sure she welcomed me when I got to Omaha. The day that Gigi stopped by my apartment for a welcome visit, I found out that she was Puerto Rican. Even though she was born in the Bronx and later on moved to California, she was Puerto Rican wherever she was. Gigi told me that being Puerto Rican was another reason why she was so happy I accepted the offer to work with her. During my first fall semester, Gigi made sure I was given the necessary information and that I met all the people that we needed to be in contact with regarding ESL and bilingual education teacher education programs. Whenever there was an event, Gigi would tell me "we'll go together," and we went to Latino banquets, several faculty meetings, community events, Latina women luncheons, documentary viewings, school districts' meetings, and more. Gigi made sure everybody knew I was her "new colleague" and that we were working together. We worked as a team on a new syllabus for our program and redesigned the new course requirements. Even when she was not feeling well, Gigi gave her all and it was a real collaboration where I never felt I was doing more than her. Besides work, she also made sure that I was not alone for my first Thanksgiving in a new city. At that time, Gigi was having a hard time holding anything in her stomach, but she still managed to eat a little bit of the *arroz con gandules* and *flan de calabaza* that I contributed. She had told me that she wanted really badly to eat arroz con gandules! The last time I saw Gigi was in December 2013 during the graduation ceremony. We took a picture together that shows how happy we were to wear our "fancy gowns"; this is the last image I have of her. On January 7, 2012 we received a message that Gigi's health had taken a turn for the worse and that her cancer was attacking her stomach, making her extremely fragile. It was heartbreaking! At our office suite we had a feeling that we were not going to see her again and that any day now we were going to receive the sad news. Gigi passed away Saturday, January 14, 2012 and left me with a feeling of emptiness. I still feel I was not able to say goodbye to my dear Gigi. It has been tough not to have her around and I have missed her terribly! I am grateful that I had her during my first semester to guide me, and I could still hear her voice telling me that she needs me. After Gigi's passing I know I have to continue her work here. Everybody loved her, because she worked with the community and was the reason behind the state now having a bilingual education endorsement. I have some big shoes to follow (not to fill) in this journey, but I have to do it also for her.

My friendship and mentorship relationship with Gigi made a huge difference as I started my first semester in a tenure track faculty position. She made sure I was "*bien cuidada*" (well taken care of) and did not leave me "*ni a sol, ni a sombra*" (day and night). I miss Gigi everyday, especially because we understood each other beyond work, she was my Puerto Rican godmother. In addition, after she passed away my workload had increased tremendously, and there are no hopes of hiring someone to replace her.

CONFESSION: IS THE TENURE TRACK FOR ME?

Cervantes-Soon (2012) describes confessions as "this type of discourse involved making themselves vulnerable by sharing stories about intimate or difficult experiences, or even what they considered shameful behaviors, and the reflections that they provoked" (p. 383). I have a confession to make: I must admit that after Gigi passed away it has not being easy to continue my tenure-track process and I have thought of quitting many times. Some of my White colleagues have tried giving me advice that even if in their minds was well intentioned, it has made me angry, frustrated, and feeling more alone than ever. As an example, the spring 2013 semester was a test to my commitment to be a teacher educator. For the first time, I had the full 12-credit teaching load, which included three classes, four undergraduate student teachers, and three graduate practicum students. This teaching load, in conjunction with my service responsibilities, made it hard to breathe or work on my research. As a result, I started complaining aloud and was scolded for complaining too much. I was advised to stop complaining, because "everyone had a lot of work." While neither my gender nor my culture was mentioned in this interaction, I can hear García's (2005) words: "I began to think more critically about the advice I was often given: to keep my mouth shut. What are the implications of such advice? How many scholars of color in academia are encouraged or forced into silence?" (p. 261). I now realized that in my colleagues' minds I was going against the Midwest culture of being nice and working hard. Sometimes I feel like my colleagues want me to become more like them, but as time passes I affirm my identity as a Latina even more. For example, although I have followed my colleagues' advice and avoid the negative complaints near White colleagues, I have not stayed silent.

As part of the requirements for the tenure and promotion documents that I turn in every fall, I have to include three personal reflections on the areas of research, teaching, and service. For my first two years I wrote very positive reflections, but for my third-year review documents, I broke my silence. In my reflections, I spelled out my responsibilities and explained why my research is suffering, why the advice of "protecting my research time" is not realistic with a ¾ load, and I expressed how I was feeling about being the only Latina faculty in the College of Education. I do not know how Gigi did all this work! In addition, I shared my need to keep connected with my Latino/a roots, to not lose myself in the tenure process, because it would be like losing who I am. Until this day, I have not received any formal feedback from those who read my documents acknowledging my words, nor the fact that I am the only Latina faculty in the College of Education. I must admit that it is disappointing when higher education institutions choose to not address the elephant in the room and take steps towards ensuring more representation of diverse faculty members (Ponjuan, 2011).

I know I still have a purpose in my PWI, and while some colleagues may feel that I am giving up and that I am looking for a new job, that is not the case. I love what I do, and I feel the need to tell my *testimonio* to confess and heal, so I can move on and be successful in this tenure-track process.

CONSEJOS: MOVING FORWARD IN THE TENURE PROCESS WITHOUT LOSING MYSELF

My parents taught me that I should surround myself with people who will support me in my personal and professional life. Therefore, I am taking the steps to surround myself with positive personal and professional relationships that support the work that I do and do not ignore the fact that I am Latina. This past fall, through the Office of Latino/Latin American Studies (OLLAS) at my institution, I was given the responsibility to chair the OLLAS Cumbre keynote session with Dr. Pedro Noguera. I was scared, but I knew it was a big honor. After the fact, I must admit that this moment was the highlight of my academic career. I was extremely happy, but it was also a wake-up call that I needed to keep my connections with OLLAS, with the Latino community, and with other Latino scholars around the country. These connections to the Latino community reaffirm my culture and make me feel at home in the Midwest.

Since then, I have attended AAHHE (American Association of Hispanics in Higher Education) as a faculty fellow, went back to AERA to reconnect with the larger teacher education community, and attended two junior faculty workshops with others who looked and talked like me. From all these opportunities, I kept receiving the same *consejo*: "Conduct research on who you are and what you love." In the past year, I have also joined a community group that meets once a month with Latino youth to help to develop the new generation of leaders. It is not an easy task to explain why I am doing this work, as it is always considered service and not scholarship, but I need to do it for my own sanity, and it is my way of seeking balance in a PWI (Ponjuan, 2011). Moreover, Tuitt, Hanna, Martinez, Salazar, and Griffin (2009) send me a reminder that

> I cannot let them change my sense of purpose or weaken my resolve to demand justice and pave the way for young people of color who might not otherwise see images of themselves in academia. I must stand in the way of disregard, dismissal, ignorance, and the steadfast desire to do things the "way they have always been done." For me, this is the key to dealing with the microaggressions and macro-oppressions that are endemic to this work—the understanding that my job, having arrived in this place, is to stand in the line of fire. (p. 70)

I am very aware that my presence as a Latina in academia entails a double responsibility. This is a difficult fact to convey to my White colleagues as I am here for both my mainstream White students and for my diverse students. I have to keep standing in the line of fire to pave the way for future generations of Latino professionals. The tenure and promotion process sends me the message to not rest assured that I have a faculty job, but I am trying to not let it control my life. My family in Puerto Rico reminds me that I still need to live, that frustration and anger will take away my happiness. My colleagues may never understand that my Puerto Rican family is part of my balance and the reason why I go home twice a year is to get the energy to continue my work in the United States.

It took two years on my tenure-track faculty position to realize that I need to own the fact that I am a Latina in academia and that even if I am the only one in the college, I have to reaffirm my identity and share it with others. One way I do this is through cooking Puerto Rican food for my students towards the end of the semester. Even though some people have called me crazy for doing this with the amount of work that I have, I know I need to continue this tradition that I started back at Penn State when I was a TA. It is a way of sharing Puerto Rican culture and making sure my students understand that Puerto Rican food is not Mexican food (it has spices, but it is not spicy). But it is also a great way to create community and relax for a bit! I love cooking, and my students appreciate my efforts. The other day a student told me to never stop cooking for my students; it helped him learned something about Puerto Rico, as he knew nothing before then. I do not make excuses anymore, and it brings me a sense of happiness and family every time I do it.

To end, my cousin the other day let me know that *there is no doubt* that I will get my tenure, that *these* people do not *know* me as they (my family) do, and that I *always* finish what I start. Her words were a reassurance that I need to continue this journey and go back to those moments when my dad called me *maestrita.* He never doubted my calling and I should believe in myself with the same conviction that he and others do.

REFERENCES

Cervantes-Soon, C. G. (2012). Testimonios of life and learning in the borderlands: Subaltern Juárez girls speak. *Equity & Excellence in Education, 45*(3), 373–391.

Delgado Bernal, D. (2008). La trenza de identidades: Weaving together my personal, professional, and communal identities. In K. P. González & R. V. Padilla (Eds.), *Doing the public good: Latina/o Scholars engage civic participation* (pp. 135–148). Sterling, VA: Stylus.

García, A. (2005). Counter stories of race and gender: Situating experiences of Latinas in the academy (Reflexiones Pedagógicas section). *Latino Studies Journal, 3*(2), 261–273.

Latina Feminist Group. (2001). *Telling to live: Latina feminist testimonios.* Durham, NC: Duke University.

Ponjuan, L. (2011). Recruiting and retaining Latino faculty members: The missing piece to Latino student success. *Thought and Action, 27,* 99–110.

Reyes, X. A., & Ríos, D. I. (2005). Dialoguing the Latina experience in higher education. *Journal of Hispanic Higher Education, 4*(4), 377–391.

Tuitt, F., Hanna, M., Martinez, L. M., Salazar, M., & Griffin, R. (2009). Faculty of color in the academy: Teaching in the line of fire. *Thought and Action, 25,* 65–74.

CHAPTER 3

ON THE TENURE TREK TO EQUANIMITY

¡Oh, Cúan Lejos LLegarás!

Vonzell Agosto

Through writing this self-reflective inquiry into the hyphens between work-life, life-work, and life-world I am crystallizing a way of walking in the world that feels good to me ethically, spiritually, and emotionally. I characterize this initial leg of my academic journey as being on the tenure trek to equanimity. My developing ideas about equanimity are framed in part as a culturally diverse discourse of thriving in academia that highlights central concepts in my educational philosophy and research program: culture, justice, and curriculum. To discuss equanimity in relationship to being on a tenure trek, I refer to the scholarship of McRae (2013) who draws on Tibetan Buddhist philosopher and yogi Patrul Rinpoche (1808–1887) to advance a feminist-Buddhist concept of equanimity. She describes equanimity as a feeling with affective and cognitive components that is cultivated through the reduction of aversion and craving in order to develop the emotional maturity, self-awareness, and openness needed to reduce bias and prejudice that interferes with loving relationships and moral judgment. Equanimity

Abriendo Puertas, Cerrando Heridas (Opening Doors, Closing Wounds), pages 21–33
Copyright © 2015 by Information Age Publishing
All rights of reproduction in any form reserved.

concerns balance as an evenness in temperament rather than evenness in effort or time expended.

In seeking equanimity rather than balance, I am heeding Caproni's (1997) claim that "you can't get there from here" (p. 46). She asks if balance is even what one should seek given that the discourse of work–life balance is shrouded in "language that promotes predictability, control, individual achievement, hierarchy of values, constant movement toward goals, and compartmentalization of life" (p. 47). I find equanimity to be more consistent with a notion of balance symbolized by the Egyptian goddess Maat rather than with the Roman goddess Justitia. While balance associated with Justitia was represented by scales of justice symbolizing the weighing of contributions to justice and injustice, balance associated with Maat involved order, truth, and justice in the universe and among people as well as the weighing of one's heart or conscience. Furthermore, images of Justitia portray her as blindfolded, while not those of Maat, who therefore more closely symbolizes the impartiality (elimination of bias), is described by McRae (2013) in a stance one cultivates rather than a position one undertakes (to act as if one is veiled or blindfolded). McRae (2013) characterizes equanimity as a practice of impartiality that eliminates bias at the interpersonal level and expands our sphere of genuine concern by removing the major psychological obstacles (i.e., craving and aversion) (McRae, 2013).

My aspiration to develop equanimity is becoming clearer to me through using *currere*, which is the Latin root of the word curriculum, signifying movement around a track as well as a phenomenological and existential approach to understanding educational experience. Unlike Pinar (1975), I am engaging the method of *currere* without having "sat zazen, the Zen Buddhist meditation" (p. 5). Instead, my trek has been informed by "working the hyphen" in inquiry with others (Fine, 1994), as well as myself. According to the life-world philosophy of Ogata Masato, one should seek connectedness: a strong sense of being connected organically to a rhizome-like life-world and to those from one's past and present (a spiritual community). Life-world is a translation of the Japanese terms "seimei sekai" (生命世界), or "inochi no sekai" (いのちの世界) (Yoneyama, 2012). It is a philosophy that provides ethical and spiritual dimensions that are not covered by the system–society perspective. Likewise, in the method of *currere*, the investigator has an obligation to speak from where she lives and make clear her biographic basis (Pinar, 1975).

My ideas about walking, working, and living are developing through reflection on my positionality and the relationships I have had with people and contexts, past and present. The people, places, and relationships invoked, explicitly and implicitly, in this self-reflective inquiry are shaping me in the current moment (Smith, 2013). Moreover, the distance between the researcher and subject (I, me) is bridged and a clearer understanding of the present is gained by outlining the past, present, and future (Pinar, 1975).

My roots inform my educational trajectory from teacher to aspiring doctoral student and professor/scholar. I am a woman who identifies as mixed-race and multiethnic with a hyphenated African-American/Black and Mexican American heritage that includes creole roots from New Orleans. While kith and kin of Latino descent are central in this reflection on how I am coming to think about and seek equanimity across work, life, and world, honoring them should not be understood as the devaluation or neglect of people and ideas from other racial and/or ethnic groups who have contributed enormously to my personal and professional growth. In the fashion of *currere,* my narrative flows from reflection on events and relationships into my analyses of them to affect the development of my thinking about equanimity, or as I have learned to say in Black English Vernacular: "stay cool." To communicate this trek I use additional languages of beauty, from the whimsical rhymes of Dr. Seuss (in Spanish and English; 1990, 1993) to concepts invoked in Buddhist and Chicana feminist philosophy.

HOW FAR I HAVE COME TO BE HERE

Almost a decade ago I deliberated about whether or not to remain a high school teacher or leave it to pursue graduate studies. My friend Roman, who is also multiracial/ethnic (Mexican-American and White), had been accepted into graduate school and received a fellowship that was paying for his tuition and providing him a stipend. As more of a whim than the pursuit of a life's dream, I sought a similar arrangement. Roman gave me his graduate record examination (GRE) note cards and soon after I was accepted (to my surprise) into two doctoral programs. However, when it came time to decide whether or not to leave teaching, I weighed the decision more heavily, for it meant that I would be leaving Latino males in the hallways. Those who I urged to class each day, while most other teachers passed by them, might be left posturing against their lockers. They, like I, were in a position to consider Dr. Seuss' questions.

Do you dare to stay out?
¿Te atreves a quedarte?
Do you dare to go in?
¿Te atreves a entrar?
¿Cuando puedes perder?
How much can you lose?
How much can you win?
¿Cuanto puedes ganar?

I entered my first semester of doctoral study in a research extensive institution with the thought that I had no clue about what was before me and whether I would succeed.

I cannot recall being told that I would go far in life. Although elders seemed to think I was smart in some way, they did not tell me with any consistency what path I should seek. Although talk of a career path was nonexistent in my family, I have to realize that I was being prepared to be a kind of person, not a kind of worker, so that no matter the career path I chose I would have the knowledge, skills, and dispositions to be in relationship with other lives (including my own) in a nondestructive way.

You have brains in your head.
You have feet in your shoes
You can steer yourself any direction you choose.
Con cerebro en tu cabeza.
Con pies en tus zapatos.
Cualquier dirección escojerás que tus pies quieran encontrar.

I was being taught to be docile: to accept the authority of adults without question and remain quiet unless spoken to. But I was also being taught to be socially skilled (listen, pay respect, be frugal). In the *Merriam-Webster Dictionary*, docile is defined as both (1) easily taught and (2) easily led or managed (docile, n.d.). While the latter definition is more commonly used today, I see both operating in schools today as educators struggle with the boundaries between them. This struggle is perhaps more prevalent today with the word *discipline* given that one of its meanings is fading into obsolescence: instruction (discipline, n.d.). The paradoxical nature of docility was demonstrated to me by the first Latina I met, my mother. She was Mexican-American, a second-generation U.S. citizen who was bilingual (Spanish/English). As far as I know she was attracted to Black/African-American men (one of whom was my father) rather than women. Although I saw her as someone with a quiet disposition, I also learned to see her as disobedient with regard to the status quo of racial politics during the time she was coming of age (1940s–1950s).

Even later, at the time of my birth, when the racial politics included the illegality of interracial marriage (at least in one state), she defied her family. Despite her mother's expectation that she would seek a Mexican or Mexican-American partner (i.e., husband), my mother did not conform. Her challenge to the racial status quo of the time is a spirit I have undertaken, which comes across in my research interests in multicultural education, participation in a global mentoring network, and preference for being in the company of people from various racial and/or ethnic groups—romantically and platonically. The hyphen between my racial-ethnic identity markers (African-American and Mexican-American) means that I am working the margins daily as a mixed-race person and as someone who sees the margins as bridges and bridges as good places to hang out—not just points of transition to and from other places.

If my mother was docile in her temperament, she was less so in her praxis. According to *Merriam-Webster Dictionary*, "temperament" is defined as "the constitution of a substance, body, or organism with respect to the mixture or balance of its elements, qualities, or parts" (temperament, n.d.). Through her life I have been taught to attune to temperament as a constellation of elements that constitutes the substance of one's character and consider the body as racialized, gendered, classed, and organized within a larger set of structures (i.e., organizations and institutions such as marriage, education, or society). I find the word *temperament* to be closer to what I mean by equanimity and relevant to praxis: a way of walking in the world. I wonder if by some rhizomatic meander I have come to land on the body and organisms/organizations as characterized by Deleuze (1969) or Deleuze and Guattari (1980): a body without organs. At least I am certain I have returned to Moraga (1981) and Anzaldúa (1987) and their articulation of a theory of the flesh based on the physical realities experienced by women of color: a theory conducive to forming a society in which they can heal. My return to their scholarship is characteristic of the method of *currere* in which one attempts to extract the existential meaning of the present to create a fuller portrait of the curriculum of one's life that includes the physical self (Pinar, 1975).

THEORY OF THE FLESH

During the second semester of my first year of teaching as an assistant professor in a research extensive university, a student informant disclosed to me that other students in the Master's level course had questioned if I was Black. In hallway discussions some expressed uncertainty about my race and ethnicity and tried to determine it through analyzing the texture of my hair. I subscribe to the racial/ethnic identifiers Black/African-American with Creole roots in New Orleans and Mexican-American: biracial and multiethnic. According to the informant, on one occasion a fellow student left class asking classmates if I was married. The student noted that I mentioned having a child but they did not see a wedding ring on the index finger of my left hand. Even though I was an assistant professor and well past my teenage years, their comments and questions revived my memory of stereotypes about unwed teenage girls of color (especially Latinas and African Americans). I recalled my determination as a teenager to avoid becoming an example of the stereotype featured in public service announcements (PSAs): poor Black/Mexican teenagers who become pregnant and undereducated mothers. I felt the students' comments were building into a role and I was being typecast as the unwed mother with my child as the bastard son. My trust in students had been challenged and I felt a painful loss after teaching youth (high school, undergraduate level) the prior two decades with joy.

And when you're in a slump,
You're not in for much fun.
Cuando en la bajada estés,
divertida la cosa no la será,
Un-slumping yourself is not easily done.
Y des-bajarte ardua empresa resultará.

My soul was wounded upon hearing that these and more scathing comments (communicated by another informant) were being circulated by students (which the first informant labeled racist). As a first-year assistant professor, my hazing signified a "struggle of the flesh, and struggle of borders, an inner war" (Anzaldúa, 1987, p. 100). The body, in general, provides a site from which to theorize the "flesh and blood experiences of the woman of color" (Moraga, 1981, p. 23). A sense of self-doubt clouded my thinking and I grew conscious of my fingernails. I questioned whether I should polish them or avoid polishing them for fear the polish would peel and students' disgust for me could be provoked and attributed to my body rather than my race, ethnicity, and gender: to my less than pristine nails. A sense of dull heaviness arose and I looked down at my nails in judgment and fought back the extension of that sensation to my lips, toes, buttocks, and so on. Such moments remind me how permeable the hyphen between work and life can be. The sensation of being assaulted traveled from their comments on my hair and index finger toward my fingernails, thereby illustrating the idea of the body subject: the direct relationship between the human body and its world (Buttimer, 1976).

I recall having the sensation of dull heaviness come and urge me to look at my fingernails while playing volleyball. This instance was particularly disturbing since the volleyball court was my refuge from the academic institution and I had not identified any institutional space that would allow me to express these sensations as I felt them. The discourse in the institution regarding the annual review process and teaching narratives emphasized reflection and change in response to various demands and expectations. However, there was risk in attributing the low ratings of my teaching to others' racial bias. I continue to feel the burden of having to internalize the problem so that I can reflect on areas where I need to improve and taking full responsibility for those who enter the classroom prejudging me as incompetent, unwed, and too smart to be a woman of color. Over time, I have come to know the types of students who find me problematic (by gender, class, race, intellectual experience, and ideological leanings). If a divide truly existed between the work of teaching and life, then the effects would not enter other spaces and places, nor matter in the materiality of my annual evaluation to affect my income and professional status.

During my first year as an assistant professor I developed a refrain: recovery through resubmission. It communicates my determination to harness whatever energy I have left after being rejected and redirect it into the same or a different activity where I would like to be successful (another publication, proposal, course development). Even though this approach helps me to work through disappointment and redirect it into resilience, it does not liberate me from the pressures of having to perform. "[T]here is a deep alienation in the experience of constantly living to perform" (Lynch, 2010, p. 55). Additionally, recovery through resubmission serves as a strategy in my pursuit of life-work and life-world equanimity. For instance, recovery from the semester described above led me to analyze the role of the gym, how working out mattered. I found that spin class (stationary bike riding to music) allows me to release negative energy; yoga allows me to relax into a brief nap; volleyball allows me the connectedness that comes from working collaboratively as part of a team; and lifting weights allows me to develop strength and stamina. Practice that involves healing, energy, naps, connectedness, strength, and stamina has been critical in helping me mediate the intensities that have been provoked in me during the first five years of my tenure trek.

Fortunately, I have taught many students who have embraced me and my teaching, even in that semester. They helped me to heal the wounds. As that particular course section was ending, another student read from the book by Dr. Seuss, *Oh, the Places You'll Go!* (1990). She offered an inspirational tale in which a former teacher encouraged her to continue her education. She (a White woman), the informants (who were women of color), and a few other students in the class helped me to persist into the next semester.

¡Oh, cuan lejos llegarás! ¡Que divertido será!
Oh, the places you'll go! There is fun to be done!
Hay puntos que anotar. Juegos que ganar.
There are points to be scored. There are games to be won.

However, it has taken a few years for some of the joy of teaching to be replenished, which is now intermittent at best. Just recently, my struggle of the flesh while teaching has been rewarded in 2014 by the Leadership for Social Justice (LSJ) Special Interest Group (SIG) of the American Education Research Association (AERA).

THE HIDDEN (IN THE CLOSET) CURRICULUM OF ACADEMIC LIVES

I had taught half the day and decided to take a late afternoon flight, which was delayed. Therefore, I arrived after the awards ceremony but was later recognized. Adding to the celebration of the moment was that my dear friend Frank was taking minutes as the SIG's secretary. We had met ten years ago in graduate school during a seminar he co-taught on diversity and educational leadership. Soon after that, we were sitting at the table as graduate student representatives as part of the student government. Frank is a man of Mexican descent whose spirit I feel is intensely healing. Through meeting him I was able to bridge my personal and academic lives in the transition from educator in a secondary school with a racially diverse student, staff, and faculty to doctoral student on a campus with a student population that was predominantly White.

It was in a seminar Frank led where I first saw a White woman cry after watching someone shout accusations of racism in a video. I was stunned at her reaction and wondered why she was crying when the people of color in the class were not, and why she did not hold back tears as I had. I was also perturbed by the event, her explanation (a feeling of helplessness and uncertainty about what do about racism), and that much attention went to comforting her rather than those who were holding back tears. I did not speak but listened instead, as did Frank, who was the facilitator and model. I was challenged to check my biases, show restraint in order to work toward understanding through dialogue, and calm myself. "Whenever we are able to respond to a situation without reacting out of feelings of craving or aversion, we are exhibiting equanimity" (McCrae, 2013, p. 452). Overall, the seminar also challenged my perception that educational leadership was an academic and professional field devoid of concerns for diversity and social justice. Having such a friend, mentor, role model, and ally allowed me to transition my focus from work-life to academic-life and adjust to the social and academic demands of graduate school. Frank was instrumental in helping me develop equanimity across life, work, and world. He is also the only one in my academic community who has met my previous partner—Chris.

Chris is Puerto Rican. It is from her that I gained my surname Agosto. Over the first ten years of our relationship, we loved deeply and hated one another nearly as intensely. Across the next ten years we settled into a relationship for which I have not found a name that seems appropriate. Sometime during the first ten years, I came home one day after having a difficult week of teaching and meetings concerning a student whose violence was directed against students and adults. Chris said I could quit my job if I wanted to and not worry about paying bills. Although I did not quit, I will always remember that feeling of calm that came with knowing I had a choice of leaving if I wanted to leave but also realizing that I wanted to stay. Equanimity "has a clear affective component, which is the light and expansive feeling of calm and peace" (McCrae, 2013, p. 453). That is the kind of calm I seek today on the tenure trek, which has more to do with my perception and deliberation about opportunities I take or make. My survival in academia is coming through the development of my perceptual ability to know and respond to external and internal cues about where to direct my energies and how to be affected by energies coming at me. I seek to maintain equanimity despite varying intensities and regardless of the im/balance in the quality or quantity of the workload that faces me.

Nunca olvides ser diestro y hábil.
Just never forget to be dexterous and deft.
Y nunca enredes tu pie derecho con el izquierdo.
And never mix up your right foot with your left.

Although these prior experiences while teaching and studying illustrate moments in my coming to embrace equanimity over balance, the current moment (as I prepare to submit my application for tenure and promotion at the end of my fifth year as an assistant professor) comes with a clearer understanding of how these prior experiences are feeding my story of persisting on the tenure track. More troublesome in this story of persistence are the forces that I feel pulling me to be a particular kind of person: one who is careless.

CARE-LESSNESS AND CARE-FULLNESS

In the academy, care is valued when it is professionalized rather than personalized (Lynch, 2010). Lynch (2010) describes how the new managerialism of higher education has intensified the need for a care-less form of competitive individualism in which the "idealized worker is one that is available 24/7 without ties or responsibilities that will hinder her or his productive capacities" (p. 57). The emphasis on workers without a care (who are care-less) has disproportionately negative consequences for women in academia, who tend to be the primary caretakers of friends and family members. "It is assumed that even the care of one's own emotional wellbeing is incidental" (p. 57). In contrast, care-fullness is more inclusive of one's professional and personal life. Yet, in order to maintain care-fullness, I must seek calm amid competing professional and personal demands.

While I was a high school teacher, I read the *Celestine Prophecy*, which reinforced my belief that energy exists between the organic and inorganic and between the living and the dead. I still believe that all energy circulates as part of the universe—not just the university. From that point of view I am never alone, and any pain I cause or bad vibes I give out will likely resonate out into the universe to affect me and others. Both care and justice are intertwined ethics in my attempt to participate in the cosmic community while embracing an academic role. So when I started to face pressures related to external yet internalized demands (publish or perish), I had some confidence that community and energy (positivity, asset perspectives, activity) would offer life support in order for me to persist in what I was beginning to define as my life's work. This perspective is congruent with the life-world philosophy that favors connectedness and communicates the tensions between individual initiatives and institutional pressures (Elliott, Katagiri, & Sawai, 2012). Fortunately, my previous experience had prepared me to enter academia by first scouting out my community to support my well-being. From there I was able to start collaborative research projects through which I have built a support system through good work and working relationships. Also important in my persistence are personal relationships.

My first year on the tenure trek was situated in an agreement between me and Cornelio (the father of my son). Since I had provided the majority of care for our son for the first three years while completing my dissertation and job search, Cornelio agreed to take over being the primary caretaker of our child and home for the next three years. Cornelio left his family and relocated to Florida, meaning the care and acculturation that he and my child had been receiving from family was interrupted. For the first time, Cornelio was leaving his family to live in another state. This was not insignificant for him or his family who have a strong tradition of family gathering and find kinship invaluable. These customs and cultural assets are as strong as depicted in many broad-stroke descriptions of Latino culture (or more specifically for Cornelio—Chicano culture).

The support that Cornelio has provided to me while starting this leg of my career is immeasurable. For the first three years I had minimal responsibilities at home and spent very little time with him or my child. While the tenure clock was ticking, so was the period of me being free of cares (careless) at home. Despite the freedom this arrangement provided, I also awoke each day during years two and three in a fright—counting my publications and checking the calendar. I did not know what stress felt like before I became an assistant professor. In addition to starting many days with pain in my shoulder blade from typing, a hoarse throat from being exhausted, and feeling upset about not being able to clear my mind enough to get an adequate amount of sleep, I knew that he was sacrificing his own career goals. Though he was bonding with his child, his other personal and professional connections were growing more distant. I treated the first three years on the tenure clock as if the mid-tenure review would be my tenure and promotion review to be scheduled for the sixth year. Knowing that I would have to take more responsibility at home meant that I worked with the expectation that I had three years to build a foundation of scholarship that would support my productivity as I transitioned back to doing homework. Honestly, adding to the pressure, I thought my contract would be terminated at mid-tenure if I did not have two to three publications per year, among other concerns I had.

In year three, a friend/colleague asked why I kept saying the university will let me go and why I refused to hang photos in my home. Through our discussion it became clear that my fears were unreasonable given the history of the institution and my productivity up to that point. However, I felt little concern from the institution that I was not caring for me or my family outside of maintaining my position or ensuring that my contract and career would continue. I began to question who I was working for and what I wanted to feel like en route to becoming tenured. The demands to provide service to the field and institution, produce scholarship, write grants, and teach were ever present and I suspect will continue to be so. In year four and five I needed to reconnect with me and my family to ask us what really mattered and how I might care-fully about life-world–work-life.

Pisa con cuidado y gran tacto
Step with care and great tact
y recuerda esto: La vida es un gran juego de equilibrio.
and remember that Life's a Great Balancing Act.

Today, I am much more aware that in addition to gender bias, forces such as neoliberalism influence institutions of higher education in ways that support its commercialization and urge care-lessness as a moral imperative (Lynch, 2010). I take my cue going forward from those who have shown me care (Roman, Frank, Chris, Cornelio) and from McRae (2013), who reminds me that in "properly cultivated equanimity, the love we have for our family members does not decrease but rather serves as a standard to which we raise others" (p. 458). I also have more clarity about the relationship between presence and service, its commoditization, and how it comes with a price tag. To colleagues who request more of my "presence" in the office (2013 annual review) and more service to the institution (as a responsible citizen), I say I have done that and better for I have gained some presence of mind, which helps me to act constructively and direct my energy toward building an international presence. Demands to be present locally and care-less with regard to the amount of service I render take a toll on the care I give to the larger community, myself, and family. Care-fullness comes from being present with those for whom caring and just relations are central. Equanimity supports a life-world of care-fullness for the universe—not just the university. It braces me to work within a system that can be counterproductive to that which it asks of me: to be research productive. Despite the competing demands and forces that would diminish my sense of care (make me care-less) in order that I serve the institution, my inner battle to maintain composure is greater. Acquiring the capacity to sustain calmness or evenness of temperament is congruent with care and justice for it (dis)positions me to challenge neoliberal forces that reduce care to a commodity, gendered biases that benefit men over women, and discourses of care that neglect the value in expressions of care I am giving to and receiving from those outside or marginalized inside the academy. Care-fullness can be a vehicle for developing the emotional maturity, self-awareness, and openness needed to reduce the bias and prejudice that interferes with loving relationships and moral judgment. A tenure trek to equanimity is at minimum a journey to express the full range of care that goes into establishing a career.

REFERENCES

Anzaldúa, G. (1987). *Borderlands/la frontera: The new mestiza.* San Francisco, CA: Aunt Lute Books.

Buttimer, A. (1976). Grasping the dynamism of lifeworld. *Annals of the Association of American Geographers, 66*(2), 277–292.

Caproni, P. J. (1997). Work/life balance: You can't get there from here. *Journal of Applied Behavioral Science, 33*(1), 46–56.

Deleuze, G. (1969). *The logic of sense* (M. Lester with C. Stivale, Trans., 1990). New York, NY: Columbia University Press.

Deleuze, G., & Guattari, F. (1980). *A thousand plateaus* (B. Massumi, Trans.), Minneapolis: University of Minnesota Press.

Discipline. (n.d.). In *Merriam-Webster's online dictionary.* Retrieved from http://www.merriam-webster.com/dictionary/discipline

Docile. (n.d.). In *Merriam-Webster's online dictionary.* Retrieved from http://www.merriam-webster.com/dictionary/docile

Dr. Seuss. (1990). *Oh, the places you'll go.* New York, NY: Random House.

Dr. Seuss. (1993). *¡Oh, cúan lejos llegarás!* (A. Marcuse, Trans.). Lyndhurst, NJ: Lectorum Publications.

Elliott, A., Katagiri, M., & Sawai, A. (2012). The new individualism and contemporary Japan: Theoretical avenues and the Japanese new individualist path. *Journal for the Theory of Social Behaviour, 42*(4), 425–443. doi: 10.1111/j.1468-5914.2012.00496.x

Fine, M. (1994). Working the hyphens: Reinventing the self and other in qualitative research. In N. Denzin, & Y. Lincoln (Eds.), *Handbook of qualitative research* (pp. 70–82). Newbury Park, CA: Sage.

Lynch, K. (2010). Carelessness: A hidden doxa of higher education. *Arts and Humanities in Higher Education, 9*(1), 54–67.

McRae, E. (2013). Equanimity and intimacy: A Buddhist-feminist approach to the elimination of bias. *Sophia, 52*(3), 447–462.

Moraga, C. (1981). La güera. In C. Moraga & G. Anzaldúa (Eds.). *This bridge called our backs: Writings by radical women of color* (pp. 27–34). New York, NY: Kitchen Table Women of Color Press.

Pinar, W. F. (1975, April). *The method of "currere."* Paper presented at the Annual Meeting of the American Research Association, Washington, DC. Retrieved from http://eric.ed.gov/PDFS/ED104766.pdf

Redfield, J. (1993). *The celestine prophecy.* New York, NY: Warner Books.

Smith, B. (2013). Currere and critical pedagogy: Think critically about self-reflective methods. *Transnational Curriculum Inquiry, 10*(2), 3–16.

Temperament. (n.d.). In *Merriam-Webster's online dictionary.* Retrieved from http://www.merriam-webster.com/dictionary/temperament

Yoneyama, S. (2012). Life-world: Beyond Fukushima and Minamata 「いのちの世界」：フクシマとミナマタを超えて. *The Asia-Pacific Journal: Japan Focus, 42*(2), 1–24.

CHAPTER 4

BEING A LATINA IN THE SOUTH

Being "The Other" of "The Others" in the Academic World

Paula Guerra

Right before graduating with my doctorate in curriculum and instruction for mathematics teacher education, I attended a retreat where, I still believe, I got the best advice for new professors I could have gotten. The retreat focused on Latinos/as and how they learn mathematics, the experiences they have, the socialization that leads them to perform the way they do in mathematics, and best practices. The advice came to me from a panel of other professors who were finishing their first year in academia. Their words made so much sense, and their experiences resonated with me. I could understand completely where they were coming from, and I could see where I was going. In this chapter I will describe the result of not following that advice, as well as the ways in which I have been able to balance my impulses with other practices that I am sure those giving the advice would have approved.

Abriendo Puertas, Cerrando Heridas (Opening Doors, Closing Wounds), pages 35–44
Copyright © 2015 by Information Age Publishing
All rights of reproduction in any form reserved.

WHO I AM AND WHERE I COME FROM

I believe my position as a mathematics educator and a Latina is quite unique and beneficial at times; at other times it has seemed as if I was jumping hurdles. Yet jumping hurdles is not all that bad if one completes the race on time, and sometimes one even breaks a record. I was the first in my family to graduate from college, and I am now the first to have master's and doctoral degrees. A woman in mathematics and mathematics education was already an advantage back in my country, where I never had issues finding places to teach. I had choices. I had advantages. Those advantages kept growing once I entered academia, but they also brought bigger responsibilities, bigger risks, and bigger reactions of approval or disapproval from others in academia. Yet, with all that, it was easy to see that being a woman who is not White, knows English, and can do mathematics opened doors since day one, when I was awarded a fellowship by the Organization of American States (OAS) to come to the United States (US) and complete a master's degree.

During my interview for the scholarship, it was clear that it did not matter how well I could do or teach mathematics; it was important that I knew English well. I remember one of the interviewers mentioning that they had just interviewed someone who was highly skilled, who had said he spoke the "language of math" and believed that to be enough. The interviewer made it clear to me that this person was not going to be funded by OAS. Finally my love for the Beatles and American sitcoms was paying back, since I could have a conversation in English, and I also made sure they knew I could pass the TOEFL and GRE tests.

Mathematics and language skills were useful when I was offered a research assistant position to complete my doctorate. Also my strong beliefs in social justice, combined with my teaching practices and will to do research in urban schools, which are populated with Latinos/as in the Southwest of the U.S., made me a good candidate for more financial support to complete my doctorate. So, just like that, I was able to receive higher education at a well-known school in the U.S. for free. There were signs that everything was not always going to be that easy. I may have not been illegal at a small school in a big urban center, but sometimes I was reminded that, in some people's eyes, I was not all that different from the undocumented. Not that I wanted to be. But I did want to make a difference for me and for Latinos/as who were not as lucky as I was. Those signs came from different directions, and I often tried to shut them down.

So I did not believe what my boss at graduate school—one of them anyway—said about me getting job interviews so schools could check off the "Latina box." I believed my skills were needed today in teacher preparation programs, and I had something unique and valuable to offer. I did not think

I was going to be hired just so the school could check a box, after which I would be "the Latina" of the bunch. But at this point in my career I could not pretend that people like my boss were not out there, and I had to begin considering things differently. I knew that once I was out of school in an academic position, I had to be careful with my moves and how I was going to teach and develop my research agenda. So at the retreat I mentioned, when this new professor told us his secret to success, it made sense to me.

THE WISDOM

What this professor said (and I will reveal the wisdom now) was that as new professors we should stay away from being innovative. "Do not try to do something too different," he said. "Until you are tenured, do not call attention to yourself and freak out the students and the other professors." It was sort of sad, but it made complete sense to me. It was the end of innocence to hear someone else say it, but it had crossed my mind. It was like having someone else rip off the Band-Aid.

Everyone at the retreat wanted to make a change. I wanted to make a change. But it was very clear to us that working toward that change in the most efficient ways we could imagine would probably "call attention to us." And this was at every level for me. I realized that my work for social justice was going to raise eyebrows from day one. But I also knew (although it was probably not as clear to me then) that my work toward better ways of teaching mathematics could be one of those "curious" things that maybe older professors, set on their ways, might reject.

But all of us in that room had to be "strategic" about it: We had to secure for ourselves a position where we could experiment and show others that our ideas worked even if they would "freak out" many people at first. That position, that Promised Land, is called "tenure." Achieving tenure, we knew, depended on our blending in somehow; and then again, we needed to be "strategic." I left that retreat thinking that those fears that I had begun having were reasonable, yet I had a fairly good answer for them. Blend in. Be "strategic." And do not call attention to yourself. All of that while doing your best job at an assistant professor position, serving all students—and (in my case) the students of my students, as I work with preservice teachers. This advice was of double relevance for me, being not only a Latina, but also international faculty. So I began my first year of teaching as an assistant professor in a state university in the South of the United States.

I was an assistant professor at a university in the Deep South, certainly a good place not to try to rock the boat from day one. It was a traditional place where at the first orientation we, the new hires, were told that "honestly" it was going to be a little hard to make friends unless you practiced a sport or belonged to a church. I discovered, with time, that one of those activities was more praised than the other. Belonging to a church and religion in general is a very important part of the community. Colleagues and students alike think of it as a higher form of relating to others in the South. Not being religious, and being more of a follower than a player of organized sports, I was a little scared. But, also "honestly," I thought the person who had said this was exaggerating, generalizing his experience about things he liked doing and the ways he related to people. So I moved on with an open mind to my first week at school, where I would meet other professors in my department.

HOW I DID NOT FOLLOW THE ADVICE

I could easily identify a good number of professors in different areas who were (like me) interested in social justice and equity. Most of them, I realized, had been either recently hired or hired at the same time as me. I was still the only Latina. I did not think about it much then. I thought about my job and how issues of language, and particularly interest in Latinos/as and their schooling, were going to be "my thing." In retrospect, being the only Latina did not make me the only one capable of studying those issues. But I do believe that teaching Latinos/as and doing research on Latinos/as can benefit from the mind of a Latina. So I was more than fine with that situation. There were a couple of other faculty members of international origin, and that was, back then, interesting. Later on I would see working with international faculty a relief and a necessity. But all of these colleagues made me feel comfortable, and their liking what I had to say was important.

They, too, wanted to make a difference, and they were also interested in social justice and equity, even applying lenses and asking questions I had not thought about. I believe some of my questions and lenses were also new to them, and that is how I was "the Latina" of the group. I was concerned with the mathematics schooling of Latinos/as and especially Latinas. And I was bringing Latino critical theory (LatCrit) to the table as an everyday thing. So the exchanges with these new "friends in academia" were good and looked promising. Yet they were not able to hide from me that they were not the only ones in the college or department, and that having the numbers does not always mean having a voice. I found that then, more than ever, I was not to "do something too different" from what was being done already. Yet I had my answer. I had the strategy. I was set for success. Then, the faculty who made me feel the most comfortable approached me. They had a plan, a new project. And they wanted me to be a part of it.

That is how I first broke my rule, and how I decided to participate in the organization of—and teaching in—a special cohort of preservice teachers in their senior year, with a social justice theme. Social justice was being taught by a Latina to a class of mostly White girls from the South. And even though this one course taught me a lot about my position as a Latina teaching mathematics methods classes in the South, I still did it again. The second time I was a leader for a similar cohort with teaching English language learners (ELLs) as a theme.

Teaching mathematics methods to preservice teachers can be challenging on its own. I have encountered not only a lack of mathematical knowledge from preservice teachers, but also a less-than-positive attitude toward the content area. This attitude is likely a result of that lack of knowledge combined with poor experiences as students that they are willing to reproduce as teachers. If this situation seems challenging, adding to it social justice and equity, and all this coming from a non-White woman, had very "enlightening" results.

At first sight, students may be confused about where I come from. Even after speaking and showing my accent, still no one is certain. Truth is, just by saying the name of my country, students still may not know where I am from. Without me clearly stating my Latina and my South American origin, I have been asked whether I am Italian or from East Europe. Just by my accent I have been asked whether I am from Brazil, although my looks indicate to them I am not. And some have been even surprised and thinking I am joking when I say where I come from, most likely because of their lack of knowledge about the different countries in South America. But in a few classes I am pretty sure it is clear where I come from, given my practice of sharing experiences I had as a teacher, and my strong interest in social justice and the schooling of Latinos/as. This means a few classes in, students are certain of their position towards me.

At the end of the semester when I taught the social justice group, I learned that White middle-class female students were not likely to trust me with their experiences and have genuine conversations in class. This cohort had three out of four professors who were females and were not White. The only professor who was able to have conversations about issues of social justice in her class was the White female literacy professor. I learned a great deal about resistance, and especially resistance to what I represented to my students as a Latina. My class was filled with "politically correct" statements from my students, as well as their trying to guess what I wanted to hear. Sometimes that meant hearing them say some "positive" comments about Latino families and their involvement in the mathematics education of their children, followed by a negative similar comment about another race, such as African Americans. Other times, not fully aware of the implications of what they were saying, they allowed me directly to see what they really thought of Latinos/as and their children.

The challenging situations that I proposed to them in class, modeling the type of emancipatory education that Freire (1970) talked about, appeared to have led them only to say that I did not focus enough on the mathematics. Conversations in class leaning toward social justice and mathematics were either monologues or long periods of silence. I was not the only one seeing this reality. An Asian professor in the group was getting a similar response from students. And an African American professor saw some of it, although the students communicated with her more. But none of us was able to be part of conversations like the White female professor in the group, who described to us conversations students were having in her class which the rest of us wished we could have been a part of. They might not always have shown the level of critique we would have liked, but we wanted to at least expose the students' ideals and put them out there for discussion.

AND I KEPT ON GOING . . .

Something very similar happened with the ELL group. This group was yet another experiment I decided to do, negating the advice I was given—it seemed to be so long ago at this point, only a year after that retreat. This group in particular challenged my English and claimed to be unable to understand the scope of assignments, how deep they should go into certain issues, and the level of analysis expected. It was not rare for students to roll their eyes at me as I described the assignments over again. Their final statement was that I needed to focus more on "activities" that they could use instead of constantly talking about "meaningful mathematics teaching." Even when I called students out for their disrespectful attitude, they were quick to reject my meeting request and instead emailed my chair, a White male, explaining how hard it was to understand me and my goals for the class. Even when they finally met with me (at the suggestion of the chair), they described being in a situation in which they felt they could not communicate with me, and not because of language, but for lack of a common ground.

That common ground, which we were meant to build as a new space where my students would critique their previous views of Latinos/as and their families—as Latinos/as make up a good number of the ELL students they will be educating—meant more than translating key vocabulary words; it also meant getting to know the culture of the ELL students, having respect for them, and reaching out to the families as the valuable resources they are. Instead, my chair told me that perhaps I should learn more about the White culture of my female students. He said that multicultural education meant for me to be sensitive to their culture, and maybe even be more apologetic for my accent.

WHERE I DID NOT FIND SUPPORT

Such experiences as these made me once again feel that, even if I wanted to blend in and be "White," I would still face some rejection from students with whom I did not share a common background, culture, or even values. Not only that, but I would probably be invited to be less Latina and maintain a demeanor by which perhaps I would try to blend in; yet still I would be rejected. But I am not even close to trying to "pass as White" or be White. My focus has always been to promote changes in education that lead us all to accept people for who they are. In a department that claims to educate teachers to teach in a more global and multicultural society, being reminded that I had to be more aware of my students' White culture, and adjust to it, was at the very least discouraging. So where did I find the energy and gain the interest to go back into the fight? First, I will delineate some places where I thought that I would find that encouragement and even understanding, only to realize quickly that I was wrong.

The first of these places was in class, as a student. My well-intentioned White professors who taught me a lot about theory could not see how they failed in their own practice. I once read Ellsworth (1997) talking about this issue. It is possible for White folks to not only understand but also practice what they teach about. But this is not always the case. It was clear to me that even with those informed professors we still had to walk an extra mile to be at the same level as White students.

It was hard for me to take their place as well, so I could not blame the professors for not taking mine. They wanted to provide a space for our voices and skills to be heard and seen, but sometimes they did not know what that would look like, or what that would mean. I often think of it in terms of Susanita's approach to helping the poor in Quino's *Mafalda*. More academically, it reminds me of the attempts by Freire's oppressor to liberate the oppressed.

I did not find support, either, in other groups that I believed might have experienced something like what I experienced, such as African American colleagues. Keeping in mind where I taught, and knowing there was an important group of African American professors in the department and college, I thought they would be the safety net I needed—or they would be the people I could go to with my concerns, who would understand me without my having to spell it out. I was wrong once again. Perhaps we are all so focused on our particular situations that we cannot break the mold we have created for ourselves to understand others who are even a little different. How can we talk about not stereotyping others when we do it ourselves and we even stereotype ourselves by not being able to see how similar we are with one another, and focus on differences? In a mix that probably bothers other people too, I find good intentions mixed with distrust. But it does not always have to be that way. In fact, I did find people who helped me in and out of the office to balance things out and to see the good there is out there as well.

WHERE I FINALLY FOUND SUPPORT

I found the network that I needed. I found the people to go to in order to voice my concerns, fears, and innovative ideas. These people would have been other Latinos/as at my school if there were any. Every time I took part in the Center for the Mathematics Education of Latinos/as (CEMELA) retreats, I found a big support system where explanations were not necessary. Given the lack of other Latinos/as in my department and college, however, I found that other international faculty were the "go to" in times of doubt or excitement for new projects. These were my tools for achieving balance: international faculty at my department and college and CEMELA.

In CEMELA I found an outlet for the work I am passionate about. CEMELA is not only concerned with teaching and learning mathematics, but it is a center for Latinos/as. There is a joy that comes along with anything I do that I think will change and improve the quality of education of Latino children. CEMELA faculty are committed to ensuring Latino children have access to quality mathematics education. Latinos/as or not, members of CEMELA have been able to blur those lines that could divide them, and no one thinks of himself or herself as a "liberator" of others; we are all on the same side. The people I have met there give me hope. And when I say there are some who are not Latinos/as, I mean that they are from all over the world and from all kinds of cultures. It may be that a group accepting of anyone and everyone just because we have the same goal makes people humble and ready to open up to give to and take from others. It is a similar experience with the diverse group of people I work at my college.

In my department and college, just like in CEMELA, it almost does not matter where the international faculty come from. There are not other Latinos/as in that group—not Latinos/as of international origin or born in the U.S. And I make the distinction because Latinos/as born in the U.S. not always have to deal with critiques to their accent, and they are likely to understand certain "American discourses" and "American ways" to do simple things, that we, people of international background, still have to learn and remember each time. It is sometimes simple things, like waiting for the waiter to seat you in a restaurant, and be ready for the times they come to ask you if "everything is OK." But those small things, when you do not know them, earn you surprised and sometimes disapproving looks. In that network at my department, I count people from every continent. Different races, religions, genders, ages, and sexual orientations may make for a group that looks eclectic, yet we have a clear identity. And probably because we expect to have very little in common, we celebrate those things that we do share.

The things we have in common are various. It has always amazed me how, it seems, my culture has so much in common with those of my Korean and Turkish friends. Sometimes I wonder if this searching and finding of a common ground with them serves as a way for us to comfort each other. The comfort is knowing there is nothing wrong with our culture and that it is all right to talk about the things we do differently, because these do not make us bad or weird. Instead, maybe we can try and learn. And I am talking about small things: what we do when we get sick, or the way we go from one part of the city to another. More often than not, there are commonalities, and we know that this person who grew up on the other side of the world understands. This is so different from my first encounter with the White culture at the college where I graduated, where in the very first meeting held on campus, an international student meeting, we were told not to spit and burp on campus. I think at that very moment all of us, international students, started a community where we would accept each other with our differences and our commonalities.

But one other thing that my international colleagues and I happen to have in common is the relationships we build with our White students and the American faculty. Those relationships are often very similar. It is with these colleagues that I find a safe place to talk about my experiences, share my ideas, and confide my concerns. They also help me check myself; and with their understanding, which they have from a position similar to my own, I feel valued and cared for as a human being. It is with them that I can proudly say I am a Latina without wondering whether they think I should apologize for that. These are the colleagues I can call "friends" first, who help me cope with the not-so-great parts of my work and personal life as well, because our experiences outside of school also happen to be similar. But it is not all about "coping": they are my friends, and they make me feel more connected with the world. And the more I know about them, the more they also know about me, my country, and my culture. And I believe that is what globalization should be about: feeling connected with people with whom at first we thought we had nothing in common. It is from that connection that I draw the happiness to continue fighting and working for social justice and the strength to do so even when the conditions are less than favorable.

REFERENCES

Ellsworth, E. (1997). Double binds of whiteness. In M. Fine, L. Weis, L.C. Powell & L. Mun Wong (Eds.), *Off White: Readings on race, power, and society* (pp. 259–269). New York, NY: Routledge.

Freire, P. (1970). *Pedagogy of the oppressed* (M. Bergman Ramos, trans.). New York, NY: Continuum.
Quino, & Davis, J. (2004). *Toda Mafalda* (8 edition). De La Flor.

CHAPTER 5

EVERYTHING I NEEDED TO KNOW TO SUCCEED IN ACADEMIA I LEARNED AS A MIGRANT WORKER

An Autoethnographic Account

Raymond V. Padilla

INTRODUCTION

This chapter is an autoethnographic account of my growing up as a migrant worker and winding up as an academic. The disparity between the point of origin and the final destination is so great that the journey merits some reflection to see what insights we might gain. There seems to be much that can be learned from our lives, our histories, and our stories. In the Latino tradition, personal narratives often are called *testimonios*. To provide a *testimonio* is to bear witness to lived experience. It is a way to turn personal experience into shared community history.

I'll start with a very short autobiography based on photographs—a kind of "photo bio" or narrated "selfie"—so that you may know something about

Abriendo Puertas, Cerrando Heridas (Opening Doors, Closing Wounds), pages 45–61
Copyright © 2015 by Information Age Publishing
All rights of reproduction in any form reserved.

me, the storyteller. Then I will sketch, in the manner of Durkheim, a general framework for discussing the similarities between migrant worker experiences and life as an academic. Elaboration of details and some examples will put a little meat on the framework and, hopefully, make my case.

SHORT PHOTO BIO

For the purpose at hand, my autobiography can be presented in eight photos and one drawing. Photo 1 shows me as a baby. This picture was taken so that my father, who at the time was working in the U.S. as a Mexican *bracero*, could see his new son. I was born in the state of Jalisco, Mexico in the middle of the Battle of the Bulge during World War II while my father was a guest worker in the U.S. In those days, Mexicans were invited into the U.S. as guests so that they could do important work while the U.S. was embroiled in world war. It's ironic that Mexicans have kept on coming ever since, even as the U.S. has withdrawn the welcome mat to a large extent.

Photo 1

While in junior high school (Photo 2) I lived in Austin, Texas, the winter respite from our summer migrant travels in the Midwest. I attended Allan Junior High School in Austin, Texas and lived in Montopolis, easily the most impoverished neighborhood in Austin. I wrote a short narrative about my experiences in junior high school in a book that Kenneth Gonzalez and I edited (Gonzalez & Padilla, 2008).

Photo 2

Being poor and temporarily out of college to earn some money, in May of 1966 I got drafted by the U.S. Army during the Vietnam War (Photo 3). I guess that I didn't have the pull or the savvy to get into the National Guard. Going to Canada to avoid the draft was not in the tool kit of a barrio boy.

Photo 3

Photo 4 shows me as an undergraduate student at the University of Michigan where I studied after I was discharged from the Army. I earned a bachelor's degree in Spanish language and literature. I also met my wife (Mary) at the university (Photo 5). At the time there were only about a half dozen Chicano undergraduates at the University of Michigan, and I was active in organizing them into a group called Chicanos at Michigan (CAM).

Photo 4

Photo 5

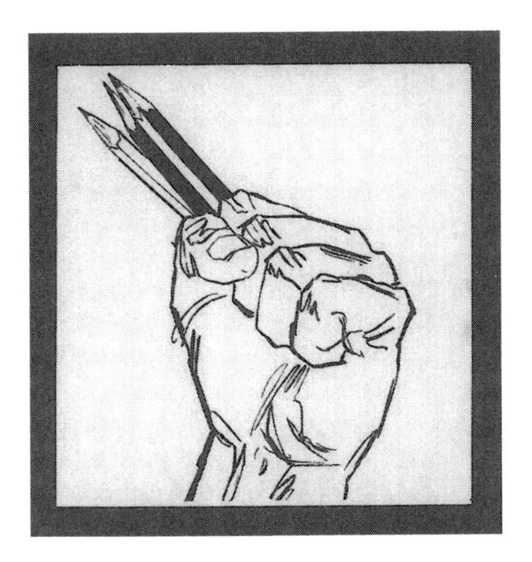

Figure 5.1

After graduating from the University of Michigan, I was hired by the university as the first Chicano recruiter in that institution. Together with other Chicano/Latino recruiters in the state, we created the Association of Chicanos for College Admissions (ACCA). Figure 5.1 shows the logo of the association. Think: "Acá está la papa!" (The good stuff is here!) Ramiro Gonzalez of Delta College (also a Vietnam veteran) did the drawing. This drawing portrays well the energy and idealism of the Chicano movement of the 1960s and early 1970s that spread like wildfire throughout the United States.

While working as an admissions counselor and recruiter at the University of Michigan, I found my calling and decided to pursue doctoral studies in higher education. Photo 6 shows me as a graduate student during the early 1970s at the University of California at Berkeley where I earned a PhD in higher education administration.

Photo 6

After graduation from UC Berkeley and doing a short stint at the Michigan Department of Education as a higher education consultant, I became a professor at Eastern Michigan University (EMU) and also Director of Bilingual-Bicultural Teacher Education Programs. Photo 7 shows me with a student while I was working at EMU. Finally, Photo 8 shows me as a retired old man telling you this story.

Photo 7

Photo 8

ACADEMIC SUCCESS AND THE MIGRANT WORKER EXPERIENCE

What does it mean to be successful in academia? For me success in academia means to master and carry out at least two of the three main activities

- Values
- Knowledge
- Skills
- Attitude

Figure 5.2 Drivers of academic success.

characteristic of academia: teaching, research, and service to the profession and the community. As a student, success in academia means that one excels in one's studies and graduates. As a professor, it means competence as a teacher, productivity in creating new knowledge, and rendering service to the profession and the larger community.

So what is it that drives success in academia either as student or professor? To keep things simple, let us agree for now on a short list of academic success drivers. As shown in Figure 5.2, the list includes values, knowledge, skills, and attitude. Let's look briefly at each of these success drivers.

VALUES

Figure 5.3 shows some of the relevant values that I acquired as a migrant worker. These values generally refer to character and comportment. Let's examine each of these acquired values.

- *Bien hecho. Ser bien hecho* means that a person performs actions in a thoughtful and competent manner. Someone who is raised to be *bien hecho* is not permitted to be slothful, sloppy, or incompetent. "Either do it right or don't do it at all" more or less wraps up the idea of being *bien hecho.*

- Ser bien hecho (Competence)
- Ser bien educado (Civility)
- Ser dadivoso (Generosity)
- Ser trabajador (Hard working)
- Tener respeto (Respect)
- Ser gente de palabra (Keeping one's word)
- Ser honesto (Honesty)
- Tener verguenza (Shame)
- Tener honor (Honor)
- Ser valiente (Courage)

Figure 5.3 Values acquired as a migrant worker.

- *Bien educado. Ser bien educado* refers to a person who is, above all else, civil. It also connotes a high level of schooling but schooling doesn't always guarantee civility. And lack of schooling does not always entail lack of civility. This value demands both schooling and civility.
- *Dadivoso. Ser dadivoso* means that a person is generous. One is generous to family and friends, but also to the community and even to strangers. To be *dadivoso* is to give in a disinterested manner—in the sense that giving is an end in itself and is not done for self-interest.
- *Trabajador. Ser trabajador* requires one to be a hard worker. No grumbling. No complaining. Just do it. And do it right. Work hard even when the boss is not looking. Work hard in order to feed yourself and your family. *Trabaja duro para comer caliente* (Work hard to eat hot food). Work hard because life itself is hard work.
- *Respeto. Tener respeto* means that one is respectful of people and things. Respect applies to parents, family, friends, the community, and strangers. Respect for and from another person is always the initial presumption. Such respect is lost only by one's own bad behavior. To lose respect is a serious matter, relegating one to the lowest rung of the social hierarchy. Hence, having and preserving respect (as well as showing it to others) is an integral part of social life.
- *Gente de palabra. Ser gente de palabra* means that one keeps one's word. Therefore, what you say is what you mean and what you mean is what you say. You are bound by your word. This value is in stark contrast to the Anglo value of "get it in writing." In Anglo culture, if it is not in writing, it means little or nothing. Verbal agreements are problematic. Not so when one is bound by the value of being *gente de palabra.* If you agree to it verbally, you are held to it. You also hold yourself (and others) to a verbal agreement.
- *Honesto. Ser honesto* is being honest in word and deed. One must be truthful. Stealing from others is a dishonor to oneself and one's family. Dishonest people are to be avoided. Note the applicability of this value to scholarship: As every freshman in college is taught, don't plagiarize (and in graduate school, don't "cook" the data).
- *Vergüenza. Tener vergüenza* entails the notion of shame. The auxiliary verb is *tener,* which translates as "to have." What the expression means, though, is "having the capacity for feeling shame." Someone who doesn't have this capacity for shame is called *sin vergüenza,* meaning shameless. You don't want to behave in a manner that causes others to call you *sin vergüenza.*
- *Honor. Tener honor* is another of those qualities that you can "have" (*tener*) or not. Honor is a big deal in Hispanic culture in general, and Mexican migrant workers are no exception. Children are expected to honor their parents. They also must not bring dishonor to

the family. On the contrary, bringing honor to the family is positive. Honor also can have a problematic side: To protect honor one does what one has to do. Sometimes this gets you in trouble with the police. At other times maintaining honor can make you a war hero. The number of Chicano warriors receiving the Congressional Medal of Honor is proportionately higher than the proportion of Chicanos in the general population. See the value of *valiente* next.

- *Valiente. Ser valiente* means that one has courage. Cowardliness is frowned upon. You must stand up for what you believe and speak your mind. You must defend what is yours when others attack. This is especially true for protecting family, friends, community, and nation. You don't go around making trouble, but you don't back down when trouble finds you.

It doesn't take much reflection to understand how values such as these contribute to success in academia. If you acquire these values, migrant worker or not, you have a pretty good chance of succeeding in academic work. Of course, having these values alone will not guarantee academic success. After all, there has to be an educational opportunity structure available and accessible so that someone can excel in it. But when you combine the two, abiding values and educational opportunity, the chances for academic success are greatly enhanced.

KNOWLEDGE

The next driver of academic success on the list is knowledge. We can think of knowledge as ideas, facts, theories, and so forth. We can even think of knowledge as plain data or information. It turns out, though, that knowledge is the central feature of academic life. As an academic, one constantly acquires, teaches, or produces knowledge. Knowledge needs to be compiled, critiqued, and published. Indeed, knowledge is what makes the academic world go 'round.

You might be wondering, what kind of knowledge could one garner as a farm worker that would be helpful in the academic world? Good question. It took me a long time to figure out that the answer is in language itself. As it turns out, at the highest levels of the academy the most important activity is assessing the trustworthiness of knowledge. This is what allows us to agree (or not) on what the facts are and which theories we will consider as credible.

But it turns out that this assaying of knowledge has some language dependency. And even though I didn't know it at the time, as a Spanish-speaking migrant worker I was being linguistically prepared to detect later, in a remarkable way, the language dependency of knowledge validation. Here is what I mean. In English to know is to know positively and absolutely. On the other hand, in Spanish there are two distinct ways of knowing, as expressed by the Spanish verbs *saber* and *conocer*. So what is the difference between the two?

Suppose that a Spanish-speaking person is in a school and wants to know about a student named Juan García. The person might go to a Spanish speaking Latino counselor and ask, "*¿Quien es Juan García?*" (Who is Juan García?). The answer might come back: "*Se de él pero no lo conozco.*" Now what are we to make of this response if we translate it into English? Surely it would not be an accurate translation to say, "I know him but I do not know him." What's the problem here? The problem appears to be that in Spanish there are two quite different ways of knowing that are distinguished by the words *saber* and *conocer*, as already noted. *Saber* is accurately translated into English by the verb "to know," but what about *conocer*?

Conocer implies a more personal, interactive, and relational kind of knowing, a situated knowing that depends on personal experience. To observe someone or something is to know (in the sense of *saber*) about the person or thing, but it is not *conocer*. To know people or places interactively and relationally involves *conocer*. *Conocer* implies a contextualization or mutuality of knowing, a knowing that is achieved in a relationship that is reciprocal between the knowing parties. Thus, *conocer* cannot be absolute knowing because it is premised on a relationship between the knower and the known and the relationship cannot be one of objectivity. Rather, it must be one of interconnectivity, interactivity, and perhaps even intersubjectivity. *Conocer* thus opens a new epistemological space that is outside the Anglo epistemology of absolute, objectivist knowing. *Conocer* type knowing makes no claim to universality or objectivist foundations. Consequently, universal (nomothetic) knowledge is outside the scope of *conocer*. Yet it is interesting that *conocer* type knowing may be used to validate *saber* type knowing, as in the expression "*Se donde vive porque lo conozco.*" (I know where he lives because I am acquainted with [i.e., I know] him.)

These may seem like academic distinctions, but the exclusive reliance by today's U.S. educational institutions on *saber* type knowing has resulted in a culture of measurement that is threatening to engulf all other perspectives throughout the country and to overwhelm broader approaches to education. The culture of measurement is leading schools to distorted practices that predetermine the life chances of children on the basis of single-score, high-stakes tests that only recognize *saber* type knowledge (McNeil & Valenzuela, 2000). The *conocer* type of knowledge, which in the context of schooling can be understood as resulting from a pedagogic relationship between the student and the teacher, the student and the parents, and the student and the community, is almost completely ignored by the culture of measurement. Instead, the culture of measurement can be seen as promoting a mechanistic type of teaching (usually to the test) that in the end is profoundly antidemocratic and inimical to the transcultural foundations of civil society and of the Latino community in particular. Multiple measures in educational assessments (Valenzuela, 2002) that are based on both *saber* and *conocer* types of knowledge would be a powerful safeguard against the harmful effects of the culture of measurement and its penchant for high-stakes, single-score testing.

The bifurcated epistemological space of Latino culture must be taken into account in educating Latino students. All school knowledge cannot be crammed into the limited span of *saber* type knowing. *Conocer* type knowledge should be a fundamental part of Latino pedagogy so that students can learn both nomothetic (*saber*) as well as relational (*conocer*) knowledge.

My bilingual and bicultural background as a migrant person also allowed me, over time, to see how Spanish and English can be contrasted on their suppositions regarding the nature of being. In English there can be only one ontological state, which is described by the verb "to be." In Spanish, ontology is bifurcated and the two distinct states of being are designated by the Spanish words *ser* and *estar*. *Ser* is correctly translated into English by the verb "to be." "To be" refers to absolute, continuous being that has no conditions placed on it. Hence, "to be or not to be" is the only possible question. What about *estar*?

Estar denotes conditional, contingent, or temporary being. *Estoy enfermo* means "I am sick," but sickness is presumed to be temporary and something that will not exist forever, hence the use of the *estar* form of "to be." **Soy enfermo* is not a proper expression in Spanish because sickness cannot be permanent or without contingency. On the other hand, *soy mujer* means "I am a woman" and uses the *ser* form of "to be." The expression **estoy mujer* is not permitted because presumably the characteristic of being a woman is permanent and not contingent once established.

The hegemony of English-oriented ontology has distorted the way that educational institutions function. Limited to an ontology of absolute being (*ser*), Anglo culture often supposes that human cultures exist (in the sense of *ser*) in an evolutionarily determined hierarchy (see Menchaca, 1999, for a discussion of the racialization of Mexicans by the U.S. after 1848). Thus, from an Anglocentric perspective, cultures can be arranged in an order of absolute superiority and inferiority. This results in a worldview that announces the superiority of Anglo culture and demands the righteous imposition of this culture on all "foreign" peoples, while exterminating all "foreign" languages and cultures. Educational and other institutions operating under the sway of this worldview implement assimilationist practices whose goal is to absorb all languages, cultures, and peoples into a "melting pot" of Eurocentric people and culture. Those people who are seen as not susceptible to assimilation are regarded as targets for destruction, enslavement, or erasure (Menchaca, 1997). In this context, teaching adopts a subtractive stance (Valenzuela, 1999). The goal is to extract and subtract from students all "foreign" language and cultural elements and replace them with "superior" Anglo language and culture. The curriculum is infused with Anglo-centered history and culture, and there is the systematic erasure of the histories, languages, and cultures of all other groups across the land (Macedo, 1994; Menchaca, 1999; Padilla, 1993; Perez, 1999).

Latino education should include the ontology of both *ser* and *estar.* Under being as *estar,* human existence is seen as a historical, contingent, and changing set of relationships between various groups and cultures. All languages and cultures are seen as having inherent value and as needing resources in order to thrive. Under the sway of *estar* ontology, schools and other institutions recognize, embrace, and celebrate the variety of languages, cultures, and peoples across the land. They accept those who are different and promote the value of *convivencia,* that is, the notion of "live and let live." Teachers appreciate and share different languages and cultures; they practice additive pedagogy by adding language and cultural resources to what students already possess. The curriculum emphasizes multiple languages, cultures, and histories so that students from various groups can see themselves positively in what they study.

As can be seen from this brief excursion into knowledge, facts and figures are important elements of knowledge, but making and validating knowledge claims can indeed depend significantly on cultural and linguistic perspectives. As a migrant worker, I was exposed to contrasting cultures that later, as an academic, allowed me to see knowledge claims and validation in a broader context than some of my monolingual and monocultural colleagues.

SKILLS

The next item in our list of academic success drivers is skills. Surely, you might wonder, skillfully hoeing cotton cannot possibly contribute to academic success. This may well be true, but there are many other skills that I developed as a migrant worker that have direct relevance to academic success (Figure 5.4). Let's examine each in turn.

- Thinking outside the box
- Working with what you've got
- Honing a sense of strategy
- Hold your fire (timing)
- Vigilance
- Work smart and pace yourself
- Escarmiento (experiential learning)

Figure 5.4 Skills that drive academic success.

Thinking Outside the Box

Migrant workers face many challenges in their constantly changing environment. To face these challenges, it is often necessary to think outside of the box. My mother longed to own a house. My parents finally made a deal with a farmer to have the farmer finance a couple of lots, which my parents could then pay back in annual installments after the harvest season. The farmer also included in the deal a couple of old dwellings that could be torn down and the materials re-used to build our house. This is recycling at its finest. My dad and siblings did all of the demolition work and most of the house building. After all this, my mother finally had her house.

Working With What You've Got

If you have only lemons then make some lemonade. At least that is what an old saying advocates. Migrant workers and their families don't have a whole lot to work with. When my dad finally bought his own used pickup truck in Michigan, he needed to furnish it with a cover over the truck bed when we were ready to return to Texas. For migrant workers, there is never enough money to just have somebody do this or that for you. So my dad went into the woods and cut down a number of saplings. He used the sapling wood (after he had softened it with fire) to make the arched braces that would hold up a tarp over the truck bed. As a kid I saw him go through the whole rigmarole. But it worked. He created a covered wagon effect with few expenditures and lots of work and ingenuity. In this instance, "Just do it!" is the valuable lesson and skill that I picked up on the migrant stream.

Honing a Sense of Strategy

Life rewards those who have a good sense of strategy. One has to plan ahead, see what's coming, know what to expect. What is your game plan to come out ahead? Farmworkers often are paid on a piece rate. The more work you do, the more you get paid. But crops do not grow evenly. In a cherry orchard, for example, some trees may have a heavy load of cherries while other are sparsely loaded. If you get the tree with the heavy load of fruit, you can make more money. The same is true for many other crops. The unspoken rule is that trees are assigned in sequence and whoever gets first to the tree gets to pick it. Having a large family, my dad would deploy us individually so that we could capture more of the heavily loaded fruit trees. That's strategy at work. You might be amazed at how many strategies are in play out in the fields. The same is true for academic fields.

Hold Your Fire (Timing)

If you are what is called a "loose cannon," you will fire your volleys willy-nilly into the horizon and see what happens. Not so if you have a good sense of timing and know how to hold your fire and where to fire at exactly the right time. When some other worker did something that was suspicious, my dad would bring it to our attention but caution that nothing needed to be done at that time. "*Ya me lo eché en la bolsa,*" he would say (He is in my pocket already.) Or he might say, "*Cuando el va yo ya vengo.*" (When he is going I am coming back already.) All this business of timing and strategic deployment of knowledge is quite handy in the academic world as well.

Vigilance

Having a keen sense of your surroundings is essential for survival as a migrant worker. You can't fall asleep at the switch. "*El cangrejo que se duerme se lo lleva la corriente,*" is something that my dad used to say. (A sleeping crawfish is swept away by the current.) You have to be a keen observer of your environment. See who your friends are and who they are not. Take note of opportunities and challenges. Be aware of things and events around you. In academia, these notions (when applied to institutions) fall under the rubric of "environmental scanning." My dad was a master at scanning the environment. I had little trouble understanding the concept of an "environmental scan" when I ran into it many years later in the field of higher education. Vigilance also can make you proactive. Too many students fail in academia because they are not sufficiently vigilant and proactive.

Work Smart and Pace Yourself

If you are going to be chopping cotton for eight or ten hours a day, you need to pace yourself. Working at a steady pace is important because migrant workers usually don't get breaks. And you can't just stop or quit. When I was in the fields, we were lucky to get a bathroom let alone a break. A half hour lunch and no breaks makes for a long day. And chopping with a hoe takes a lot of energy. Try it in the garden sometime. So learning how to work at a steady pace is a valuable skill. I was a full-time doctoral student. When it came time to writing the dissertation, I put my migrant skill of working steady to a new use. Every day, five days a week, I would get up, have breakfast, and at eight o'clock sharp I would sit at my typewriter and start working on my dissertation. My neighbors in the adjacent student housing apartments would hear the clacking of my electric typewriter. They expressed wonder at how predictably and steadily I was working. I figured that even if I only wrote one page a day, that would be five pages a week and 20 pages per month. After a few months my dissertation would be completed. And indeed that turned out to be the case.

Escarmiento (Experiential Learning)

Escarmiento is a wonderful word in Spanish that is not easily translated into English, at least by a single word. *Escarmiento* has to do with learning. In English, learning is conventionally seen as a positive experience. It is often thought that learning should be interesting and fun. That kind of positive learning is called *aprender* in Spanish. But there is also a different kind of learning that in Spanish is conveyed by the word *escarmiento*. *Escarmiento* means that one learns from negative experiences. In English this notion is captured by the expression "I hope you learned your lesson." The idea also is captured somewhat by the expression "learn from your mistakes." *Escarmiento* means that if you did something that was not right and you learned your lesson, then some good came out of the negative experience. The worst of all possible outcomes is that you did something bad and still didn't learn your lesson. That may well put you in the category of *pendejo* or fool.

Escarmiento is quite valuable in academia. Especially as a researcher, you can gain a lot of knowledge from failure so that eventually you can get things right. When I studied student success in academia, I noticed that freshmen in college sometimes were failing because they did not recognize or appreciate *escarmiento*. They would behave badly and then not adjust their behavior in a positive direction. For example, when a student is off to college and away from home and parental supervision, the student has to learn how to control the consumption of alcohol. If the student cannot learn from one or two bad experiences with alcohol, the student is likely to fail and drop out. In Spanish we say, "*No escarmentó*!" (S/he didn't learn their lesson.)

As a migrant worker, I was admonished with "*Escarmienta*!" (Learn your lesson!). As a student and academic I put that skill to good use and tried to learn lessons from negative experiences. Better still, I learned not to repeat mistakes if at all possible.

ATTITUDE

The final item in the list of drivers of academic success is attitude. Attitude includes notions of having a positive self-image and knowing who you are and where you come from. Attitude makes you proud of your roots and allows you to express your personality. Attitude can protect you from the slings and arrows of others and from the sting of adversity. Attitude means, "*Si se puede!*" (Yes, we can!). It is said that a picture is worth a thousand words, so take a look at Photo 9. This photo was taken in Michigan during the 1950s when I lived in a migrant camp many years ago. My older sister is on the extreme left. You think those guys have attitude? Change a few things and they would be right at home at a frat TGIF on any university campus.

Photo 9

In addition to pictures, which show physical bearing, attitude also is quite apparent in what people say. Here is one of my mother's many admonitions: "*Si te caes no te quedes aplastao en el culo. . . . Levántate y sigue adelante,*" which loosely translated means, "If you fall don't stay on your butt, get up and keep going."

Sayings or *dichos* often convey plenty of attitude. When someone says, "*Con pendejos ni a bañarte porque pierden el jabón*" (With fools, don't even share the bath because they'll lose the soap), they mean that you should not hang around stupid people.

Another *dicho* says: "*Pocos pelos pero bien peinados*" (Just a few hairs, but they're well combed), which means that you should strive to have some class.

And apropos of academia there is this saying: "*Pa pendejo no se estudia,*" which simply notes the obvious fact that "no study is required to be stupid."

The migrant fields and camps are full of *dichos* that cover many situations in life. But they also convey a certain attitude toward life and the world. With *dichos* one gets to make pronouncements about the world and to see one's own life and behavior in a broader community context. In academia, the wisdom of the *dichos* can come in handy and shield you from the nonsense that sometimes swirls around campus.

Finally, we can turn to music as another source and shaper of attitude. As a migrant worker I was raised in a world of fusion music that included *rancheras, boleros, corridos,* tropical rhythms, *norteño,* and *tejano* music—but also country and western music, popular music, blues, and, of course, rock and roll. It is hard to beat Mexican music when it comes to attitude. Just listen to an old recording of Jorge Negrete singing *Yo Soy Mexicano.* Now that's attitude. Who in Mex-America doesn't know at least the refrain of *El Rey* by José Alfredo Jimenez ("*pero sigo siendo el rey*"—"still I continue to be the king")? And how about Miguel y Miguel singing *Cruz de Madera*? Now there's poverty speaking with real attitude. So physical bearing, *dichos,* music, and similar cultural elements provided a migrant kid like me with the positive attitude that I needed to succeed in academia.

After all, "*El que es buen gallo en cualquier gallinero canta,*" which proclaims that "a good rooster will crow in any chicken coop," whether that coop be a strawberry patch or an Ivy League campus. *Y si te corren* (and if they run you off), well, "*De mejores gallineros me han corrido,*" which acknowledges that "I've been run off of better chicken coops."

When I was involved in the field of bilingual education as a professional, it struck me as somewhat odd that Mexican American students were then characterized by some educators as having a negative self-image. I never saw that in the fields. That's because there was plenty of attitude to go around.

CONCLUSION AND CAVEATS

In concluding this chapter, some caveats are in order. I don't mean to argue that becoming a migrant worker is the preferred or required route to academic success. Nor do I mean to imply that all migrant workers will be successful in academia. I also do not want to argue that the knowledge, values, skills, and attitudes that promote academic success are available only through participation in migrant labor.

What I do want to point out is that one's social and economic status ought not to be the basis for either automatic exclusion or privileged inclusion. We must provide educational opportunities for students from all walks of life. That *mocoso* kid working out in the fields may be learning valuable lessons that will lead to academic success if we will but provide the opportunity. If the students dare to dream, we should dare to provide.

REFERENCES

Gonzalez, K. P., & Padilla, R. V. (Eds.). (2008). *Doing the public good. Latina/o scholars engage civic participation.* Sterling, VA: Stylus.

McNeil, L. M., & Valenzuela, A. (2000). *The harmful impact of the TAAS system of testing in Texas: Beneath the accountability rhetoric.* Houston, TX: Rice University. Center for Education. Occasional Papers, Vol. 1, Issue 1.

Macedo, D. (1994). *Literacies of power. What Americans are not allowed to know.* Boulder, CO: Westview Press.

Menchaca, M. (1997). Early racist discourses: The roots of deficit thinking. In Valencia, R., (Ed.), *The evolution of deficit thinking. Educational thought and practice* (pp. 13–40). Washington, DC: Falmer Press.

Menchaca, M. (1999). The Treaty of Guadalupe Hidalgo and the racialization of the Mexican population. In J. S. Moreno (Ed.), *The elusive quest for equality. 150 years of Chicano/Chicana education* (pp. 3–29). Cambridge, MA: Harvard Educational Review.

Padilla, G. M. (1993). *My history, not yours. The formation of Mexican American autobiography.* Madison, WI: University of Wisconsin Press.

Perez, E. (1999). *The decolonial imaginary: Writing Chicanas into history.* Bloomington, IN: Indiana University Press.

Valenzuela, A. (1999). *Subtractive schooling. U.S.–Mexican youth and the politics of caring.* Albany, NY: State University of New York Press.

Valenzuela, A. (2002). High-stakes testing and U.S.-Mexican youth in Texas: The case for multiple compensatory criteria for assessment. *Harvard Journal of Hispanic Policy, 14,* 97–116.

CHAPTER 6

OF AND WITH

Stories of Belonging and Forging Multiple Latino/a Identities in Four Voices

Mónica Byrne-Jiménez, Adriana Villavicencio, Rosa Rivera-McCutchen, and Chris Torres

The idea that the Latino/a community is one, large, monolithic group has pretty much been dispelled from mainstream media and thought. The growing political power of Latino/a voters highlights the differences—by region, country of origin, race—within our community. Add that to the waves of *Latino Diaspora* (Hamann, Wortham, & Murillo, 2002), which has transported families to areas of the country where Latinos/as had seldom ventured, the realities of "growing up" Latino/a in the United States are increasingly complex. In most urban areas, you can walk into a Latino/a market or listen to Spanish-language radio that caters to Mexican, Dominican, Salvadoran, and Ecuadorian palates and audiences. This diversity within the Latino/a community and the development of a Pan-Latino/a consciousness is our future.

Abriendo Puertas, Cerrando Heridas (Opening Doors, Closing Wounds), pages 63–73
Copyright © 2015 by Information Age Publishing
All rights of reproduction in any form reserved.

Yet our understanding of the Latino experience as faculty in education leadership has limited spaces for sharing diverse stories. The study of Latino faculty experiences has spanned decades (i.e., De la Luz Reyes & Halcón, 1988; Verdugo, 1995) and continues to be a necessary area of inquiry. Many of these explorations of Latinos in academia, however, come from two strands: (1) studies with Chicano scholars (i.e., Vllenas, Godinez, Bernal, & Elenes, 2006) or (2) studies in which the term "Latino" is broadly defined (i.e., Urrieta & Chavez, 2010). These both contribute to the development of a global understanding of the Latino/a experience, yet they overlook the subtle and important differences in our individual lives. In perhaps a strange twist of fate, a Pan-Latino/a consciousness will arise, not from a universal approach to our community, but from a deep exploration and honoring of our differences.

Our chapter is one such exploration of what we call "multiple Latino/a identities" and how these shape—and are shaped by—diversity within the Latino community. There are four "voices" represented here. Three of us are women and one is a man. Two are biracial, all of us represent multiples cultures. Two of us were raised (mostly) on the east coast, one on the west coast, and one not in the contiguous United States. Our individual paths have been tricky and complex. For this chapter we sat around a virtual table—and one real one—to talk our stories, laugh, commiserate, authorize, and strengthen each other. This *charla* is a beginning.

OUR STORIES

In this section we share our personal histories growing up and finding our way(s) in a range of geographies and communities. Questions of identity and belonging repeatedly in all our stories and how we negotiate intra- and interpersonal relations.

Pilgrimages

A pilgrimage is a long journey. A long journey to a sacred place. Growing up in upstate New York in the late 1970s, far from the warmth of extended family and community, 14th Street in New York City was the site of our pilgrimages. Twice a year we would go to *la ciudad* in search of the supplies that would make our home like those my mother and father grew up in thousands of miles away. After carefully surveying each aisle and shelf in Casa Moneo, my mother would carefully select her wares: *tomate verde, chorizo, tortillas, papa seca, rocoto,* and more. On the other side of the store my father would look through the latest records, books, and news. If we were well-behaved we might get fresh *churros* for the ride home. On the return trip home, our car would smell like a *mercado* and we would listen to music, laughing, and making sure that we didn't get any sugar from the *churros* on the car seats. The trunk, packed with boxes of those things essential to our Latino home, would last us for the next several months.

I remember those pilgrimages like they were yesterday: The strangeness, yet familiarity, of the smell and sounds. The comfort with which the strangers and my parents spoke in quick Spanish. The colors. The threads of a world that I vaguely knew but recognized as home.

I was born in Louisiana to a Peruvian father and a Mexican mother. "Pemex," my father would call us, the best of two proud and magical cultures. I had inherited the "European" coloring from my father's side of the family, whereas my brother shared my mother's *mestizaje*. We moved around quite a bit growing up, until we landed in the Hudson Valley when I was nine. I saw us as tumbleweeds and was unaccustomed to putting down roots outside the four walls of our home. When my parents decided to stay, every day became a pilgrimage: from the small, all White Catholic school where I was "Mawnica," to my home and family, where I slipped into the comfort of *my* name, "Mónica." With time and practice, I became skilled in making these daily treks, though I was never quite sure if the sacred place was the school where I was told my future lay or at home where the past sheltered me. I was skilled, I was quiet and compliant and "like them," so I was easily accepted at school. At home I led a secret life, where I learned and was appreciative of the lessons my parents taught me.

My arrival at an Ivy League university signaled another pilgrimage. In search of a Latino community, I joined groups and sought out others "like me." My development was political and intellectual and rapid. I began to identify as *Chicana*—and still do. I sought to learn the history of my people and how I came to be. There were no ethnic studies programs at the time and so I cobbled together classes on Latin American history, politics, literature, anthropology, with courses on European intellectual thought and North American history. In those days, I grew and formed deep bonds with those around me, and yet somehow I remained different. Unlike most of my friends, I was raised in a small, middle-class, mostly white, semi-agricultural part of New York. From a young age I had traveled to both México and Peru. My English was standard, the nuns saw to that, and my Spanish was proper, my parents saw to *that*. At home, the use of *Chicana* hurt my father who felt that I was dismissing his "half." My mother was angered at the slight to my father. Both my parents became impatient with my insistence that racial politics were everywhere. Back on campus, my *compañeros* openly accepted me as friend and leader, but when mixing with groups from other universities many questioned my "Brown-ness," suspicious of my light skin and my accent-less Spanish. The pilgrimage was difficult as I struggled to find a sacred place.

Several years after college I began to work in NYC public schools as I bilingual teacher. With my master's in hand and some experience in the "Little Mexico" section of Detroit, I respectfully entered the classroom. My students in the Bronx were Dominican and Puerto Rican, with a few *Mexicanos* and *Columbianos*. I taught all the core courses and I taught them how to make pilgrimages of their own: to the library, to Central Park, to the museums of art, to places and spaces they didn't think they could go. We often laughed over differing dialects and the faux pas I would unwittingly make. On Friday afternoons, we would push the desks back and they would teach me how to dance. And, of course, there were my lessons in humility and persistence, sheer stubbornness and pride, lessons in strength and hope. For the first time in my life, I think, the classroom became the sacred place.

When I began my doctoral studies in educational leadership, I entered a space where it was made clear that I did not belong. It was made clear that *none* of us who were "practitioners" belonged. And so relying on my early skills, I entered stealth mode, put my head down, and just did the work. I revealed myself to the only Latino faculty in the program, but his tenure was short-lived and he was gone a year later. I plowed through my coursework, with my eyes on the *premio*, thankful for the occasional helping hand from faculty and friends. When I began my doctoral studies, I intended to return to work in public schools. As my dissertation neared completion I was surprised to realize that my interests were steering me towards academia. And so I began the search for a faculty position. Thrilled when I received my first offer, I packed up my bags and moved to teach in a program that focused on urban leadership. Talking once with my new Latina colleague and chair of the search committee, she said that she had asked my academic references what it had been like to have a young, Latina scholar in their classes, and one said that they never thought of me as a Latina. An indictment, on the one hand, of their assumptions and blindness, but also a clear testament to how highly skilled I was in moving between worlds and hiding my true identity when necessary. I know some would call this a "privilege," but I always felt the burden of not being who I was. When I returned for my graduation, I remember spelling my name out phonetically on the little card that you hand to the announcer. My parents were in the audience and I wanted to make sure they heard my name pronounced correctly and that everyone there knew I was Latina. In that moment, on that stage, a brief sacred place.

What Are You?

"What are you?" Three words containing a dictionary full of subtext. A simple question masking a complicated set of assumptions, preconceptions, and locked-and-loaded stereotypes. A thousand years of colonization, immigration, and alienation delivered in half a second.

Typically, I answer: Ecuadorian. Other times, people guess... but rarely correctly. It's not an insult to be mistaken for another ethnicity. I also acknowledge the privilege that comes along with an obscure or even invisible ethnicity in certain environments. But to be honest, that moment stings. The next moment, I may brush it off... but in *that* moment, I feel unknown, unrecognized, like I'm wearing the wrong uniform.

Like many other Latinas the world over, I don't fit the (sometimes ridiculous) stereotypes of Latinas commonly displayed in movies, on television, or in the collective consciousness of many Americans. But sometimes, I wish I could wear some kind of a badge, maybe a visible stamp that indicates what I am. I want to ask them, Why can't you see me? Don't you know who I am? I'm the daughter of pioneers from Guayaquil who immigrated in the 60s with half-formed plans and fully-stocked ambitions. I'm the daughter of a man who led dozens of Ecuadorians to jobs in factories and restaurants washing dishes, so they could make better wages for their children. Born from a woman—a warrior in the face of poverty and abandonment—who serves *su gente* (whether they are documented or not) at a worn oak desk in a business she started more than 20 years ago. I am the descendent of the man who wrote the state song for Manabi, Ecuador where my grandmother was born and raised 13 children. I've been there—to Junin—many times, clenched the soil between my toes, felt at home on the porches of the *finca* that my *abuelita* used to grow chocolate on. I speak in English, but I think in Spanish when I'm in love, when I make love, when passion swells in my breast and pulses in my blood. I move in Spanish when Salsa plays, when *los cumbias me lavantan* and the steady *pum pum del merengue* rouses every cell in my body until my heart beats with the rhythm. When the soul of the Incas is resurrected in the music of Peru, Ecuador, and Columbia (before we stopped calling each other brothers and sisters), and the *quena* flutes haunt me with genetic memories of painful displacement in the most beautiful expressions of soulful somber I have ever heard.

They don't see those things, the people who ask WHAT ARE YOU, the students I used to teach in Bushwick who called me "the White lady" on my first day, the White banker guys who think I just look "exotic," my Black neighbors who think my Black husband married a white woman, the Latinas who think I'm not one of them.

Because I have not always been visible or identifiable even by other Latinos, my cultural identity for two decades was very much a personal one—limited by an understanding of *self* as an individual, but not as *self* in community with a shared heritage, common struggles, or collective values. As a college student, I felt like an outsider sitting next to my predominantly White peers, so much more well-read than I was, so free in their ability to assert their perspectives and intellectual prowess. I could only do it in writing, too embarrassed I would say something in the wrong way. But I also felt like an outsider among Latino groups on campus (many Chicano or Caribbean), feeling like I wasn't quite Latino enough because I didn't talk like they did and didn't have the vocabulary of ethnic struggle they had already acquired—though perhaps even they might have struggled with feelings of not belonging in ways I never did.

Spanish Harlem

My whole life, I have felt like an "other"... I never quite belonged. Not Black enough to go "Down South" for the summer like my neighborhood friends, not Puerto Rican enough (or city enough?) to feel at home in the Bronx or El Barrio, where my extended family lived. And most certainly NOT Puerto Rican enough for the island.

I grew up in Queens, NY, way out in an area named Laurelton (labeled the "boondocks" by my city family). My parents, both with striking Taino features, spoke to us in Spanish, and my father insisted that we only speak to one another in Spanish. I still hear him bellowing from an upstairs corner in the house "*¡Hábla en Español!*" when he would miraculously hear my sisters and me speaking English in hushed voices. We made our weekly pilgrimages to see *Mamá y Papá,* my father's parents, or *Abuela y Abuelo.* We'd kiss them and ask for their *bendición* (or risk getting in serious trouble). I'm told that when I started kindergarten, I only spoke Spanish. I felt Puerto Rican.

And yet... my father often stated that he was Black (and I was too young to understand the distinctions between race and ethnicity, and the political statement he was making). In elementary and middle school, I learned "Lift Every Voice and Sing," the Black National Anthem, and we sang that at every assembly. My friends were all Black. I believed I was Black, too. But... not quite. I was exotic: my hair was different and I could speak Spanish.

It wasn't until I reached high school, where there were more Latinos/as, that I started to feel torn about who I felt most comfortable with. My Spanish was limited, and my Latino friends were first generation whereas I was second... my parents' homeland was El Bárrio. I tried hanging with the Latinos, but feeling like a fake, I gravitated to my Black peers.

The issue of identity came up once more when I went off to college at the predominantly White University of Rochester in upstate New York. My sister, a junior, was the president of the Latino organization. I became immersed in the organization's activities, and two years later I also became the president. Under our leadership, we cultivated an unprecedented working partnership with the Black Student Union. Even as a leader in the Latino/a organization, my instinct (and my sister's) was to unite with Black students.

Still, I pledged a historically Black sorority. Though there were no Latina sororities on my campus at the time, it never once occurred to me that I should seek to establish one (as others eventually did). I didn't feel a void; I simply felt at home with my Black sisters. One night while pledging, the pledges were asked to sing "Lift Every Voice and Sing," and I was the only one who knew the words. My pledge name, "Spanish Harlem," was given to me by my big sisters as a witty nod to my identity as a Puerto Rican who sometimes knew more about Black history than some of my line sisters. As I reflect on it now, it is a profound symbol of my in-between-ness, my challenges with identity. Not surprisingly, when I read W. E. B. DuBois' *The Souls of Black Folk* (1903) in my sophomore year in college, the concept of "double-consciousness" resonated so deeply for me. My identity has never solely been about who I felt I was (if I even knew what that was); it has also always been defined/shaped by how others saw me.

Being Latino

What does it mean to be considered Latino? This question typically lies beneath the surface of my mind. Yet it shapes my identity, the choices I make, and the risks I take.

Growing up in Hawaii, I never thought of myself as Latino. On an island where being biracial and part Asian is the norm, I thought little of my racial and ethnic identity beyond Chinese New Year dinners and the delicious *panadijas* and *pasteles* that my grandparents made. I was raised in a middle-class family where English was the only language. I learned Spanish in high school but was afraid of speaking it. Back then, I was simply afraid of making mistakes, not about whether others would think I was Latino enough.

College brought my "otherness" to the forefront. I'd never been to the east coast or on a college visit, so arriving on campus a few days before the start of the semester was a huge culture shock for someone accustomed to being part of a racial/ethnic majority. I'd never heard of Exeter or Deerfield, but quickly learned that these kids were at ease and intimidating. I retreated into my comfort zone and befriended the other Hawaii kids. This was the first time I began to explicitly think about race, class, and culture. After making several close non-Hawaii friends, I found my own college niche but didn't reflect much on how my own racial and ethnic identity shaped my experiences.

That changed when I began teaching in the Bronx. Like many other young graduates searching for meaning, I had a desire to "give back" to underserved communities, and this time it was impossible to avoid my ethnic background. Because of my last name, families from the Dominican Republic, Cuba, Puerto Rico, and Honduras expected me to speak Spanish. I explained that I was Puerto Rican and, with some embarrassment, that I could speak Spanish "un poquito." I talked about *arroz con gandules* and other food I loved in an attempt to identify myself as an "authentic" Puerto-Rican/Latino. But I didn't *feel* authentic, and I'm still not sure what being authentic means, or what it should mean. Regardless, interacting with these families gave me a true appreciation for the intersection of race, class, and culture in urban schools that served as an entry point into doctoral studies.

OUR WORK

Here we relate our experiences as "academics," how that shapes our work, and our thinking about our work. The questions that arose in our stories continue to have an impact on our lives as teachers, scholars, and members of the Latino/a academic community.

Pilgrimages Continued

The *peregrinaje*, or pilgrimage, continues even as I enter and am accepted into formal academic spaces. Those spaces, however, continue to be uncertain terrain. It is important to me now, as never before, that my Latino and non-Latino colleagues *see* me as a Latina. The "stealth" tactics that I learned from a young age are distasteful to me now, though I recognize their importance in my academic success. The need to correct the pronunciation of my name is ever-present, the importance of reaching out to Latino/as continues, my research agenda around Latinos/as in "non-traditional" contexts evolves. My teaching/advising, perhaps most of all, is a constant invitation to students to make their own pilgrimages, to find their way. And in the larger discussions that we share as Latino/a scholars, I try to carve out room for diverse voices and experiences, particularly for emerging Latina scholars.

As a "senior" scholar I continue to make pilgrimages, some long, some short, some easy, some hard. I've learned that the pilgrimage can be to a sacred space or in search of one or the journey *is* the sacred space. And sometimes that sacred space is the quiet inside and the pilgrimage is to oneself. For Latinos in academia, those spaces are few and hard to find, often fraught with loneliness and doubt. I've come to realize that while differences within our community exist, they become less important as we take the road together. We must recognize the parts of the journey that we can take together and support each other for the parts of the journey that we must take alone.

Who I Am

I noted a similar struggle to find my place when I entered doctoral studies after teaching for five years. I would waver between feeling frustrated at my White peers and colleagues who just didn't "get it" and feeling set apart from Latino scholars who were pursuing research questions about Latino students, immigration, and English language learners. My students had been predominantly Black. My immigrant students were from Africa and Haiti, and my Latino students (who often identified as Black Latinos) were 3rd or 4th generation American . . . which is not to say they didn't face their own cultural challenges. At conferences and certain academic gatherings, I would wonder if I was still not Latino enough because my research never focused on "our" students.

It wasn't until I finished my doctoral studies, began to do the research I do now—focused on improving opportunities for all low income students of color—that the personal became political. It wasn't until I became a leader at an organization called Being Latino—a platform that connects people across the Latino community—that my individual identity became communal. It was a time when my circle of friends and colleagues began to include others to whom I felt intimately connected by our Latino-ness. And I was now more powerfully able to draw from our collective histories and trajectories to say something meaningful about Latino students and all students who, because of racism, discrimination, and the persistence of inequity, lack the opportunities to succeed.

People still ask the question—*what are you*—but for the most part because of these connections, this *hermandad*, I no longer feel invisible. It is a cliché to say we all want to be heard. I would add we also want to be seen . . . not only as *what* we are but *who* we are collectively and as individuals. *Soy Ecuadoriana, y somos Latinos.*

Being Hybrid

My hybrid identity has shaped my scholarship and my navigation of the world of academia in ways that continue to challenge me. I am a Puerto Rican in a Hispanic-serving institution, in a predominantly White unit. The field of educational leadership, although becoming more diverse, is also overwhelmingly White. Already an outsider by virtue of my ethnic identity, the fact that my doctoral degree is not in educational leadership has sometimes contributed to my sense that I don't "belong."

Yet as I continue to settle into and feel comfortable in my skin, I've learned to seek out sustenance for all parts of my identity: the Puerto Rican Studies Association Bi-annual Meeting, *charlas* at UCEA, and yes, congregations of Black men and women in academia.

And as I've followed my passions in my research, I realize that my scholarship mirrors my sense of identity: I am drawn to examine the collective experiences of Black and Latinas/os in urban middle and high school settings. My scholarship merges the identities that make me who I am.

Seeking Authenticity

Authenticity became something I grappled with as an emerging scholar as well. Studying issues of race and class in African American and Latino communities made me an even more passionate advocate for social justice and at the same time more acutely aware that I did not share the lived experiences of many low-income communities of color. I had opportunities to explicitly study racial/gender identity and its influence on schooling for my dissertation, yet I felt nagging doubt. Can I study that which I have not really experienced? Would I be able to connect with the topic and with others on a personal level? Would I risk revealing myself as an "outsider" to communities of color?

As a new academic, I am increasingly aware of racial dynamics and disparities not only within K–12 education, but also in higher education. Again, I find myself negotiating these same questions: Who am I? Am I a Latino scholar just because I am part Puerto Rican? How do others perceive me? How do these perceptions influence the way others view me and my work, and the choices I make about what work to engage in? How can I connect with other Latino scholars when I am unsure of this question of authenticity?

OUR THOUGHTS

This *charla* serves several important goals, for us and for the field. First, it highlights the development of an ethnic and academic identity within nested and complex contexts. Latino scholars must navigate identity politics in their own academic settings and in the larger Latino academic community. Second, it addresses the delicate relationships among Latino faculty. These relationships, forged out of common goals, must be carefully nurtured over time. The continued exploration of these relationships is vital to individual and community development. Third, by offering alternate perspectives of the "Latino" experience, this chapter provides insight into how personal identities are constructed, fractured, and *reforged* within a seemingly monolithic and monocultural group. In addition, the weaving of individual stories and joint reflection allows for a more in-depth exploration of these experiences by highlighting where our narratives intersect and diverge. Fourth, this chapter addresses a little discussed issue: intragroup expectations. Latino scholars enter the academic space from multiple backgrounds, different research agendas, and a range of understandings of community. When these differences are not openly discussed and shared—and in some instance ignored—among Latino scholars, the possibility exists for miscommunication, isolation, and increased balkanization. This erasure of individual differences weakens the entire community. Lastly, by offering multiple Latino/a voices, we highlight the need to continue to engage faculty—of all races and ethnicities—in discussions around identity development and the experiences of Latinos/as in education more broadly. We believe that the reflections offered here would be of interest to Latinos in and preparing to enter the field.

This notion of a Pan-Latino/a consciousness is one that must continue to be explored in research, theory, and conversation. As faculty in educational leadership, we are sensitive to the importance of context, bringing disparate communities together, and the importance of a common vision. Yet we seem to hesitate when addressing personal contexts and diversity within our own community. We offer our stories as one piece of the larger puzzle with the hope that it helps others share their stories and helps others to listen.

REFERENCES

De la Luz Reyes, M., & Halcon, J. J. (1988). Racism in academia: The old wolf revisited. *Harvard Educational Review, 58*(3), 299–315.

Du Bois, W. E. B. (1903). *The souls of Black folk.* New York, NY: Bantam Classic.

Hamann, E. T., Wortham, S. E. F., & Murillo, Jr., E. G. (2002). Education and policy in the new Latino diaspora. In S. E. F. Wortham, E. G. Murillo, Jr., & E. T. Hamann (Eds.), *Education in the new Latino diaspora: Policy and the politics of identity* (pp. 1–16). Westport, CT: Ablex Publishing.

Urrieta, L., & Chavez, R. C. (2010). Latin@ faculty in academelandia. In E. G. Murillo, Jr., S. Villenas, & R. T. Galván (Eds.), *Handbook of Latinos and education: Theory, research, and practice* (pp. 219–231). New York, NY: Routledge.

Verdugo, R. R. (1995). Racial stratification and the use of Hispanic faculty as role models: Theory, policy, and practice. *The Journal of Higher Education, 66,* 669–685.

Villenas, S. A., Godinez, F. E., Bernal, D. D., & Elenes, C. A. (2006). Chicanas/Latinas building bridges. In D. Delgado Bernal, A. Elenes, F. Godinez, & S. Villenas (Eds.), *Chicana/Latina education in everyday life: Feminista perspectives on pedagogy and epistemology* (pp. 1–9). Albany: State University of New York Press.

CHAPTER 7

FINDING AND DEFINING YOURSELF IN THE COMPANY OF OTHERS

Israel Aguilar, Juan Nino, and Dessynie Edwards

As three UCEA Barbara Jackson scholars, we each consider the social justice work we do and/or teach about a moral imperative or nonnegotiable, yet the work we do is often contested by those we call friends, colleagues, students, and even family. In fact, it would be safe to say that the social justice work we do and teach about is difficult, unfinished, messy (Aguilar, 2012), and perhaps even lonely. While it is possible (and necessary!) to empower those around us by helping each develop a sense of democratic responsibility, the very institution(s) we occupy on a daily basis such as universities, K–12 schools, nonprofits, churches, and other sites of learning play a significant role in either advancing or diminishing our efforts to be socially just and/or facilitate/teach social justice. Despite the challenges we, the authors of this chapter, face while pursuing social justice as a research agenda and way of life, we continually find and define ourselves in the company of others as a purposeful way to ameliorate inequities (discrimination/alienation) that result when institutional structures perpetuate normativity and when individuals enact deficit thinking. As a result of developing a com-

Abriendo Puertas, Cerrando Heridas (Opening Doors, Closing Wounds), pages 75–84
Copyright © 2015 by Information Age Publishing
All rights of reproduction in any form reserved.

mon agenda, we have expanded the possibilities for informing research and practice in our respective contexts.

Moreover, all of us have learned that as scholars of color we simply do not exist in isolation and have continued working together in order to understand and navigate around inequities fueled by binary logic, privilege, and other forms of oppression so that we can have an equal opportunity to earn tenure, earn respect, and earn promotion. As such, the process of turning to one another and tapping into our synergy is important; however, before we look to one another we find it necessary to first understand ourselves individually through *me-search* or autoethnography (Preston, 2011; Sykes, 2014) to then be better able to yield *research* that is meaningful and contributes to the development of new epistemologies, which will help transform roles, identities, perspectives, networks, and institutions in ways that promote change and improvement throughout the P–20 educational system and beyond. Furthermore, while our common agenda is conducive to collaborative scholarship, we also acknowledge that our innate differences in identity also play a significant role in the work and in the knowledge we produce individually and collectively. Essentially, working with others who are similar *and* working with others who are different has given us each more leverage as leaders, as scholars, and as educators. This is a plus! However, negotiating differences in identity while attempting to develop networks is not always welcome in all contexts. Unfortunately, there are pitfalls along the way that can affect one personally and professionally.

Yet it is our hope that sharing parts of our collective and individual stories (complete with possibilities and pitfalls) will help to facilitate individual change and inspire social justice work by encouraging other scholars of color to also find and define themselves in the company of others in order to explore individual and collective ingenuity. Also, our individual *testimonios* offer a counternarrative to the age-old tale that scholars of color are absent from academe because they do not exist or make up such a small percentage of academics that they are insignificant. Moreover, we aim to interrupt images of the Ivory Tower, Latino masculinity, school leadership, identity, and even traditional ways of knowing. By conceptualizing our experiences as *testimonios*, we aim to stimulate others' creativity and productivity within their respective organizations so that organizations and the folks who occupy them can be more inclusive of *the other.*

In this chapter, we each take turns individually discussing a particular concept while leading and learning for social justice (work–life balance, personal identity, and ideologies). As current scholar-practitioners, we also discuss the overlap of our individual identities and highlight the fluidity of the self. We contextualize our scholarship, beliefs, and practices in relation to our intersectionality, or power/political dynamic, which are brought upon by the intersection of multiple identities. Warner and Shields (2013) maintain that one's difference (i.e., race) does not carry more meaning or weight than any other form of difference (i.e., gender). Instead, all of the differences make up one's identity because a single form of difference does not exist in isolation from the rest.

In the first *testimonio,* Nino tells how his past experience has shaped his identity, which contributes to his actions, beliefs, and expectations as a social justice scholar.

TESTIMONIO 1: NINO

I grew up in a border community of the Rio Grande Valley. Childhood was normal until I was eight years old when my family became migrant workers. For five years, my family and I would leave the comforts of home and relocate to West Texas in search of work. Even though I only worked for four hours each day, I saw the challenges of work, including some injustices. In was during my years of a migrant worker that I started to learn the value of *familia,* of friends, and of education.

For years, my friends never realized I was a migrant. I was in advanced classes and started and ended school with everyone else. My parents valued education and did not want for my siblings or me to miss out on any school days, so we would migrate when school ended and return home before school began. While the perils of the fields were eminent on a daily basis, my parents provided my brothers and me with an experience I still cherish today. For example, I learned to appreciate the value of knowledge by appreciating the process of learning, and I started to question why migrant people were viewed as workers, not thinkers.

During my school years I carried many labels, some earned while others given. In elementary, I was labeled as a limited English proficient (LEP) student, yet I was also the male student in my elementary school with the highest GPA. In high school, I was the victim of deficit thinking because of another label: migrant student. For example, I was enrolled in a reading class all migrant students were required by administration to take because of their alleged vulnerability and at-risk status. Garza (2007) reminds us that migrant children are labeled as culturally disadvantaged and severely at-risk because of low expectations of a deficit thinking society. As such, a counselor did not enroll me into an advanced curriculum, which was for students in medical pathways. The counselor insisted I stay in a remedial reading class, even after the reading teacher recommended I be removed from this course. It was the passion, advocacy, and equity lens of this teacher that helped me move from this course and into an honors English class. I graduated with honors from the high school and was awarded several scholarships from major universities. However, I did not want to leave home, so I decided to pursue a bachelor's degree from a local university.

After obtaining my degree I applied for a teaching position in my hometown. I was recommended by several school principals to be hired, but I chose to teach at the same school where I graduated. After my second year, I was assigned as the English as a second language (ESL) science teacher because I apparently understood the students more. My colleagues reminded me of my former LEP and migrant labels and often suggested I was the best option for "these students." As an ESL science teacher I found myself as the only advocate for ESL and migrant students. I voiced my concerns about several issues, including when I saw a lack of funding and resources available. In addition to standing alone and questioning inequitable practice, I sought assistance from the principal, who, to my dismay, was not interested in becoming a voice for the marginalized students. Instead, she wanted to satisfy the superintendent's mission—"increase scores."

In an attempt to work at the systems level, I earned a master's degree and became an assistant principal. I joined the leadership team of a high school with high ambitions and hopes of creating equitable programs for all students to succeed. Again, my assignments focused on the ESL population and the special education groups. I questioned some inequitable practices, especially those that involved the inappropriate use of funds to pay for teachers not servicing the ESL nor the special education students. I addressed my concern with the assistant superintendent of curriculum and instruction along with directors of both federal programs, yet my equity issue was not well received. They insisted that my role was to maintain and implement best practices to ensure that the ESL students' test scores increased, not to create programs that hindered the plans of the district.

Rather than give up and be complicit in the subjection of more students, I resigned from my school leadership position and enrolled full-time to earn a doctoral degree with an emphasis on social justice. Over the course of three years, I was engaged in much research and scholarship that I felt prepared to join the ranks of academia. Completing two internships and participating in local, national and international studies provided a clearer picture of what I wanted to do with my PhD. However, earning a position in academe was not easy. I was interviewed by three Tier I universities, but no job offers from any came through. Again, I did not give up.

I returned to public education in the capacity of a district office support member where I visited several schools on a daily basis, monitoring instruction. What I witnessed on a daily basis was far more of a concern than what I had experienced as a student who was treated differently because of language or what I had seen being done to students because they were different. Teachers, principals, and central office could not articulate the purpose of education other than to pass a state test. The more I questioned, the more they alienated me. Again, I was a threat to the status quo! Despite this, I continued to pursue the professoriate as a way to continue to work at the systems level for social justice.

I understand the intersections of my differences and how they influence my work. As such, I question everything I do and posit the same to my students, colleagues, and friends. At times, I make those around me feel uncomfortable, as humans tend to surround themselves with the familial, but challenging people and systems is necessary to interrupt deficit thinking, binary logic, and other forms of oppression such as classism to instill change.

While I have studied and taught (now work, too!) in central Texas, the place I call my home is a secluded area in the southernmost part of Texas. Anzaldúa (1999) referred to this geographical region as "una herida abierta" (an open wound) (p. 25) where the intersections of interest, cultures, people, and power live. As a *mestizo* and a scholar, I understand the complexity of life in which labels do create meanings. I do not believe there is a single framework that can nail down the identity of a person, people, or place. As a Hispanic male, growing up in a land of two *fronteras*, or borderlands (Anzaldúa, 1999), Texas and Mexico, my agency as a scholar and researcher has been influenced by unique social, cultural, and historical experiences to create a unique intersectionality (*mestizo*). This results in an individual living *in between* two cultures. For Anzaldúa, to live between two cultures is to experience ambiguity on a daily basis. As a *mestizo,* one is "free to create one's own" identity grounded on the alienation from the two cultures (Velazco & Trianosky, 2010, p. 288). Today, my intersectionality as a mestizo continues to inform my leadership, research, and practice. Being a Latino educational leader for social justice invites me to conduct qualitative research using ethnographic techniques, multiple theories, and various epistemologies so that I can help others better understand that school systems are living systems that are complex and evolving, just like humans who work in them.

In the following *testimonio,* Edwards explains how work–life balance is never in sync; instead, it is in constant flux, for her identify as a woman (married with children), biracial (African America/Latina), scholar-practitioner, and district leader all compete for different amounts of time, of energy, and of soul.

TESTIMONIO 2: EDWARDS

"Your job is not for someone with children and a family!" This statement encompasses a dialectic of oppression (Collins, 2009) meant to assign minority women like myself to subordinate spaces where we struggle to fulfill the demands of work, of life roles, and of personal responsibilities. In order to feel and be successful, I conceptualize work–life balance differently, for it is a fractured ideal in contemporary popular culture that has created very real tensions for minority mothers who are also professionals, scholars, and leaders.

As a biracial woman, mother, wife, school district executive leader, and doctoral student, I have struggled to achieve a balance between my work and life obligations. As such, balancing or paying equal amounts of attention to each of my roles is impossible. For example, I spend all of my weekends with my husband and three children at our home in South Texas while my weekdays are consumed by more than 70 hours of work at my district leadership job in North Texas (I work and live in two different cities that are 275 miles apart). My work/life landscape is uniquely navigated by both a car and airplane, as my numerous arrivals and departures still result in only two days with my family and five days at my workplace. I am also challenged to carve out time to devote to the intellectually rigorous thinking and writing of my doctoral dissertation and other research projects. If I am lucky, I can squeeze in a hair appointment and/or other personal hobbies such as reading a magazine. Regrettably, achieving a balance between my work and life experiences is an ideal I have woefully failed to accomplish for the past two years; therefore, it would be safe to say that I regret neglecting some priorities over others.

Yet I recognize the uniqueness of my participation in the diverse expressions of the American work experience, as Collins (2009) contended that Black women as a group in the United States "live in a different world from that of people who are not Black and female" (Collins, 2009, p. 27). The concept of intersectionality was coined by Black legal scholar, Kimberley Crenshaw (1989), to describe the multiple oppressions experienced by Black women. Crenshaw (1989) argued that Black women are discriminated against in ways that do not distinctly fit into the legal categories of "racism" or sexism," but these oppressions are an intersection of both racism and sexism.

My experiences as a biracial woman, mother, wife, school district executive, and emerging scholar have stimulated my understanding of the intersectionality of race, gender, class, and the ideal of a work-life balance. My consciousness of race and gender intersections has assisted with my understanding of my existence, connections between my experiences, and my thinking about these experiences. Gwaltney (1980) noted that the mind of the man and the woman is the same, "but this business of living makes women use their minds in ways that men don't even have to think about" (Gwaltney, 1980, p. 33). I contend that my struggle with the ideal of work–life balance is situated in the intersectionality of my experiences. In other words, just like I cannot isolate one identity over another, I cannot isolate one priority, role, or job over another, which is why I find that work-life is always already in a constant flux. It is then my job to not feel too guilty when I feel I am neglecting one priority for another.

"Your job is not for someone with children and a family!" suggests I created the imbalance between work and life by choosing to work and have a family. On the contrary, I see this statement loaded with inequitable expectations. Also, I see a balance act as oppressive because I see my intersection of race and gender and that of work and life as fluid, never balanced, and always in flux. I am a mother and wife, just as much as I am Black woman, school leader or scholar; accepting this paradox and living with the tension that may exist because others around me don't understand it is an ontological stance I accept.

The following *testimonio* illustrates how Aguilar sees his head, heart, and body, which makes up his identity as a 21st century scholar.

TESTIMONIO 3: AGUILAR

From the age of 9 to about 15 years of age, I was sexually abused on multiple occasions by a male neighbor and a male relative. The two individuals made me watch pornography with them and then forced me to perform sexual acts with them. As a child, I did not know what to think of this, so I did not tell anyone, including my parents. Perhaps I was embarrassed and scared of speaking out even though the two individuals never threatened me or resorted to blackmail. Ironically, I do remember feeling a sense of forgiveness for my attackers. Perhaps it was my strong Christian conviction that helped me to forgive.

Eventually, I did build up the courage to ask one of individuals about a year after the abuse stopped why they abused me. I wanted some closure. "I don't know why, "he said. "My uncle abused me, too." Despite this confession, this still did not answer my question. During the years while the abuse occurred, I remember wanting to commit suicide on several occasions or run away so that my family would not feel negligent. Incidentally, I felt responsible for the abuse after some time, especially because the sensation and the experience began to feel natural over the years so that I began to welcome the sexual encounters. Essentially, I stopped fighting. Again, I was nine years old when this started!

Rather than seek professional guidance or counseling in order to cope with the abuse, I tried to better understand who I was by listening to my heart and trying to reclaim some form of sexual identity. After all, I was maturing and developing needs. Over the years, I explored relationships with both males and females. By listening to my heart, I found that love is love, regardless of one's biological sex. Today, I continue to listen to my heart, and I am in a relationship with a woman. Articulating my identity as a bisexual man for myself was a task for me, especially to tell the woman I love. Nonetheless, she accepts my sexual identity, and I am proud to say that I do not live with any tension in my heart. I wear my heart on my sleeve and keep my head high, especially because I recognize that my sexuality may not be welcome in all contexts as some do not accept variations in identity. Despite this invisible disclaimer many institutions may have and despite definitions of Latino masculinity, I am proud of the identity I inhabit.

In addition to my sexuality that plays a significant part of my identity, my body and mind also have significant roles. As a wellness enthusiast, it would be an understatement to say that I watch what I eat or that I am conscious of calories. However, I did not always worry about my body. In fact, in 2001 I graduated from high school weighing 250 pounds because I did not respect my body. I went on feeling unhealthy and unmotivated in college. My mission was later clear: lose weight! Over time, I developed healthier habits and did lose weight.

Before relocating to central Texas in 2007, my father was diagnosed with rectal cancer and about that same time my mother's diabetes was spiraling out of control. Both my brothers also were battling high blood pressure and high levels of cholesterol. I figured I too would become another statistic if I did not maintain a proactive approach to wellness and take advantage of my physical ability. Along with Niño, I pursued wellness as a way of life. I held him accountable and he held me accountable to high health standards.

I began lifting weights, running, and eating more nutritious and organic meals. My mission for achieving wellness was also fueled by my desire to be desired, especially because I did not feel *sexy*. By reading and studying wellness and exercising I saw the potential physical strength I possessed. Soon thereafter, I recognized that a healthier body afforded me the energy and courage to speak up and confidence to be recognized as a holder of knowledge. Before, I did nothing to attract attention to myself, and I stayed quiet all the time.

As part of accelerating my development of more strength and endurance I began to experiment with different diets and consumed supplements that interrupted my natural ability to sleep and control my temper. In order to sleep, I took another set of supplements. Practically addicted to sleeping aids and mood enhancers, I did not realize I was inadvertently destroying my body. Fortunately, I came to my senses and with the help of a friend I was able to see the problem. Today, the possibility of reaching maximum wellness is still alive, yet if I had allowed myself to succumb to pitfalls along the way I would not be here today. Moreover, I am proud to say that my body and physical ability are major parts of my identity because like sexuality, a body is also fluid. I am sure others would agree, especially if they like sweets like me!

It was important to discuss my heart and body before my mind because I have spent my entire life developing my mind (formal schooling, graduate studies, biblical studies). Yet developing my thinking processes and aptitude has allowed me to be a fast, critical, and creative thinker who seeks to work at the nexus of theory and practice. Perhaps that is why after I graduated with a PhD, I spent some time as a school administrator in a large urban school district in north Texas. By applying my knowledge of theory I was able to introduce a social justice perspective on a campus through professional development and help facilitate the understanding of deficit thinking, racism, classism, and other types of oppression that are often prevalent in organizations. I did so by helping staff members problematize their own beliefs. Once the staff saw how one could be complicit in the subjection of others, staff members saw their practice differently (Pennington, 2007). While I may have a mind I am confident about, I cannot define who I am without simultaneously also acknowledging my body, my sexuality, my religion, my language, or my ability.

By understanding who I am through *me-search* or *autoethnography*, I know differences that I possess and thus see value in differences I have and those that others have. Moreover, having this perspective helps me teach aspiring school principals about the value of multiple differences others have, including students and teachers. This is conducive to creating more equitable K–12 schools. Also, because I subscribe to intersectionality, I do research with others who have the same moral orientation. In this way, we all assist in the effort to give voice to historically marginalized groups, including ourselves. For example, this chapter with Edwards and Nino is a testament to the fact that even those with a variation in identity are productive, determined, and accomplished. Because these scholars give me strength and additional resources to work around pitfalls such as phobias, privilege, binary logic, and other forms of oppression I encounter daily for identifying with difference from the norm, I hope to earn tenure and promotion by continuing to find and define myself in the company of others such as my colleagues. Together, we navigate around institutional structures set up to keep folks out who look like us, who feel like us, who love like us, and who teach like us. I have a stronger heart, healthier body, and sharper mind because of the company I keep—others who also seek social justice. At the same time, these qualities help me be a better leader, educator, and researcher who can better develop the next generation of scholars of color for social justice.

CONCLUSION

Our individual and collective *testimonios* communicate that we each have encountered both possibilities and pitfalls along the paths to tenure and personal development. Thankfully, we help each other navigate academe and the systems and structures in it. We maintain that it is up to each of us as academics to foster the relationship between *me-search* and *research* so that inquiry is better informed and so that we can develop more effective leaders who exhibit an equity lens. Doing so will help us open doors for others. In the end, this very work/scholarship is the one that will not only help us achieve tenure and promotion while feeding our soul, but also shape experiences for other Latinos in the future.

REFERENCES

Aguilar, I. (2012). *From absolute spaces to inclusive environments: A case study of teacher leadership.* Unpublished doctoral dissertation. Texas State University. Retrieved from ProQuest.

Anzaldúa, G. (1999). *Borderlands/ La frontera: The new mestiza* (2nd ed.). San Francisco, CA: Aunt Lute Books.

Collins, P. H. (2009). *Black feminist thought: Knowledge, consciousness, and the politics of empowerment* (2nd ed.). New York, NY: Routledge.

Crenshaw, K. (1989). Demarginalizing the intersection of race and sex: A Black feminist critique of antidiscrimination doctrine, feminist theory and antiracist politics. *The University of Chicago Legal Forum, 140,* 139–167.

Garza, E. (2007). A study of migrant children in the U.S. In Soto, L. D. (Ed.), *The Praege handbook of Latino education in the U.S.* (pp. 307–314). Westport, CT: Praeger.

Gwaltney, J. L. (1980). *Drylongso, A self-portrait of Black America.* New York, NY: Vintage.

Pennington, J. L. (2007). Silence in the classroom/whispers in the halls: Autoethnography as pedagogy in White pre-service teacher education. *Race, Ethnicity And Education, 10*(1), 93–113.

Preston, A. (2011). Using autoethnography to explore and critically reflect upon changing identity. *Adult Learner: The Irish Journal Of Adult And Community Education,* 110–125.

Sykes, B. E. (2014). Transformative autoethnography: An examination of cultural identity and its implications for learners. *Adult Learning, 25*(1), 3–10.

Velazco, G., & Trianosky. (2010). *Mestizaje* and Hispanic identity. In S. Nuccetelli, O. Schutte, & O. Bueno (Eds.), *A companion to Latin American philosophy* (pp. 283–296). West Sussex, UK: Wiley-Blackwell.

Warner, L., & Shields, S. (2013). The intersections of sexuality, gender, and race: Identity research at the crossroads. *Sex Roles, 68*(11/12), 803–810.

CHAPTER 8

TESTIMONIO FOR LIVING AND LEARNING IN ACADEMIA

Caring for Mind, Body, and Soul

Susana Hernández and Leslie D. Gonzales

Testimonio is described by Delgado-Bernal, Burciaga, and Flores (2012) as a methodological strategy often employed by women of color to disrupt majoritarian narratives and create a sense of solidarity among individuals who might share similar experiences of marginalization, isolation, and oppression. In relation to academia, creating such solidarity is especially important, as it can serve as a source of affirmation and legitimization for women of color who remain highly underrepresented as producers of knowledge within academe (Sotello Viernes Turner, González, & Wong, 2011).

In this way, *testimonio* requires the simultaneous opening of hearts and minds. While a narrator offers a listener a peek into the inner, often hidden contours of her life, she must take a position of vulnerability. The listener, on the other hand, must humbly open herself up to learn, see, feel, and recognize this shared experience as knowledge. To be vulnerable and to be

Abriendo Puertas, Cerrando Heridas (Opening Doors, Closing Wounds), pages 85–93
Copyright © 2015 by Information Age Publishing
All rights of reproduction in any form reserved.

humble can be difficult; it can push us to unfamiliar, uncomfortable, and maybe painful places, but over the next few minutes, we ask you to listen to our stories, to imagine yourself in these experiences, and to consider how our experience/knowledge is connected to larger matters of in/equities that persist inside the institution of higher education.

Before moving on, we must admit that when we began work on this chapter, we had little writing experience with *testimonio.* We worried and asked, "Can we do this?" As any well-trained scholars would do, we downloaded articles and identified book chapters. We highlighted and took notes, and had conversations about our learning. And then we suddenly realized that we have long employed *testimonio* without knowing it. Indeed, *testimonio* is how we live as friends journeying inside academia; what we mean is that we consistently listen to and share with one another, affirm and counsel one another. In this way, *testimonio* is at the heart of our friendship.

With this in mind, in this chapter we provide entrée to our shared *testimonio.* We want to document for ourselves, for one another, and for others, our experiences as we navigated into and now inside of academia and to show how powerful it can be when two (or more) people build community by believing and trusting in one another. We believe this is an important contribution because as women of color, first-generation-college students-turned-academics from working-class "no-collar families" (Turner, 2002), our historical locations in the broader socio-political-economic structures has always positioned us at the margins. Being at the margins has meant confronting, sometimes side-stepping, and very often struggling in the face of deeply institutionalized barriers such as inadequate school funding *and* deeply racist *or* classist schooling experiences that dismiss, or at least fail to validate, the unique cultural histories and "funds of knowledge" (Rios-Aguilar, Kiyama, Gravitt, & Moll, 2011) that our families inscribed into our hands, hearts, and heads. And yet, we are here; we occupy a space within the academic community that very few Latinas, and women of color more generally, have occupied despite the long history of higher education in the U.S. It is important that we share our journey with others and to describe how our experiences, some of which we highlight through the *testimonio* we share, have allowed us to move through this unfamiliar promising space.

In the immediate pages that follow, we document a brief description of the identities we hold as daughters, academics, and students, among others. In doing so, we describe some of the difficult moments we have confronted in our journey into and inside of academia. And although one of the most important affordances of *testimonio* is the disruption of majoritarian narratives and the revealing of counterstories, *testimonio* is also about resistance and resiliency, hope, and possibility, which we always find in our friendship. We conclude this chapter by describing moments we have shared that have left us with indelible marks, wisdom that transcends time and space, and fuel for our minds, bodies, and souls. These moments enable our intellectual production and emotional whole-heartedness to carry out our work in this space we are so privileged to occupy.

YO SOY HIJA DE MIS PADRES

I am Susana Hernández, the daughter of immigrant parents, Apolonio y Obdulia Marin. I always begin an introduction of myself by acknowledging my parents. Growing up in a Mexican working-class community in Los Angeles, I knew my place in the world. Holding my father's hand as he proudly carried my Winnie the Pooh backpack to school, we would say *"buenos dias"* to Doña Maria as she watered her lawn and I skipped across the pavement eager to get to school. As a little brown girl, I was so proud of who I was, proud of my hard-working Mexican immigrant parents who labored tirelessly to provide for my two brothers and me. My love for school and learning was fueled by my parents' sacrifices. My father would come home from work at 11:30 p.m. in his dark blue uniform, with "Tony" on his chest, that would shield his burn marks on his tanned skin, and would say *"ya acuestate mija, es tarde."* My mother, Lula, who would wake up at 3:00 a.m. to get to her factory job to work ten long hours would rush home to get us to baseball practice. The costs that my parents paid to support my schooling are engrained in my memory and sustained me throughout my educational experiences as a student and now as a faculty member.

I am a reflection of their sacrifices, hopes and dreams, and relentless hard work. My parents' perseverance and strength is what continues to inspire, motivate, and encourage me to surpass the difficult moments in the academy. As a first-year assistant professor, my parents are so proud of me. I recall the moment I brought my mom and dad to campus to show them my office. Nothing would prepare me for my mom's reaction. The tears streaming down her face, as she gasped for air, and walked through the wooden door into my *oficina.* "*¡Mija¡,*" she exclaimed, and with a warm embrace, I knew how incredibly proud she was of what *we* had accomplished, a position in the professoriate.

In this first year, I am reminded that although I have reached this new position, it's oddly new and yet strangely familiar. The familiar feelings of self-doubt, of thinking, feeling, do I belong? The feelings in my gut physically impair me from thinking clearly because I'm wondering how is it that I made it through the academy to be in this privileged space yet I do not (yet) feel like I am welcome. These are the feelings that I felt as a graduate student and that I thought would go away once I became a professor. The feelings of being an impostor, the constant negotiations of my time and effort, and the ever so implicit and often explicit reminders that sexism, ageism, and racism are alive and well in the academy.

In my first year, I have lost track of the countless times I've been told "you look so young, you're a professor?" To which I think, what is a professor supposed to look like? Or what is so difficult to accept, that I, me, *la hija de mis padres* can be a professor? The comment itself, to some, may seem flattering, or complementary, but when this comment is made during a budget meeting, or in discussions over curriculum, I have to question if the comment is intended to remind me I'm not supposed to be here. That I don't "look" like a professor, and get mistaken for a student because somehow, the little brown girl, who so joyfully skipped to school, skipped her way to the budget meeting.

Reminders of my parents and the costs they have paid—the burn marks on their arms, the fact that they are not given the decency to be called by their name at work are reminders that I must stay. Although my competence is often questioned and challenged in nonproductive ways, my resilience to navigate this new space as an academic is fortified by the reminders of my family and the many sacrifices they made and continue to make so that I, the daughter of immigrant parents, can be *la profesora.*

I AM ENOUGH

Like my dear friend, Susana, my story must also begin with my parents. My name is Leslie D. Gonzales. My father, Thomas Gonzales, whom I call "Father Bear," has and will always be my most steadfast advisor and friend. My father has a brilliant mind; he could have been an engineer of any sort. From Father Bear, I learned that I could be anything I wanted, as long as I was willing to work. My mother, Louise—better known as Lulu among family—is like many women who married to get out of her childhood home and go somewhere different. Through her identity, wholly tied to her children, my mother taught me the beauty, but also the dangers of selfless love; this lesson has helped me realize the importance of self-care. Although they are no longer married, our life as a family began in what I remember as a dusty little town. In fact, I can still feel the dirt on my face and see it creased into my clothes after a long day of play.

And then, I must remind myself that this image in my mind is not so accurate, and the town was not really so dusty. Instead, the dirt I imagine on my face is a memento of the long dirt road that ran along side the train tracks, which separated me, in so many ways, from the community on the other side. This community, which was predominantly White and mostly solid middle class, held assumptions about people like me and families like mine. I would soon learn that these assumptions meant that birthday party invitations were sometimes contingent on my last name and whether or not I could explain what I "was." It made no difference that I only spoke, read, and wrote in English since my parents had, with heavy hearts, decided that my learning Spanish might not be the best choice in the northern Texan context where we lived.

I continued to learn hard lessons in middle school when I developed in ways that differed from most of the other girls in class. Teased relentlessly, made to feel shameful, often, my only prayer request was to look more like the other girls in my class. Thus, race, class, and body have always been salient to my experience and are inscribed into my view of the world. The lineage of my intellectual work—whether in the classroom, in my research, or in my service—is anchored in these experiences. However, not until I was 21 did I know how to name this.

Specifically, during the writing of my political science Master's thesis, I discovered Anzaldúa, Castillo, and Moraga. For the first time, I learned that there were women of color who were also writers: These women had written and theorized and provided me with an entire language to make sense of my world. Forming knowledge through and with my experience, I weaved conventional political science literature with the scholarship produced by these women of color, who articulated questions and told stories much like the ones that I had long held in my head. I quickly learned that the academic world lacks the affinity for the kind of eclecticism that represented my life, and indeed, my intellectual production. Eventually, I wandered into higher education hoping to find a place for my ways of knowing in a more interdisciplinary field.

Today, I have managed to take the whole of who I am and develop intellectual work based on questions of power, legitimacy, and knowledge production. Yet, like Susana, and so many women of color, I struggle with imposturous feelings and questions.

Perhaps, the most difficult manifestation of this is related to my identity as a Latina academic who lacks fluency in Spanish. When in the company of my Latino/a colleagues at a conference, I listen to the smooth and beautiful sound of their Spanish. Anxiously, in my mind, I perform the translation tricks in my head: Spanish to English when listening, English to Spanish when talking. My responses are always jumbled, never smooth. I wonder, "Am I enough? Please let it be enough." And, I have to remind myself, *I am always who I always am,* and yes, I am enough. I will always be a woman loved dearly by her proud working-class family, who taught her the lesson of hard work and who chose to forego Spanish in hopes of easing my schooling experience. I will always be a trained political scientist who delved deeply into sociology and then into critical cultural studies, meaning all of this will always be in my work because it is part of me.

TESTIMONIO AT THE HEART OF FRIENDSHIP: SUSTENANCE AND SPACES OF SOLIDARITY

As promised, we have shared with you some of the inner contours of our lives: the pride and joy we share with our parents, the stumbling through educational institutions and communities who question our very presence. Now, we describe how our friendship, which we have to come to recognize as a long-running *testimonio*, has provided a source of sustenance for us. Just as we highlighted key moments in our journey into and inside of academia, we frame the following section around key moments in our *testimonio* in the attempt to capture the interactions that have nurtured our bodies, minds, and souls.

Nurturing the Body: Ways of Knowing and Self-Care

For as long as I can remember, I have had a keen awareness of my feelings, yet it was not until a recent conversation with Leslie that I realized my body is my way of knowing. Leslie helped me make sense of my body as a way of understanding the world. The feelings of self-doubt, and of feeling unwelcomed, which I expressed earlier, are usually experienced and felt as aches, as sharp pains in my gut, that tell me something is not okay. My sense of self has long been understood through my body. As a young-looking, petite scholar, comments about my body and small physical stature are often made in passing and disguised in jest. When describing my feelings to Leslie, she didn't laugh. Instead, she listened, affirmed my feelings, and what I most value, she felt my frustration.

In that moment, she helped me realize one way of knowing is through my body. I breathed. In that breath, I exhaled. In that breath, I began to make sense that my feelings are real, valuable, and critical to my self and my wholeness. In that moment, Leslie allowed me to gain a new awareness of myself, of privileging and honoring all of who I am, and all of what I feel. I realized that through my vulnerability, through sharing my feelings with Leslie, I could experience healing. Acknowledging and reclaiming my pain was the catalyst to help me remain resilient throughout the first year as a professor. My scars may not be physically visible like my father's, or concealable with my blouse, but the healing has allowed my body to be shielded from future remarks and attacks on my competence. In the following section, Leslie describes the perception of her body.

As mentioned earlier, race, gender, and body have long dominated my sense of self. As an academic, the story has been no different. While I see my body as a vehicle that allows me to enjoy life with my daughter and husband, I, like many women of color (Sulé, 2011), struggle to manage this aspect of image inside academia. It is an eerily similar feeling to the one I had as a middle-school student. Recently, though, Susana helped me think of my body in a very different way.

It was during one of our regular conversations, over coffee: We began to talk generally about health and self-care. Susana excitedly praised me for lifting weights. She kindly made reference to a photo of me competing in a small fitness event back home. Embarrassed, I told Susana how bothered I was when an acquaintance posted the picture. With a look of surprise, Susana praised me, told me that it was inspirational to see the commitment to my health, but perhaps most importantly, Susana praised the body for its strength—the same body for which I had relentlessly been teased. I am not sure that I expressed to Susana, at that moment, how powerful her words were to me, but this moment helped me begin to reshape how I feel about my body. Rather than try to cover the body that demonstrates my commitment to health, and work, and above all to life, I am working toward being proud of it. The body, as Susana noted, presents us with ways of knowing. It may carry scars or be tired from too many sleepless nights. It might be filled with muscles, and it might signal your familial lineage. In all these ways, the body is the physical home to the soul and the mind, and it is a powerful illustration of one's life and experiences.

Soul: Understanding without Words

In *testimonio,* you share experience as knowledge and often stumble onto memories that have hung with you for reasons you have yet to address. One night, Leslie and I were thinking about our approach to this chapter. We knew that the first draft was not what we wanted it to be; we realized that we had yet to really make ourselves vulnerable in writing. We remained rather hidden. We talked through the importance of situating oneself and one's history in such work, which led us directly into a conversation about our parents.

With a surprising sense of urgency, I said "Leslie, I cannot talk about myself without talking about my parents, but I have to name them. I have to name my father and my mother: my mother, who works in a factory who is never given the respect to be called by her first name." Leslie looked back at me, and I immediately knew she understood the importance of naming my parents.

Our working-class origins have translated into and are anchored in a formidable work ethic and a deep sense of pride for our families. It has also instilled in us a way of seeing the world and being alert to actions or norms that others might simply take for granted. As I talked to Leslie about my parents, I saw that she understood how class, academic identity, and academia, overall, intersect, often pulling us in different ways.

In fact, I understood Susana's experience well. I extended the conversation by recounting a moment when all of these ideas and history came to the fore. It was during one of my first academic conferences as a new faculty member. As one of the dinner socials came to a close, a few colleagues and I hung around to finish hors-d'oeuvres. I looked around and noticed that many plates and napkins had been left behind. The cleaning crew came into the room and began to pick up all the left over plates. Almost naturally I also began to clean the tables, stacking plates and tossing out the used cups. I remember looking over to my colleagues and seeing the unease on his face. One of my colleagues told me, "Don't do that. You don't have to." I responded, "No, it's okay. It is so rude not to clean up after yourself." The exchange was uncomfortable. My colleagues were *clearly* uncomfortable. However, all I could see was my mom, who has worked many jobs in housekeeping and cooking. The men and women cleaning up the dirty plates and cups were images of my mother, and although I know I did not have to, I did anyways, for the same reasons, I believe, that Susana has to name her parents when documenting her journey.

Mind: You are a Knower... Your Intellectual Production Matters

Through our friendship, through our vulnerable exchanges of ideas and feelings, we have realized the power of *testimonio* to affirm one another as thinkers, knowers, scholars, and theorizers. The broader socio-political-economic structures we described are the backdrop in our minds and in our hearts and we utilize our friendship, our *testimonio*, to affirm and sustain our intellectual production.

We understand, however, that our intellectual production is inextricably linked to our histories, our bodies, and our spirit. For us, this understanding has come mostly through our friendship, through many moments and conversations where we have gained deeper understandings of the questions we seek to answer and the affirmation that they are important. In this way, our friendship has served as a long-running *testimonio* where we reveal painful experiences, construct powerful counterstories, and provide a source of sustenance for one another.

CLOSING THOUGHTS

In this chapter, our aim was to provide our *testimonio*. This meant situating our historical locations and journey into academia as well as some of our experiences in academe, so far, so that others who might have a similar background or experience might know that they are not alone. In the spirit of *testimonio,* though, we wanted to highlight the possibility of resistance and resilience, and we especially wanted to show how *testimonio* engenders space for solidarity. As many of our colleagues in this book have highlighted, such solidarity is an essential step if academe is ever to become a welcoming space for scholars of color and underrepresented scholars overall. To have such solidarity means having a space to turn to for affirmation and legitimization (Murakami, Núñez, & Cuero, 2010). It also means that scholars, especially women scholars of color, will be more likely to remain within academe to teach future generations, produce and disseminate knowledge, and serve communities as well as the profession. Although we often navigate our academic work places as the only (or one of few) women of color, and while our families might have limited understanding about what it means to be an academic, the promise of *testimonio* among women of color scholars is immeasurable.

REFERENCES

Delgado-Bernal, D., Burciaga, R., & Flores, J. C. (2012). Chicana/Latina testimonios: Mapping the methodological, pedagogical, and political. *Equity & Excellence in Education, 45*(3), 363–372. DOI: 10.1080/10665684.2012.698149

Murakami, E., Nuñez, A.-M., & Cuero, K. (2010). Latin@ advocacy in the hyphen: Faculty identity and commitment in a Hispanic-Serving Institution. *International Journal of Qualitative Studies in Education, 23*(6), 699–717.

Rios-Aguilar, C., Kiyama, J. M., Gravitt, M., & Moll, L. C. (2011). Funds of knowledge for the poor and forms of capital for the rich? A capital approach to examining funds of knowledge. *Theory and Research in Education, 9*(2), 163–184.

Sotello Viernes Turner, C., González, J., & Wong, K. (2011). Faculty women of color: The critical nexus of race and gender. *Journal of Diversity in Higher Education, 4*(4), 199–211.

Sulé, V. T. (2011). Restructuring the master's tools: Black female and Latina faculty navigating and contributing in classrooms through oppositional positions. *Equity & Excellence in Education, 44*(2), 169–187.

Turner, C. S. (2002). Women of color in academe: Living with multiple marginality. *Journal of Higher Education 73*(1), 74–93.

PART II

HIGHER EDUCATION STRUCTURES

CHAPTER 9

INTRODUCTION TO PART II

Work–Life Balance within Higher Education Structures

Gloria M. Rodriguez

As I set out to write this introductory chapter, I couldn't help but view my involvement in this Latina/o work–life balance volume as alternately ironic and hypocritical. As the self-described "problem child" co-editor who encountered numerous work–life balance challenges this year in meeting all the self-imposed organizational and editorial deadlines, it became something of a quest to bring this work to fruition—including the writing of this introduction! To be very honest with our readers, I have never really experienced work–life balance as a Chicana faculty member in a research-intensive, predominantly White institution of higher education—never. Moreover, since I spent the better part of a decade being one of only three Latinas in my school of education and due to the other two women being involved in academic work outside our school or in administrative roles, I typically felt quite alone. I very often assumed the notion of work–life balance was reserved for those with whatever forms of privilege were necessary to secure it, including the ability to put oneself (and only one's own

Abriendo Puertas, Cerrando Heridas (Opening Doors, Closing Wounds), pages 97–101
Copyright © 2015 by Information Age Publishing
All rights of reproduction in any form reserved.

needs) first in all situations. Given that I had set out to contribute to the transformation of higher education to better reflect and respond to the strengths and needs of Latinas/os and other communities of color, I believed I could not allow myself to reflect too deeply or too often on just how out of balance the work–life scenario was for me. However, as readers will come to appreciate from the contributing authors in this section (and truly, throughout this volume), it is well worth pointing out that there is nothing particularly "balanced" about the pervasiveness of institutionalized racism, sexism, homophobia, classism, heteronormativity, and whatever we call the bias against single parents or other caregiving/family structures—to name just a few of the invisible (to those with privilege in these dimensions) sources of oppression that we endure as active participants in higher education institutions. Thus, rather than internalize the sense of failure that accompanies the persistent impact of institutionalized biases, which drain our energies for the things we most love about being academics, this section's contributors allow us to see how even within the structures of higher education one can find inspiration and reconnection to one's personal and "big picture" missions, as well as a commitment to not just strive for but to *take action toward* obtaining work–life balance.

To draw upon my roots as a Chicana raised in a family of farmworkers with a keen understanding of the need to leave the world better than how we found it, I would suggest that what our contributing authors are offering here are some perspectives and strategies for sustainability. Indeed, throughout the *testimonios* in this section, our authors invite us to consider that we have to be intentional and mindful of not only the giving of one's best efforts to accomplish individual and collective goals in the short term, but we also are called upon to seek work–life balance as a sustainability strategy that supports the long-term aspiration of higher education transformation. In my own experience, this individual/collective and short/long-term orientation to my work as an academic has not always been well understood by many of my colleagues and, in fact, has been viewed as my not having a clear focus in my scholarly endeavors. I believe I'm quite focused—on equity and social justice in and through higher education—but I'm not immune to the detriments of social isolation. When one is the lone representative of a particular marginalized group in any given campus committee, initiative, or even classroom, the social isolation becomes an enduring source of work–life *imbalance*, as noted by Jesse Perez Mendez in the first chapter of this section. Perez Mendez also points out, however, that being at the proverbial table still provides the opportunity to advocate for and otherwise support the broader mission of expanding that representation, thereby sustaining for the long term the positive impact that any one of us might achieve through our contributions in the short term.

Lilliana Patricia Saldaña, Felicia Castro Villarreal, and Erica Sosa in the second chapter help us to acknowledge the pressures toward conformity as a particular obstacle in the pursuit of work-life balance for Latina academics. In Castro Villarreal's *testimonio*, her explication of the paradox of both meeting high *and* interrupting low expectations that many Latina faculty members contend with in negotiating their professional and home identities is an insightful observation of academic life. As noted in the other *testimonios*, as well, Saldaña et al. describe richly how work–life balance is often centered on dilemmas of maintaining one's beliefs, values, and agency as human beings, even as one navigates the processes of tenure and promotion that typically demand distinct forms of institutional agency. Moreover, Margarita Jimenez-Silva, Maria Avalos, and Claudia Cervantes-Soon also echo some of the challenges inherent in balancing the multiple and often competing expectations of work and family life in their respective *testimonio* chapters, especially the beliefs and values that undergird the roles they have taken on as academics and as parents and caregivers. At times, achieving a sense of balance for these and perhaps other authors in this section has involved a negotiation of their sense of belonging—and dealing with the difficulties of not quite fitting into the norms of either conventional spouse/parent/family member or of the traditional academic.

In very powerful accounts of the dilemmas that emerge in clarifying what it means to "fit in" as faculty members under quite variable circumstances, several authors point to the need to build community with students, colleagues, and family. Linda Prieto invites us in the third chapter to think about how to combat the impact of social isolation through conscientious community-building in all aspects of one's academic and personal life. Juan Carrillo and Cervantes-Soon also share some moving experiences about the balancing of career opportunities with feelings of disconnection from one's cultural roots, practices, and "sacred spaces" that allow Latinas/os and other historically marginalized groups to thrive. These authors point to very tangible university and departmental policies and structures that accommodate child-rearing and pretenure research activity that can serve to facilitate the much-needed supports that ensure that one's productivity as a scholar does not come at the expense of that which keeps one grounded, energized, and connected to one's cultural or spiritual roots. As a protective strategy to combat social isolation, these authors demonstrate through their *testimonios* that engaging in community building renders greater opportunities for Latina/o faculty to find their place as academics, even as they constantly negotiate multiple identities and conflicting roles and priorities.

To further deepen our understanding of the complexities of finding one's place as Latina/o academics in the context of securing work–life balance, Sylvia Martinez identifies the need to embrace mentoring support for oneself and as part of the work we do for others. Learning how to navigate any given institution's processes for tenure and promotion proved to be crucial learning curves for several authors, and this often entailed developing the ability and will to seek out the resources needed to secure professional advancement. As readers make their way through the multiple *testimonios* shared by authors Laura Cortez, Melissa A. Martinez, Danielle Alsandor, Aurora Chang, and Anjalé D. Welton, we also come to appreciate the shared experiences with early career entrée into the spaces of academic networks, conferences, and mentor/mentee relationships. As these authors vividly describe their internal reflective sense-making as they were introduced to the various activities that surround our professional lives as scholars, I was reminded of my own early experiences attempting to participate alone in a conference featuring research in school finance. Given the predominance of scholars presenting large-scale quantitative work—indeed, the type of work I was trained in graduate school to conduct and also privilege—as I presented qualitative case study research, it was made infinitely clear to me by the gentleman in my session who fell asleep very noticeably during my presentation that the norms of this field were firmly established. It became deeply concerning that my success as a scholar rested on the ability to engage meaningfully with peers in my field who might one day be called upon to review my tenure dossier. However, my identity as a Chicana scholar seeking to improve the dismal conditions faced by my community through my scholarship would not be easy to negotiate in this crowd. Very much in resonance with the approaches that Cortez et al. have embraced, I strongly believe that my mentoring of graduate students to collaborate in their conference proposals and presentations of their scholarly work stems very directly from my worst experiences in attempting to navigate these venues in the expected, individualistic manner.

It is striking that in every chapter in this section, one finds examples of how adversity experienced by the authors inspired the commitments they carry about how to create more access, expand existing opportunities for academic careers, and generally foster a more inclusive, welcoming, and humane professional environment for new generations of Latina/o scholars and those representing other historically marginalized groups. Having a purpose such as these for our pursuits as Latina/o academics—indeed, as human beings, as well—is a critical theme that permeates the *testimonios* shared in this section. It is important to consider that for many of the contributing authors, the purpose they each bring to their individual scholarly pursuits is often tied to a broader, shared purpose on behalf of communities with whom they each identify personally, professionally, and/or politically. In other words, teaching, research, service, and family/community undertakings are the spaces and venues for practices that are carried out in alignment with one's purpose as a Latina/o academic, community leader, scholar activist, mentor, spouse/partner, parent/caregiver, brother/sister, daughter/son.

The development and embracing of purpose within the context of seeking work–life balance thus can be understood as a centering or prioritizing strategy among Latina/o scholars. In my experience, for example, having a clear sense of purpose *that I have defined for myself* allows me to know when (and how) to say "no" to various requests for my time and involvement and also provides me with clear evidence of when I am "on track" and when I have gone far astray in the purpose that informs my actions. Sometimes, the evidence presents itself in the forms of insomnia, reaching 5:00 p.m. each weekday and realizing I'm just now starting my own to-do list because I've attended to others' lists first, or being told by a physician that I have high blood pressure and I'm too sedentary. Revisiting my purpose means I'm forced to ask myself *why* I do what I do as a professor, so that I can create a healthier balance between that which *only* I can do and that which others *could* do in my stead but are happy to delegate to me. In addition, having a clear sense of purpose has also helped me guard against being ego-driven in my career-long pursuits. Not that academia is a glamorous life by any stretch of the imagination (here, I suspect some readers may conjure up images of known scholars who actually do seem glamorous to the rest of us!), but, perhaps because that is true, if the only reason for saying "yes" is to feed one's ego or boost the self-esteem, I have come to appreciate how quickly these low stakes devolve into petty politics, alienation, and in my case, a draining of energy, lots of hurt feelings, and betrayals of trust.

Humility, gratitude, love—these are terms that readers will find throughout the compelling *testimonios* of this section's authors, terms made all the more powerful by their conspicuous absence in the more conventional discourse of academics within the university environment. The authors are folks we respect deeply when we read their scholarly writing or in person if we happen to meet them at their conference presentations. Being entrusted with their *testimonios*, however, is a truly humbling experience. It is also painfully affirming in that we have all survived and endured the microaggressions and overt verbal assaults and general ignorance toward our cultural practices, beliefs and values, and deep commitments to our families and communities. I believe that readers, especially those who are either in the midst of similar experiences or attempting to bounce back from them, will find encouragement in the articulation of healing and self-care strategies that the authors share with us: running half-marathons; practicing yoga; including family in work events whenever possible; embracing meditation, prayer, and/or other spiritual practices; and creating family and community as a form of resistance to the social isolation of academia. That they utilize these strategies in the midst of both "giving back" *and* "paying it forward" is a testament to their strength, commitment, and generosity—and for their enduring presence, we can all be grateful.

CHAPTER 10

SGT. PEPPER'S LONELY HEARTS CLUB

Latino Administrators in Higher Education

Jesse Perez Mendez

The journey that most Latinos undertake in academia has been well-documented, either navigating the waters as a student (Berlak & Moyenda, 2001; Hagedorn, Chi, Cepeda, & McClain, 2007; Orfield, Losen, Wald, & Swanson, 2004) or as a faculty member (Delgado Bernal & Villapando, 2002; Delgado-Romero, Flores, Gloria, Arrendendo, & Castellanos, 2003; Turner & Myers, 2000) at predominantly White institutions (PWIs). However, the experiences of Latino administrators in higher education in their environment warrant more attention in the literature (Haro & Lara, 2003).

The present state of Latino administrators in higher education illustrates that more work needs to be done, considering long-reaching implications on institutions serving Latino populations. Latino administrators are instrumental in creating a hospitable and inclusive environment for Latino students and faculty alike as being powerbrokers on their campuses

Abriendo Puertas, Cerrando Heridas (Opening Doors, Closing Wounds), pages 103–112
Copyright © 2015 by Information Age Publishing
All rights of reproduction in any form reserved.

(Bensimon & Tierney, 1992/1993). In addition, from an institutional perspective, the number of administrators of color serves as a marker for institutional commitment to diversity (Jackson, 2001). And the general population of Latinos in the United States is growing at an extraordinary rate and recently overtook African Americans as the largest minority block in the country and on college campuses (Fry, 2011). In fact, the Pew Research Center projects Latinos constituting a majority in some states in the near future (Lopez, 2014). However, higher education has been slow to react to this demographic change, even though more Latinos are graduating from high schools in higher numbers (Fry & Taylor, 2013).

With an increasing Latino population, much attention has been directed toward the plight of students and faculty of color in academia, but there remains limited literature addressing the state of administrators of color at PWIs (Jackson & Flowers, 2003), much less Latino administrators. This chapter will serve as an opportunity to contribute to the literature by sharing my administrative experience at a community college and land grant institution in the following sections of this chapter.

Obviously, I am cognizant that my narrative harbors generalizability limitations, and I am hopeful that my contribution is not interpreted as self-serving or self-congratulatory. My intention is to empower others by sharing my own experience and my approach in achieving some semblance of balance along the way. Whereas the focus of the chapter centers on administrative life, there are some strong nexuses with my previous life as an untenured faculty member that provides some context. Throughout the next few pages, my comments will be labeled as *en el reloj, en el comité,* and *en la carrera.*

EN EL RELOJ

Receiving that phone call in the afternoon in the spring of 2005 was exciting and terrifying at the same time. I thoroughly enjoyed my campus interview in Stillwater and met some great people in the college. Although I was on the cusp of accepting my first tenure-track position after being an adjunct at another research institution and community college, a part of me was partly terrified at what lay ahead in academia and the possibility of being rejected for tenure. However, with any anxiety, it's a personal choice in how we channel it. Unbridled or unaccounted for, this anxiety can run amok in your psyche and self-esteem, but the other, more positive alternative is to use it as motivation and challenge yourself.

In addition, there was also the environment to consider. I was stepping foot on a campus that I hadn't even considered as a possibility before my interview, but the diversity dynamics of the institution mirrored other institutions that I have attended in the past. Throughout my entire graduate experience, it wasn't until my dissertation phase where I had my first Latino faculty mentor who graciously served on my advisory committee. Whether hardened by these past experiences at PWIs, I didn't label the new environment as hostile; I think that any new atmosphere tests one's resolve and raises doubt in one's ability to be successful. In addition, my transition into the new environment was eased by the presence of some key mentors, including but not limited to the program coordinator of my home department and some key administrators in the college, namely an associate dean of Native American descent in addition to a first-year colleague and friend of Latin American decent. Outside of the college, the Hispanic staff and faculty organization on campus lacked any faculty involvement, tenured or tenure-track. Even with these very supportive colleagues, my social circle was mostly void of any Latino tenured faculty colleagues who could have provided mentorship. Short of that, within my own college, I had to be my own mentor and most staunch advocate.

One of the larger challenges on the tenure track was to decline requests of my time. Being one of the few Latino faculty on campus, I can personally attest to the experience of faculty of color—I was put in countless situations where I was asked to speak on behalf of other people of color who were stakeholders on campus. Personally it can and has generated some internal trepidation, mainly because I don't have the mandate to speak for all of those who share my cultural background, but I recognized the importance of having our perspective present in campus dialogues. It is just a larger time commitment when on the tenure track. Once tenure was achieved and the tick-tock of the clock ceased, I found it easier to commit to diversity initiatives on campus. However, it remains a beautiful obligation that should be balanced as either a faculty member or administrator of color.

EN EL COMITÉ

My experience as a governor-appointed regent for a public community college was as unexpected as it was rewarding. Some boards within the state require that particular service areas be represented by a regent who resides in that area. While watching a baseball game at my institution, I received a phone call from a state senator of my district who knew of my research background, inquiring whether I would be interested in serving as a regent for a public community college given my academic background and where I resided. The community college was a three-campus PWI that served the northern part of the state with more than 5,000 enrolled. Each campus served a city that would be best described as rural. Being a second-year assistant professor at that time and a faculty member at a comprehensive research university that was also a PWI within the same state, I was hesitant at first to serve in this capacity. I had visions of being in politically compromised positions during my five-year term as an untenured faculty member. However, after reflecting more, I saw this as an opportunity to impact higher education directly, given the role that community colleges play in postsecondary access and my own attitude toward social uplift responsibility of higher education.

My term on the board was a very fulfilling one. The state senate confirmation process was admittedly an anxiety-producing experience, but an educational one. Board nominees present themselves before the education subcommittee in the state senate, and during the days leading up to the confirmation hearing, C-SPAN visions of personal hard-hitting questions posed to U.S. Supreme Court nominees floated in my head. I imagined questions ranging from my political leanings to my preference of cereal being casted on me by imposing senators. "Dr. Mendez, as a regent of a community college, what are your feelings about the holding of *Roe v. Wade* (1972)?" However, the reality of the process was more benign than I could have possibly imagined. After I was introduced to the subcommittee, no one had questions, and I was later dismissed. Later that week, the state senate confirmed my nomination, and I started to read more about the history of the institution that I was about to serve. It had a storied history of more than a century in serving the rural population in the northern part of the state and a sizeable Native American population.

The longstanding and distinguished president of the community college retired during my term, compelling the institution to self-reflect on its future and direction. Following his retirement, the institution underwent one presidential resignation, an interim president for a year, and the appointment of a new college president who would lead the institution for years to come. I not only had the privilege of shouldering this responsibility with the other regents, but I also had the opportunity to chair the presidential search committee during my last year on the board.

In retrospect, I had underestimated the regional profile of serving as a regent for a community college. In the beginning, I merely saw myself as a glorified administrator, providing guidance in the operation of small rural college. However, the longer I served in my term, it became apparent that the regents *meant something more* because the institution was such a huge part of the communities in which there was a branch campus. And as a regent, you, regardless of the color of your skin, represented that institution among the different stakeholders. Although it is easily deductible, it's the genuine emotional connection that the communities attach to this role and the institution that surprised and pleased me. I experienced nothing but respect, support, and the warmth of kindness from everyone associated with this hard-working rural community college.

If anything, the only uneasiness came from an aspect in which they had no control—the lack of Latino peers. Given the status of the position, I was also cognizant that I was the only regent of Latino descent in the state, and just as a faculty member, it is impossible to divorce oneself of one's Latino identity. On a fairly routine basis, the college would broach issues that would have an impact on either Latinos or other students of color on campus or in the communities, and I found myself advocating for positions with their needs in mind. Such examples would be the state of ESL programs on campus, the inclusion of diversity in administrative hiring practices, considering institutional decision-making with demographic information in mind, and monitoring presidential candidates on their approach to leadership and diversity. In addition, because the role of regent has such high social status in the communities, my identity was not lost on other Latinos on campus. On the campuses, the pictures of the regents are posted in the main hallway at all three branch campuses, and I lost count of how many Latino students have approached me randomly and mentioned how great it was to see a brown face in those hallways. It illustrates the need for more Latino stakeholders at various administrative levels of higher education, given the growing number of Latinos within the state.

My term ended during my second year as an associate professor, and during the last year of my term, I was asked to serve as an associate school head after receiving tenure. With a new dean hired and the present school head wishing to return to faculty before retirement, I applied for the position that I wouldn't have imagined assuming seven years before.

EN LA CARRERA

Within our college, we subscribe to a school structure where several programs are housed under one academic unit. After acquiring tenure and concluding my term on the board, my peers recommended my appointment in the school head position, and I was humbled by the honor. But with this responsibility, I gave myself some freedom to meander to how I identified with my administrative role and how I would undertake advocacy on a new administrative level even with the steady, kind guidance of a dean. In a rational sense, I am very much conscious about being one of the few Latino administrators on campus. But instead of being invested in the present state of that environment, I think that we have the choice in how to respond to our environment. The temptation may be to dwell on the atmosphere, using it as a lynchpin and tying our frustrations on when the administrative issues may be less than ideal. It's very easy to become bitter throughout this process. On the other hand, this energy can be utilized to persist, grow, serve the constituents of the administrative unit/college, and identify opportunities for social uplift and advocacy, while managing a balance not only with scholarship, but also any personal stress levels with this administrative life on the run.

Compared to my previous experience as a regent, the altitude of the position is obviously lower to the ground, enabling one to concentrate on more of the minutia of administrative operations. But like my time as a regent, the new role of an academic head enabled me to make the academic unit more open to diverse perspectives and, with the faculty, diversify (in the broadest sense of the word) our academic ranks with new hires. I am fortunate to work with great colleagues from different walks of life, and each of them brings something special to the equation of the academic unit.

In addition, in comparing my obligations from being an assistant professor to being an administrator, what is asked and the frequency has not changed, but the amount of disposable time I have has decreased, requiring me to be selective about my choices. Another parallel between academic and administrative life is a lack of Latino peers in my journey so far. In addition, if Latino faculty was a super-exclusive group on campus, being a Latino administrator on campus is somewhat like being the sole member of Sgt. Pepper's Lonely Hearts Club. In becoming an administrator, particularly an academic head, colleagues that you previously depended on for fellowship are no longer peers on paper. The same coping mechanisms that served as an assistant professor are employed to some degree as an administrator. You must continue to serve as your own advocate, supporter, and personal internal cheerleader. To some degree, there is a dynamic that can serve as a silver lining: serving as a mentor to junior faculty, staff, and students on campus and providing an element in their lives that you may have lacked—emotional and personal support from an experienced peer.

Issues with Balance

Niños

There are only so many hours to a day, so much given energy in our bodies, and a finite amount of emotional bandwidth in a given amount of time. There not only has to be balance within oneself but also with those closest to us, especially if you have children. In the remaining sections of this chapter, I'll briefly provide an overview of how I have integrated my children into my work and how I manage stress to maintain perspective in life.

My two children were born while I was on the tenure track. Presently my son, Elias, is a very active six-year-old boy while my thoughtful daughter is about to turn eight this May. When I made the transition to administration, I was concerned about their well-being, and I have made conscious efforts to integrate them into my work life as much as I can in addition to making time to address their needs and attend their social and athletic activities. When they were younger, I would take them to social functions at the community college. Sometimes their behavior would cooperate with the social outing, and sometimes it would not. In my current role, they are regular characters in the sitcom that is my office. They will sometimes accompany me to short visits in the late afternoon where their presence isn't a distraction. They also have attended social outings with me for the college on occasion. In ideal situations, their activities on campus are of their own. Last year, they were enrolled in a reading program in the child development center, and they regularly check out books in the library in the college of education. I do this for three reasons. First, I enjoy spending time with them and I like that they are interwoven into the different dynamics of my life. Second, I see this integration as key for the development of their cultural and social capital, an aspect that I did not have to this degree when I was a child. And third, with many faculty with children in the college, I want to make sure that the working environment is child-friendly. Of course, there are reasonable parameters of the presence of children in working environments, but I do want faculty to feel free to integrate their own children into their academic lifestyle if they choose.

Managing Stress

Additional stress is perhaps the largest element in transition from faculty to administrative life, and it's probably best to develop healthy ways to dissipate the cumulative stress that accumulates in a given period of time. For the past few years, I have been a runner, participating mostly in half-marathons. This activity provides an outlet for self-reflection, managing any cortisol levels that come with daily and administrative life, and allowing my mind to deconstruct any issues. In addition, there are added health concerns for Latinos when it comes to diabetes. According to the U.S. Department of Health and Human Services (2014), Latinos are 1.7 times more likely to be diagnosed with diabetes than non-Hispanic White adults and 1.5 times more likely to die from complications from diabetes. Like many Latinos, diabetes has a strong history with both of my parents' families. Whereas I don't know what the chances are of being diagnosed in the future, running allows me the option to at least keep this risk in check, among all of life's challenges. In addition, running provides me an opportunity to meditate, zone out, and brainstorm at the same time. There have been instances where I have developed a really great solution to an administrative issue on a long run or devised an interesting study during my runs.

Also, running and training for races also harbor positives that exceed their physical and emotional benefits—it's the positive outlook on personal improvement. It's a healthy way to compete with yourself that can be transferred to other aspects of life. In academia and administration, sometimes the perceived competition with colleagues can become such a strong, manufactured focus, which can be unhealthy and unnecessary. With running, the focus is on your pace with less regard for how your peers are advancing. The aim is to improve your personal record times, your pace, and your own well-being. With the society's emphasis on competition, placing more attention on your own personal development and inner peace is probably the healthiest approach to life.

Perspectives

On an institutional level, the recruitment, but also the retention of higher education administrators of color remains an issue for colleges and universities (Jackson, 2002; León, 2003). Some institutions have used leadership institutes to develop administrative talent (Leon & Nevarez, 2007; Raines & Alberg, 2003; Smith & Ross, 2005), but many of these initiatives are decentralized and locally devised. Instead, it will be up to us as individual Latino stakeholders to develop ourselves while identifying younger Latino stakeholders to mentor and develop our community, whether it be locally or regionally. And in that sense, we cannot rely on others to advocate for us; we will have to advocate for ourselves. As with any obligation, it's another variable that has to be negotiated in our lives.

So in this journey of advocacy, three general themes should be emphasized throughout the preceding sections of this chapter. First, the path of Latino administrators, particularly in a PWI, can be a lonely one. Relationships with peers outside your college, or even outside the university, are key in establishing support systems. Be resourceful and cultivate those relationships. Make sure to remain positive and to be your own personal internal cheerleader. Second, developing healthy ways to maintain balance is a constant challenge. If you don't take time to take care of yourself, your ability to care for others will be dramatically undercut. Although not an exclusive list, this can be done by exercise, mediation, prayer, and/or hobbies. And third, maintaining that balance not only within yourself, but with your family and children is a constant challenge. Your approach may not look like everyone else's, and you need that flexibility to tailor one that fits you and your lifestyle.

As a stakeholder in the institution despite our standing, we must accept that we have the beautiful burden of advocacy for our community, creating an inclusive environment for all using our personal experience as Latinos/Latinas, generating cultural capital for those who need it, and taking care of ourselves so that we can take care of others.

REFERENCES

Bensimon, E. M., & Tierney, W. J. (1992/1993). Shaping the vision for a multicultural campus: Strategies for administrators. *College Board Review, 166,* 4–30.

Berlak, A., & Moyenda, S. (2001). *Taking it personally: Racism in the classroom from kindergarten to college.* Philadelphia, PA: Temple University Press.

Delgado Bernal, D., & Villapando, O. (2002). An apartheid of knowledge in academia: The struggle over the "legitimate" knowledge of faculty of color. *Equity and Excellence in Education, 35,* 169–180.

Delgado-Romero, E. A., Flores, L. Y., Gloria, A. M., Arrendendo, P., & Castellanos, J. (2003). Development career challenges for Latino/a faculty in higher education. In J. Castellanos & L. Jones (Eds.), The majority in the minority: Expanding the representation of Latina/o faculty, administrators and students in higher education (pp. 257–284). Sterling, VA: Stylus Publishing.

Fry, R. (2011). *Hispanic college enrollment spikes, narrowing gaps with other groups.* Washington, DC: Pew Hispanic Center. Retrieved from http://www.pewhispanic.org/2011/08/25/hispanic-college-enrollment-spikes-narrowing-gaps-with-other-groups/

Fry, R., & Taylor, P. (2013). Hispanic high school graduates pass Whites in rate of college enrollment. Pew Research Hispanic Center. Retrieved from www.pewhispanic.org/2013/05/09/hispanic-high-school-graduates-pass-whites-in-college-enrollment/

Hagedorn, L. S., Chi, W., Cepeda, R. M., & McClain, M. (2007). An investigation of critical mass: The role of Latino representation in the successes of urban community college students. *Research in Educational Research, 48*(1), 73–90.

Haro, R., & Lara, J. F. (2003). Latinos and administrative positions in American higher education. In J. Castellanos & L. Jones (Eds.), *The majority in the minority: Expanding the representation of Latina/o faculty, administrators, and students in higher education* (pp. 153–165). Sterling, VA: Stylus.

Jackson, J. F. L. (2001). A new test for diversity: Retaining African American administrators at predominantly White institutions. In L. Jones (Ed.), *Retaining African Americans in higher education: Challenging paradigms for retaining students, faculty and administrators* (pp. 99–109). Sterling, VA: Stylus.

Jackson, J. F. L. (2002). Retention of African American administrators at predominantly White institutions: Using professional growth factors to inform the discussion. *College and University, 78,* 11–16.

Jackson, J. F. L., & Flowers, L. A. (2003). Retaining African American student affairs administrators: Voices from the field. *Journal of College Student Affairs, 22*(2), 125–136.

León, D. J. (Ed.). (2003). *Latinos in higher education.* London, UK: Elsevier.

Leon, D., & Nevarez, C. (2007). Models of leadership institutes for increasing the number of top Latino administrators in higher education. *Journal of Hispanics in Higher Education, 6,* 356–378.

Lopez, M. H. (2014, January 14). In 2014, Latinos will surpass whites as largest racial/ethnic group in California. *Pew Research Center.* Retrieved from http://www.pewresearch.org/fact-tank/2014/01/24/in-2014-latinos-will-surpass-whites-as-largest-racialethnic-group-in-california/

Orfield, G., Losen, D., Wald, J., & Swanson, C. (2004). *Losing our future: How minority youth are being left behind by the graduation rate crisis.* Cambridge, MA: The Civil Rights Project at Harvard University.

Raines, S. C., & Alberg, M. S. (2003). The role of professional development in preparing academic leaders. *New Directions for Higher Education, 2003*(124), 33–39. doi:10.1002/he.128

Roe v. Wade, 410 U.S. 113 (1973).

Smith, G. A., & Ross, M. (2005). American Council on Education Fellows Program: Celebrating 40 years of leadership development in higher education. In D. J. León (Ed.), *Lessons in leadership: Executive leadership programs for advancing diversity in higher education* (pp. 109–126). London, UK: Elsevier.

Turner, C. S., & Myers, S. L. (2000). *Faculty of color in academe: Bittersweet success.* Des Moines, IA: Longwood Division, Allyn & Bacon.

U.S. Department of Health and Human Services, Office of Minority Affairs. (2014). *Diabetes and Hispanics.* Retrieved from http://minorityhealth.hhs.gov/templates/content.aspx?lvl=2&lvlID=54&ID=3324

CHAPTER 11

CREATING WORK–LIFE BALANCE IN ACADEMIA

Family, Community, and Self-Care

Lilliana Patricia Saldaña, Felicia Castro Villarreal, and Erica Sosa

For women faculty of color, maintaining work–life balance means making everyday decisions through a mestiza consciousness that moves us in and out of opposing cultures to create new ways of being and knowing in academia (Anzaldúa, 2010). As first-generation Chicana/Latina scholars, we navigate multiple cultural terrains—the meritocratic, competitive, patriarchal, and Eurocentric culture of academia, which places research, teaching, and service demands and an institutional pressure to publish above all—and the worlds we inhabit outside of academia, namely our families and the various community spaces that provide us with spiritual and emotional nourishment. These worlds often conflict with the stress to obtain tenure and our commitment to remain fully human and whole. The boundaries between these worlds are porous as we "catch up" with our work in our homes, often to the point of exhaustion, or rigidly structure our workday with the intention of being fully present as mothers, daughters, spouses/partners, and scholar activists.

Abriendo Puertas, Cerrando Heridas (Opening Doors, Closing Wounds), pages 113–125
Copyright © 2015 by Information Age Publishing
All rights of reproduction in any form reserved.

Framed within critical race and Chicana feminist theories of everyday life, our *testimonios* speak to the challenges we face in maintaining "work-life" balance, including the ways we have worked through racial microaggressions and heteropatriarchal gender norms and expectations as Chicana/Latina junior faculty in academia (Delgado Bernal, Burciaga, & Flores Carmona, 2012; Latina Feminist Group, 2001; Medina & Luna, 2000; Solórzano & Yosso, 2000; Vasquez-Guignard, 2010; Zamudio et. al., 2011). Our *testimonios* include specific strategies of the ways in which we have "worked through" the various psychosocial and historical injuries as first-generation Chicana and Latina scholars to achieve work–life balance. Through our *testimionios,* we call for the creation of mentoring and collaboration, professional networking, safe and nurturing environments in which to express fears and insecurities, strategic planning as we work towards earning tenure, and self-care. We contend that it is through cross-disciplinary collaboration, transformational resistance (Solórzano & Delgado Bernal, 2001), and collective dialogue that we can begin to enact institutional changes that will transform the heteropatriarchal, Eurocentric, and capitalistic structures of academia that perpetuate inequalities for Chicana/Latina faculty.

FELICIA'S TESTIMONIO

For mothers in academia, finding work–life balance can feel like an uphill battle. Juggling multiple identities as a Latina, mother, and scholar, I very quickly found myself struggling to keep my head above water, but as someone who forged her identity on defying odds and exceeding expectations, failure was not an option. The professoriate and motherhood, however, beg to differ as evidenced by the underrepresentation of Latina/o scholars (<1% of U.S. scholars are Latino/a) and many female academics waiting on or deciding against parenthood (Halpern, 2008). While many working mothers report stress associated with balancing work and childcare, systemic and familial barriers unique to the academy make it especially challenging for Latina mothers to thrive as scholars. Therefore, for women academics, the reality of social and cultural norms combined with the pressures of the academy often comes to bear, resulting in fewer female academics, fewer female academics with children, fewer to attain tenure, and more females in non-tenure track positions in community colleges (Halpern, 2008; Perna, 2004; Van Anders, 2004).

My Story

The "tug of war" between family and work, the struggle to juggle it all and the emotions that accompany tough decision-making make up my inner conflicts and anxieties, my *papelitos guardados* (Latina Feminist Group,

2001). Along with this reality, I continue to contend with internalized narratives that at times motivated me and other times hindered me.

While low expectations are shared experiences in the academy, the stark contrast with high societal and cultural expectations is less examined (Ek, Quijada Cerecer, Alanis, & Rodriguez, 2010; Gutiérrez y Muhs et al., 2012). That is, in the academy, I feel as if I am always being evaluated, always surveyed for competence and the right to be here—low expectations mark many a Latina academic and scholarly experience. In my social and cultural world, by contrast, I am faced with the highest of expectations for motherhood, marriage, and childcare: hence my fearless struggle to defy expectations in the workplace and tireless pursuit to meet expectations at home.

My mother modeled for me what her mother and grandmother modeled for her, and more. She lectured on the importance of obtaining an education and being independent but also in an almost superhuman fashion, she modeled how to successfully juggle a career as a nurse, wife, and mother of three. For her, child rearing and maintaining the household was just as important as her career. With every plug for education, she emphasized the importance of caring for a family through cooking, cleaning, and taking care of Daddy. She modeled no other option but to do it all.

This insatiable desire to meet or exceed expectations, however, evolved into a need for validation. My identity began to rely heavily on what others thought of me—positive and negative. While initially negative stereotypes and the idea of defying expectations motivated me, eventually these stereotypes became fused with my identity and became central themes of my internal dialogue. I internalized all that I had experienced, all that I had read. Perceived incompetence and negative stereotypes that initially motivated me began to push me to always want and do more. My inner voice that was once instrumental to my overcoming adversity and accomplishing goals, gradually began to make me second guess myself, a preoccupation with other's perceptions of me—cognitive capacity ill spent on "what if" and "what not to do and say." My preoccupation with disconfirming stereotypes was at times paralyzing. This realization through reflection, however, was critical to silencing the voices and moving forward.

Reflection

As a Latina mother in academia finding *my* work–life balance was a process that began with self-reflection. After feeling physically and mentally exhausted at the end of each day, I took the time to reflect on what was really important to me in terms of personal and professional goals. This conscious reflection was critical to my identification of the sources of my stress, anxiety, and fears. Discovering the "function" of my behaviors and thoughts helped me to identify appropriate strategies to reach my goals. First, I tracked my journey toward becoming a professor and reflected on pivotal experiences and important people. Since becoming a professor, my life had become so fast-paced that until I couldn't manage it all, I hadn't reflected on purpose. Through introspection, I realized I was attempting to do it all in attempt to "talk back" to the oppressive narratives that I had internalized—I was doing things for all the wrong reasons. For so long, I was told that pursuing a PhD was too arduous a task and "not worth it." For so long, my dreams were ignored and even slighted, wanting to become a psychologist fell on deaf ears, so that I was running on autopilot without real purpose—without an end point. One particular oppressive narrative replayed in my mind, "That's alright, that's OK, you'll be mowing my lawn someday."

It was narratives like that, that at times motivated me and other times hindered me. Always operating like I had something to prove, I imposed too much pressure on myself and assumed others perceived me as incompetent, often misperceiving ambiguous and neutral comments as offensive or interrogative. These automatic thoughts began to impede my performance, similar to the effects of the social psychology phenomenon known as the stereotype threat, where ethnic minorities underperform as they buy in to stereotypes that they perform poorly in comparison to their Caucasian counterparts (Schmader & Johns, 2003; Steele & Aronson, 1995). The internal dialogue that initially fueled my desire to pursue my PhD turned counterproductive.

This self-examination, difficult as it was, was critical to my prioritizing and setting goals. Through reflection, I found that family and religion were of utmost importance to me but that I also had a purpose that had originated very early in my development—to serve as a role model just as my mother had been to me and to silence those oppressive narratives through service to others. Once I identified my larger goals, I was able to prioritize ways to reach those goals.

Time and Scheduling

I made a nontraditional non-eight-to-five job a traditional eight-to-five job by adhering to a rigid schedule. I arrived to the office at 8:00 a.m. and stayed until 5:00 p.m. I posted hourly, daily, and weekly goals for myself. For me, rigid self-imposed scheduling and deadlines were essential to successfully juggling my personal and professional lives. By forcing structure and rigidity, I was able to accomplish a lot and not feel as if I needed to take work home, allowing time to fulfill household and childcare responsibilities. This forced structure helped to reduce the stress and guilt that many female academics experience (Perna, 2004). This was also a way of carving space. I advanced my scholarly work through rigid scheduling and carved space through availability and visibility.

Collaborate and Seek Mentorship

Collaborate, collaborate, collaborate: Partnering with scholars with similar research interests, divergent interests, common ethnic backgrounds, and/or similar outside interests is critical to surviving in the academy. Collaboration not only increases productivity but it also provides much-needed social support.

In my experience, collaborative research groups impose social accountability and help to build and sustain momentum. When one is juggling many responsibilities and expectations, social accountability and support are essential. Aside from collaborating on research products to share data collection, entry, and the writing load, collaborative groups breed real friendships, collegiality, and a sense of "belonging." There is nothing like sharing the struggles and challenges of the academy with others who can identify with you. The idea of collaboration hinges on the notions of shared responsibility and creating space through networking and partnerships. Through collaboration you are likely to find a great mentor. Through partnerships you are likely to find the strength and courage to continue when faced with adversity and rejection. It is in meaningful relationships that you are likely to find the *communidad* you need when the essence of who you are is challenged.

Mentoring is also critical to surviving in the academy, especially for those who have been historically marginalized. Similar to my regimented schedule, I also scheduled reoccurring meeting times with mentors to discuss research projects and deadlines. Even more important than the content knowledge transmitted through the mentoring relationship is the social relationship, wisdom, and sense of "mentoring forward" that is modeled.

Utilize Resources

While resources vary by institution, it is important to utilize research and writing centers, grant support, course releases, and course buyouts to support scholarly endeavors. Freedom and perceived flexibility can be deceiving. For me, finding out about all available resources was essential to my successfully navigating the tenure process, teaching, grant writing, service expectations, and research supports. It is of utmost importance that we advocate for ourselves and exhaust each resource made available to offset those competing service and familial expectations to which women in the academy can easily fall victim.

All too often, available resources are left untapped, especially by those who have been historically marginalized. I was taught to discover my own internal resources, as to ask others was a sign of weakness. This "do it yourself" mentality led to introversion and isolation. As an undergraduate I stayed to myself, electing to write 30-page research papers rather than working in groups or delivering in class presentations. My fear of the unknown, my fear of going outside my comfort zone paralyzed me. As an early-career academic, those same fears, tendencies, and internalized narratives threatened to stop me again. Here again, reflection was key as I was able to identify patterns and see my tendency to isolate myself and not ask questions. Therefore, one of the best recommendations I have is to consciously move outside your comfort zone and tap internal and external resources to contest oppressive systems and in some cases narratives.

I offer my *testimonio* as a way to transmit knowledge, to expose my inner conflicts and anxieties in hopes of validating someone else's, and to demonstrate that storytelling is safe and an acceptable methodology. Above all, I offer my *testimonio* to transmit knowledge and share effective strategies to advance Latina mothers in the academy. My story tells of struggle and triumph aided by conscious reflection to identify goals and priorities—what I believe to be the first step toward finding *your* work–life balance.

ERICA'S TESTIMONIO

For minority faculty, the typical pressures of "publish or perish" are exacerbated by insecurities, fears of failing, and, more importantly, fears of failing and subsequently supporting a stereotype that we are in some way inferior to our majoritarian counterparts. Some of these feelings are self-inflicted. However, some arise from a divide between academia and the Latino value system. Sometimes as Latinas, we struggle to figure out how to fit the traditional academic mold in order to survive. However, appreciating differences is critical to creating a more diverse and inclusive academia. By identifying Latino values and how those align or are interpreted in academic culture, we can devise strategies for success and advancement in academia. Moreover, as Latina presence increases, we can show how these diverse values can complement and benefit academia.

Familismo versus Being Career-Oriented

I am very close to my family both physically and emotionally. I was that stereotypical Latina who wouldn't move away from home (or not for good at least). I moved away to complete my doctoral work but returned quickly to pursue my career. My current faculty position is back where my family lives, affording me opportunities to help my mother, sisters, and extended family whenever possible. I equally benefit from the support of my family as our ability to improve each other's lives is more important than fulfilling any individual self-interest. *Familismo,* the loyalty to one's nuclear and extended family, is not a burden; it is a welcomed responsibility. The family benefits from each other's presence and resources and accomplishes more as an interdependent unit.

I have learned over time that staying physically close to my family can be misinterpreted by some as being driven by fear. Mentors have urged me to not be afraid to leave the nest. Other Latina faculty at other institutions have received similar advice and criticism for decisions based on "being too afraid to be on their own." Sometimes, these decisions are based on *familismo* and not fear or weakness or insecurities.

I advise my Latino students about their future careers in the context of location and family responsibility. Sometimes considering the job market, I advise students to move away from home. However, these discussions are always done in the context of how they will be able to contribute to their family when they return. Also, I discuss other career options if they choose to stay in town. I realize their decision to stay might not be driven by fear but instead by devotion to family and their want to put their family's interests before their own. As academia acknowledges this value, we can have more fruitful conversations regarding *familismo* and professional pursuits.

Respeto versus Assertiveness

Growing up in a Mexican American home, I learned that respect is central to every relationship. Respect is shown by listening intently, waiting my turn to speak, and not questioning my elders. These gendered and cultural signs of respect can be misinterpreted in academia. Academia thrives on assertive scholars who competitively seek to be the first to discover new knowledge. We boldly propose innovative ideas, confidently lead research teams to complete tasks, and firmly defend our research against the toughest critics. This culture makes me sometimes feel like I'm in the middle of Wall Street with people shouting out bids on stocks while I sit respectfully and am outbid every time.

I realized early in my career how my respect for others was being interpreted as weakness, insecurity, and lacking professional accomplishments. At a professional conference, a young White male colleague and I were listening to a senior male faculty casually discuss his research with us. As I listened respectfully, the young male interrupted the senior researcher to discuss his own research and accomplishments in the field. I sat shocked at the disrespectful and obviously self-promoting behavior. I was sure the older faculty would be offended. However, the senior faculty seemed to welcome this as an acceptable display of assertion. By the end of the conversation, the senior faculty congratulated and set up a collaborative project with the young aspiring colleague. I stood there puzzled at what just happened. My attempt to show respect resulted in me being seen as a passive listener whereas the young White male was seen as an assertive go-getter who succeeds.

Knowing that recent research suggests confidence is more important than competence to be perceived as a leader, I've realized I need to develop this trait. Perceived lack in confidence might partially explain why Latinas earn 59% of what White men earn, even less than White women who earn 81% of what White men earn or Black women who earn 68% of what White men earn (American Association of University Women, 2013). Our inability or lack of desire to negotiate (sometimes driven by feelings that we do not need or deserve something) can leave us out on things that others feel entitled to.

Although I am confident in my skill set, I will never be good at subtly bragging about myself among academics. However, I've noticed a strength of Latina faculty is promoting each other. Many Latina faculty at my university do a great job of promoting each other's work. This keeps us in the spotlight without having to engage in some of the awkward self-promotion so valued in academia. I have also established a mentor–mentee relationship with a very successful and accomplished Latina faculty at another institution who promotes me better than I could promote myself. She invites me in on projects and to collaborate with her based on my qualifications and not self-promoting behavior.

Other institutional mechanisms can assist Latina faculty to do well despite being less likely to advocate for themselves. In our department, we use a very structured annual report system. Although most universities have an annual report, our department leadership is really good about disseminating highlights from the report to all department faculty. In a sense, our department promotes me annually for my accomplishments over the previous year. These types of approaches make it easier to recognize faculty for their competence and contributions and without relying on self-promotion.

Turning the Focus from Deficit to Strengths

Within the varying perspective in academia, support groups can help Latina faculty succeed. I have been blessed to be invited into the *hermandad* of REAL (Research for the Education and Advancement of Latin@s). REAL has been an amazing group of Latina faculty who have provided support through my pursuits as a junior faculty. They also collaborate to identify and address critical issues in education impacting Latinos. This group comprises strong women whom I respect both professionally and personally. The collaborative approach has served us well in succeeding in our professional endeavors.

Imagine an academia that embraces the best of both worlds. An academia that promotes productivity and assertiveness in the context of values such as *familismo* and *respeto* and recognizes how these values manifest themselves in our behaviors could be more inclusive. As more Latinas join higher education, perhaps we will see a shift in the academic culture. Latinas can be viewed as family-centered, collaborative, strong, and dedicated professionals. Our behaviors can be understood in the context of our values and not as signs of weakness or fear. We are strong and dedicated professionals with wonderfully diverse perspectives on the academic culture. We are in no way inferior. We can succeed. We are needed and we belong here.

LILLIANA'S TESTIMONIO: SELF-CARE AND SELF-LOVE IN ACADEMIA

As a Chicana and Chicano studies tenure-track professor committed to the transformative spirit of an academic discipline that was born out of social struggle, maintaining work–life balance comes as a challenge, particularly as the spaces between the "professional," "political," and "personal" merge, clash, or at times split into separate aspects of my life. At times, I am able to weave the three major aspects of my profession—research, teaching, and service—into a fluid methodology that speaks to my vocation as a Chicana scholar. For example, I am able to bring together my passion for critical studies in education into my pedagogical praxis (Gonzalez, 2001). Other times, I bring my teaching/learning of decolonial theory into my research. However, service to the nonacademic community is the most challenging, given the institutional pressure to publish, particularly during tenure track (Urrieta & Mendez Benavidez, 2007). As a Chicana scholar with close ties to local social justice movements, being engaged in the community means participating in nonacademic spaces of social struggle—spaces that are often invisible in academia. As a tenure-track scholar activist committed to the production of emancipatory knowledge, being involved in local social struggles requires conscious, strategic, political, and personal decision making every single day. The pressure to publish and my personal commitment to communities of struggle pull me in opposite directions as I'm left having to choose, for instance, between attending an immigrant rights protest or completing work that will count towards tenure. At the end of the day, I'm left feeling as if I've compromised one of the many parts of myself.

For me, creative and spiritual expressions like doing yoga—the ancient Sanskrit word that means "to join one point to another" or "to leave one place, space, condition, and move toward a better one"—has added lightness, vitality, and energy to a profession that can be all-consuming (as it can swallow us if we allow it to in our pursuit towards tenure) and demanding on the body/spirit/mind (Baptiste, 2004, pp. xii–xiii). In an institution that demands intellectual production and quantifies our labor, such expressions can be perceived as distractions or, worse, obstacles towards tenure.

I've come to the realization that the heavy demands of the professoriate will always be there and that we work within a capitalist-oriented institution that continuously evaluates, monitors, and quantifies what we produce as scholars, especially as institutions strive for elite tier status. Some days are teaching intensive while some are service intensive. While research (i.e., scholarly publications) carries the same weight as teaching, it prevails in our promotion towards tenure. Unlike teaching, where we are accountable to our students on a daily basis, research has the least built-in accountability in the system. Learning how to weave these three components of scholarship—teaching, research, and service—into an integrative process where each is in conversation with each other is a journey in of itself.

While I was initially resistant to practice yoga because of its colonial appropriation in the West, I decided to go outside of my comfort zone. For Chicana feminist scholars like Gloria Anzaldúa (2000), yoga extends outside of its physical dimensions. It is a fluid process that joins "the mind, the spirit, the imagination, the soul" in our writing and creative work (p. 77). It is within this spiritual and dynamic practice that I'm able to heal the split between work and life (since faculty are supposed to accept and not challenge institutional practices and ways of being that privilege White, male, and heteronormative means of producing). While I recognize the financial and social privilege I exercise in being able to join a yoga studio, I also recognize that taking care of my physical, mental, and emotional well-being is an act of resistance, particularly as diabetes runs on both sides of my family tree. In the powerful words of Caribbean-American writer and radical feminist Audre Lorde (1988, p. 132): "Caring for myself is not self-indulgence, it is self-preservation, and that is an act of political warfare."

Vinyasa yoga—as a meditative practice and spiritual alignment of body and breath—has nourished my spirit and given me permission to surrender when my body has told me to be step back from the physical and mental exhaustion of balancing the professoriate, activist scholarship, and life outside of academia. Most importantly, it has become a space of *nepantla,* the liminal and transitional space of learning alternative ways of thinking and being in the world as I connect all parts of my identities (those that are not recognized or acknowledged in academia). It is also the transformative space where I can reconnect my body, mind, and spirit. It took me years to realize that I had undergone extensive processes of fragmentation over the course of my studies as a graduate students and well into the first couple years of being a tenure-track professor, from being over-caffeinated to function and survive everyday tasks to working long, sedentary hours that forced my body to shut down when I couldn't sustain production. Each day that I enter my practice at home or with fellow yogis is an opportunity to heal the *herida* of the work–life split that often leaves women of color academics *norteadas*—confused, exhausted, and, at times, feeling out of balance and inadequate in the multiple identities we occupy as scholars, activists, daughters, and mothers.

Yoga challenges me to move into a life energy that clears my mind and spirit as I come back into my body. It awakens my consciousness and keeps me present in the institutional and social challenges that are before me so I can take strategic and creative actions within and outside academia. Even on the most exhausting days, I find myself on my mat, committed to this sacred time and space. I'm able to connect my inner consciousness with a larger universal purpose, reintegrate all aspects of my humanity, and remain present in this life-long vocation that requires self-care and self-love.

REFLECTIONS WITHIN THEORY AND CONCLUSION

As Chicana and Latina feminist methodological and pedagogical praxis (Delgado Bernal et al., 2012; Latina Feminist Group, 2001), our *testimonios* offer insight of the ways in which we (1) work through our shared fears and anxieties as first-generation women of color scholars and create identities of resilience; (2) navigate an academic culture that has historically excluded women of color; and (3) straddle community-based ways of being with an academic way of being that is becoming privatized as it assumes a masculinist, corporate model of production. Our *testimonios* illuminate the ways in which we individually and collectively enact our agency within a rigidly hierarchical, demanding, exclusionary, and, at times, institutionally violent culture towards women of color faculty. We also hope that our work generates much-needed dialogue so that others can make realistic, creative, and practical recommendations as academics/mothers/activists and take strategic action in reclaiming academia as an equitably and socially just space for women of color faculty. Perhaps, most importantly, our shared *testimonios* will serve to communicate acceptance of and recognition of storytelling as an acceptable methodology for knowledge production and social action.

REFERENCES

American Association of University Women. (2013). *The simple truth about the gender pay gap.* Retrieved from http://www.aauw.org/files/2013/03/the-simple-truth-about-the-gender-pay-gap-2013.pdf

Anzaldúa, G. E. (2000). *Interviews/Entrevistas* (A. Keating, Ed.). New York, NY: Routledge.

Anzaldúa, G. E. (2010). *Borderlands/La Frontera: The new mestiza* (4th ed). San Francisco, CA: Aunt Lute Books.

Delgado Bernal, D., Burciaga, R., & Flores Carmona, J. (2012). Chicana/Latina testimonios: Mapping the methodological, pedagogical, and political. *Equity and Excellence in Education, 45*(3), 363–372.

Ek, L. D., Quijada Cerecer, P. D., Alanis, I., & Rodriguez, M. A. (2010). I don't belong here: Chicanas/Latinas at a Hispanic serving institution creating community through Muxerista mentoring. *Equity Excellence in Education, 43*, 539–553.

Gonzalez, F. E. (2001). *Haciendo que hacer*—cultivating a Mestiza worldview and academic achievement: braiding cultural knowledge into educational research, policy, practice. *International Journal of Qualitative Research in Education, 14*(5), 641–656.

Gutierrez y Muhs, G., Niemann, Y. F., Gonzalez, C. G., & Harris, A. P. (2012). *Presumed incompetent: The intersections of race and class for women in academia.* Boulder, CO: Utah State University Press.

Halpern, D. F. (2008). Nurturing careers in psychology: Combining work and family. *Educational Psychology Review, 20*, 57–64.

Latina Feminist Group. (2000). *Telling to live: Latina feminist testimonios.* Durham, NC: Duke University Press.

Lorde, A. (1988). *A burst of light: Essays.* Ithaca, NY: Firebrand Books.

Medina, C., & Luna, G. (2001). Narratives from Latina professors in higher education. *Anthropology & Education Quarterly, 31*(1), 47–66.

O'Laughlin, E. M., & Bischoff, L. G. (2005). Balancing parenthood and academia: Work/family stress as influenced by gender and tenure status. *Journal of Family Issues, 26*(1), 79–106.

Perna, L. W. (2004). Understanding the decision to enroll in graduate school: Sex and racial/ethnic group differences. *Journal of Higher Education, 75*, 487–527.

Schmader, T., & Johns, M. (2003). Converging evidence that stereotype threat reduces working memory capacity. *Journal of Personality and social psychology, 85*(3), 440–452.

Solórzano, D., & Delgado Bernal, D. (2001). Examining transformational resistance through a critical race and Latcrit theory framework: Chicana and Chicano students in an urban context. *Urban Education, 36*(3), 308–342.

Solórzano, D., & Yosso, T. (2000). Toward a critical race theory of Chicana and Chicano education. In C. Tejeda, C. Martinez, Z. Leonardo & P. McLaren (Eds.), *Charting new terrains of Chicana(o)/Latina(o) education* (pp. 35–65). Cresskill, NJ: Hampton Press.

Steele, C. M., & Aronson, J. (1995). Stereotype threat and the intellectual test performance of African-Americans. *Journal of Personality and Social Psychology, 69*(5), 797–811.

Urrieta, L., & Mendez Benavidez, L. R. (2007). Community commitment and activist scholarship: Chicana/o professors and the practice of consciousness. *Journal of Hispanics in Higher Education, 6*(3), 222–236.

Van Anders, S. M. (2004). Why the academic pipeline leaks: Fewer men than women perceive barriers to becoming professors. *Sex Roles, 51*(9–10), 511–521.

Vasquez-Guignard, S. J. (2010). *Latina university professors, insights into the journeys of those who strive to leadership within academia.* Unpublished doctoral dissertation, Pepperdine University, Malibu, CA.

Zamudio, M. M., Russell, C., Rios, F. A., & Bridgeman, J. L. (2011). *Critical race theory matters: Education and ideology.* New York, NY: Routledge.

CHAPTER 12

DOCUMENTING THE UNDOCUMENTED

Sabidurías[1] de una Chicana in Academia

Linda Prieto

I remember sitting in one of Dr. Gary Orfield's graduate education classes at Harvard where he shared data that illustrated that of all doctoral degrees awarded in 1996, less than 3% had been earned by Chicanas/Latinos—across all disciplines. I was astonished! I assumed the figure would be low, but when presented with the reality of just how low, a feeling came over me. I was familiar with this feeling; it came from my soul, and I had learned to listen to it over time. In this context it told me if there was something I could do to maintain, or improve this statistic, then I needed to try. I was a master's student at the time and had not given any serious consideration to applying to a doctoral program or thought of earning a doctorate as a vehicle through which I would enter the academy as a tenure-track faculty. Perhaps these considerations had been elusive because I was a first-generation college student from a working-poor background, but then I began a mission. I sought advice from current doctoral students and the one that resonated most was a friend who said I should return to my home state of

Abriendo Puertas, Cerrando Heridas (Opening Doors, Closing Wounds), pages 127–136
Copyright © 2015 by Information Age Publishing
All rights of reproduction in any form reserved.

California, work for four years, and after developing more experience in the school system, then apply to a doctoral program. As it turned out, it would be three years before I applied to a doctoral program. I figured if I was unsuccessful in the application process that year, I would reapply the following year and so on until successfully admitted. As a first-generation college student, I did not feel I had much to lose but could potentially have much to offer to and much to gain from a doctoral program. After a successful application process that first year, I moved southeast nearly 1,800 miles away and enrolled at The University of Texas at Austin to begin a doctoral program in curriculum and instruction. This was a distant journey from my experiences growing up working in the agricultural fields of the central San Joaquin Valley alongside my parents and siblings.

Through these early experiences in the fields, my gratitude for my family's support and sense of responsibility to others first developed. Thus, when I struggle with work–life balance I am reminded of our time in the fields. My mother made our meals, tended to our on-the-job injuries, and worked at the same pace as my father—faster than most men. My father imparted upon us the cultural traditions of *baladas, corridos* and *rancheras mexicanas* (romantic and folk ballads and the rural traditional folk music of Mexico). His singing helped the long workdays go by faster, and when we were paid for piecework, he had us count and double count our work, which at the same time served to improve our math skills.

ENTERING THE ACADEMY

The most salient experience I have struggled with regarding work–life balance is when there is a mismatch between what I have prepared for academically and what I experience in practice as a tenure-track faculty. As I have come to learn, the intellectual endeavors are not the most challenging. Rather, the challenges arise when institutions of higher education do not live up to their stated missions or value my approaches to teaching, service, and scholarship. Currently, I serve as a tenure-track faculty at a Hispanic serving institution (HSI). I finally find myself in an academic department where I am part of a group of critical scholars of various cultural and linguistic backgrounds, all concerned with the educational needs and strengths of traditionally underserved populations. Granted, not all at the university share urgency for critical engagement with scholarship, teaching, and service, nor is the fact that we work at an HSI openly celebrated or widely known within our campus. However, it remains a significant and much recognized improvement from other institutions of higher education where I have studied and worked.

Prior to beginning employment at The University of Texas at San Antonio (UTSA) in the fall of 2013, I had already worked at two teaching institutions, one in north Texas and the other on California's central coast. As I continue to learn, each university has its own process of retention, tenure, and promotion with often unclear institutional policies and uncertain—or changing—senior and even emeritus faculty expectations. Some place greater emphasis on research over teaching or vice versa, and always, service is the least emphasized component. Another significant change to the climate of my current institution as compared to my former places of employment is that I am now part of a department with 16 other full-time tenured and tenure-track professors in the shared areas of bilingual education, second-language teaching, and Mexican American studies. I am no longer asked or expected to be and teach everything for everybody.

Yet I also hear the sometimes not so soft whispers, "Oh, that department has too many Latinas." Not both Latinos and Latinas mind you, but specifically, too many Latinas. It was pointed out to me that gender equity in our department includes the need to hire more males. Our current 64% female tenured and tenure-track faculty ratio is perceived as problematic. I wonder how fervent these conversations are across the campus and at other institutions of higher education, especially in colleges of business, science, and engineering. For example, our college of engineering includes only nine female tenured or tenure-track faculty out of 80, or 11%, and only one is Latin American—specifically, she is a Mexican national. Unfortunately what some perceive as "too many Latinas" in my academic department does not translate to equitable campus-wide or national representation of Latinas in academia.

Thus, as Chicana/Latino faculty in the academy, we must recognize that feeling that emerges from our soul and call upon the Nahual—animal spirit/shape shifter—and learn to transform and push back so that institutions of higher education fulfill their mission statements. As a matter of self-preservation, we must also recognize when it is time to leave an institution, even if that includes restarting our tenure clock. We must develop the necessary skills to create, sustain, and evolve one's "image" and work as Chicana/Latino scholars and in the process we must share *nuestra sabiduría* (our wisdom) with others. Sometimes this sharing happens as we formally and informally mentor one another; attend each other's sessions at conferences; invite each other to work on research projects, grant applications, and/or manuscripts; meet for cafecito to discuss our experiences of oppression and *sobrevivencia* (survival, transcendence, and beyond); and/or as we write our *testimonios* (politically urgent life stories) for a largely unknown audience.

> *Testimonio* then, names the workings and abuses of institutional power, the human costs, and our collective *sobrevivencia* (survival and beyond). Latina

> and women of color creative writers, artists, intellectuals, and scholar/activists make the case for the intensely political nature of our creative and professional work. Through our stories, we bear witness to our unique and collective experiences as racialized/ethnicized women in the United States. Different from the traditional genre of *testimonio*, Latina/Chicana feminist *testimoniantes* bear witness to each other as interlocutors through our own voice and authoring. (Prieto & Villenas, 2012, p. 415)

In the process, we reimagine new lives and create opportunities to expand our academic network and the reach of our sabidurías via scholarship, teaching, and service.

EXPERIENCES WITH THE TENURE PROCESS

During my time in the doctoral program, I began to develop my identity as a future tenure-track professor and scholar in education. After completing my dissertation writing year with my mentor and dissertation co-chair, Dr. Sofia Villenas, at Cornell University, I returned to Texas, but this time to San Antonio where I had two friends and classmates from my time in the doctoral program at UT–Austin. My professional aspirations at that time included securing a tenure-track position at UTSA, so I began to teach courses at the main and downtown campuses as an adjunct. To make ends meet I also taught four courses at Texas A&M University–San Antonio in the south side of San Antonio. However, it became clear that there would not be a position available in the area of bicultural-bilingual education at that time, so when I received an offer at a small teaching institution in north Texas, I accepted. I wonder how many other Latino/a faculty find themselves having to piecemeal full-time employment via adjunct positions across several institutions. I was also pregnant at the time and felt I needed more stable employment than an adjunct position might offer. What I did not know at the time was that the position I had accepted was on soft monies funded by a federal grant through the Office of English Language Acquisition (OELA) for a remaining two years. As the first in my entire and extended family to apply for a tenure-track position, I did not even know at the time what "soft monies" were or to ask if the position I was accepting was a "hard line." During my first year of employment, I was actually approached by faculty at UTSA to apply for a position in the area of bicultural-bilingual education, but I felt a sense of responsibility and obligation to the institution at which I was employed, so I thanked them and declined. As I later became aware of my tenuous situation, I wondered if the call from UTSA had been a sign that I should not have ignored. In two years I would find myself in a similar situation; more on that later.

At the university in north Texas,

> I was the only full-time faculty member in the relatively new Spanish/English bilingual education program. I had one colleague who shared a half-time appointment in bilingual education and served as the director of the program. The program offered an undergraduate degree that included preparation for teaching certification in early childhood through sixth grade (EC–6) bilingual education as well as an emphasis in bilingual education for students pursuing a master's degree in curriculum and instruction or educational leadership. (Prieto, 2015b)

Since the bilingual education program was on soft monies, my colleague and I also spent a good deal of time applying for additional grant funding. Other colleagues were also encouraged to seek external funding, but neither their programs nor their positions required external funding for existence. This presented an additional burden for me. In my second year there, I was overwhelmed by the inner conflicts between what I knew and what I was experiencing. These tensions included teaching our bilingual education teacher candidates that late-exit (during fifth or sixth grade) and two-way bilingual education programs (i.e., dual language programs) are more effective at helping emerging bilingual learners achieve academically as compared to English as a second language programs or early-exit bilingual education programs (during first or second grade but no later than third grade).

> Yet we were unable to provide them with a real world example of either program in our area. We also had to help our teacher candidates understand how to be critical of a program without criticizing their mentor teachers tasked with implementing a less effective model of bilingual education. This conflict between what I know as a bilingual education scholar—that dual language programs are the most effective forms of instruction—and what was being implemented by the school district—early-exit and ESL programs are the least effective forms of bilingual education instruction—was a difficult tension to negotiate. (Prieto, 2015b)

These professional concerns also affected me personally as I

> became conflicted over my living in this area in terms of the academic and social enrichment my child might, or might not, receive as part of the EC–12 pipeline, and if that university and community setting would be conducive to my overall professional goals. The focus of the institution was on teaching, so I became estranged from the critical engagement with research that had shaped my doctoral experience. (Prieto, 2015b)

Indeed this was a challenging and fearful time. I was fraught by the move to a new area where I knew no one, of later learning that I was hired into a position that was sustained by a federal grant that would soon expire, and of being a new mother at a university where we received an email out of the president's office telling us that children were not to be present on the university campus during business hours. These experiences posed challenges as I sought to find work–life balance in the tenure process. As the year unfolded, I also "experienced tensions between my scholarly background and interests with the realities of this university, our partner elementary schools, the overall approach by the school district to Chicana/Latino students, families, and community, and my child's experiences in early childhood settings" (Prieto, 2015b). As I attempted to focus my energies on these aspects of work–life balance, my relationship with my partner at the time also suffered. I recognize now how my professional and parenting tensions also contributed negatively to that relationship, so during that time I also became a single parent. As a matter of self-preservation I decided to move back to my home state of California where my toddler and I could at least be within driving distance of my nuclear family with which I grew up.

A SENSE OF ISOLATION

I took a job at a university on California's central coast, a visually beautiful area where my child and I lived less than 10 blocks from the coastline. I was even told by colleagues that the university leveraged the natural beauty found in the surrounding area to keep even unhappy and professionally unfulfilled faculty at the university. Unfortunately, those natural elements were not enough to maintain me at the institution beyond that first year. The institutional climate proved even more challenging than my experience in north Texas. Again, as a matter of self-preservation, I had to recognize that it was time to leave, even though it included restarting my tenure clock a second time, being further from my family, and uprooting my toddler yet again.

Before I even began the academic year, I was approached again by faculty at UTSA to apply for a new position in the area of bicultural-bilingual education. I informed them that I had just made the move to California and was about to begin my new job, so I could not see myself applying for another job, especially one that would take me away from my family and home state again. As it turns out, considering the position at UTSA was the best decision. Although again I felt a sense of responsibility and obligation to the institution at which I was employed, within a few weeks it became clear that this institution did not fully enact its mission of respecting cultural and intellectual diversity, recognizing the strengths and meeting the needs of the community, or social responsibility. When I eventually made the decision to formally leave the university, my supervisor commented on how my employment there had not been "a good match." Initially, I thought the onus was on me, or any other new person, to adjust to become "a good match" with the institution and that the institution had no responsibility to adjust to new employees or students to become a better match with us. It was not until recently that it was made clear to me that what was also happening was that the university and those within positions of power were acting in ways that did not fulfill its proclaimed mission.

As the only faculty of color in the school of education, I experienced a philosophical and cultural sense of isolation regarding my connections to community and approaches to teaching, research, and service[2]. When I was first hired, there was one other Latina in the school—a staff member, but due to the hostility in our school, she made a professional move to another area at the university before the end of the first term. When I raised my concerns with my supervisor about me being the only tenure-track faculty of color in the school, he explained that my being there already symbolized a 10% increase (from zero percent). On different occasions I was reminded of my role to fulfill a quota, and the work I did with parents of emerging bilingual learners was not valued as much as that of colleagues who worked directly with teachers and in formal classroom settings.

One day towards the end of the academic year, the dean of the school of education asked me to attend a governance meeting to report about a Latino mentoring program I was supporting with a Latino fraternity on campus and an area high school 30+ miles south of the university that served a primarily Chicana/Latino student population. I made sure to sit next to him, and when it was time for me to report, he introduced me by calling me by the wrong name. He actually called me by the name of another Latina faculty outside of our school. I looked around the room to see if anyone would correct him and finally had to comment and remind him of my name. Again, this was at the end of the school year. This incident is symbolic of not only how I was perceived as a Chicana/Latina scholar by my supervisors but also the lack of understanding of and respect towards the larger community I represent. Had I not been part of the Chicana/Latino faculty staff association and served as the faculty advisor to the student group Movimiento Estudiantil Chicano de Aztlán (MEChA) at that university I would have experienced greater levels of isolation. *Otra sabiduría* learned through this process is the importance of building a sense of community and allies for *sobrevivencia*, even if entirely outside of one's academic area and in my case, including graduate and undergraduate students.

Health has also become an area of more concern for me as I age and as a mother of a toddler. Some of the poor health outcomes I have experienced associated with racial battle fatigue include weight gain, syncope, headaches, low levels of energy, and high levels of stress. The one good thing I can point to as I reflect on my time on California's central coast was being introduced to a holistic healer by one of my ally colleagues. With the holistic healer's help I am regaining the ability to foster trust in self (what I know) and others.

As a freshman at Stanford, I remember being so frightened to learn that one of our few Chicano tenured professors on campus had suffered a stroke immediately after leaving a strenuous faculty meeting in the department of anthropology where he served as the chair. Then, after my senior year, I mourned a junior Chicana faculty member who had committed suicide after also experiencing challenges in her academic department. These were my initial exposures to how the academy isolates and discriminates against Chicana/Latino faculty in ways that damage our lives.

Thankfully, the sense of isolation experienced in north Texas and California has diminished greatly both on a personal and professional level. At UTSA I have colleagues who incorporate me into academic endeavors as well as include me in social gatherings beyond the university. I also find my colleagues to be more receptive when I reach out with research, teaching, and service ideas. These mentoring relationships serve to both induct me into and retain me at the university. Last summer, for example, colleagues and I took a group of undergraduate and graduate students to the Mujeres Activas en Letras y Cambio Social (MALCS—Women Active in Letters and Social Change) 2014 Summer Institute. At UTSA I am also supported to teach courses I want to teach and to teach them the way I know to teach them. In prior institutions I have found myself trying to strike a balance between how I know to teach and how the institution and students expect me to teach.

PREPARING TEACHER CANDIDATES

In my current bread-and-butter course, I expose undergraduate students to the cultural and linguistic diversity of our present-day U.S. public schools and alert them to the importance of developing into socially just educators on behalf of students, communities, and each other. All early childhood through 6th grade generalist teacher candidates are required to successfully complete this course. Most are female students from White middle-class backgrounds. I am charged with preparing them to understand and improve the experiences of culturally and linguistically diverse students in our public schools. Historically, this course has included examinations of sociolinguistic and sociocultural principles central to today's diverse demographics. While teaching and simultaneously reexamining the course, I am including more formal opportunities for the creation of *testimonios* by the participating teacher candidates. While my research focus to date has examined the experiences of Latina bilingual education preservice teachers, I am now working with a largely mainstream teacher candidate pool but continue to believe strongly in their potential to become agents of social justice as well. However, this can prove challenging if they do not yet see a reason why they should become social justice advocates. By providing more opportunities for the students to dialogue, I aim to help them become more self-aware of their potential role in the transformation of education—to expand their worldview beyond their experiences, to bear witness to the experiences of others, and to listen and act thoughtfully in ways that benefit all students, especially those who have historically been oppressed, underrepresented, and underserved.

However, explorations of self and systems of social dominance do not always go unchallenged. For example, a few students in my course spring semester shared in class, "If we just stop talking about race, racism will go away." Also, when a group of students presenting on the experiences of the incarcerated in America asked the class if they would incorporate children's books that included the incarcerated, such as *The Night Dad Went to Jail: What to Expect When Someone You Love Goes to Jail* by Melissa Higgins (2013), there were a number of students who voiced a resounding, "No," and expressed that if families wanted to expose children to "those types of books" it should be done at home, not in their classrooms.

As I revise the course on cultural and linguistic diversity, I also seek to continue my larger research agenda to improve and transform the education of *all* students. I *openly* examine my work from a critical perspective using life her/histories and *testimonios* informed by Chicana/Latina feminist thought. I emphasize "openly" because at prior institutions, and even in other academic departments within my current institution, it requires a great deal of energy on my part to clarify, explain, and educate colleagues as to what "critical," "life her/histories," "*testimonios*," and "Chicana/Latina feminist thought" all mean. Even during this current academic year, I was cautioned not to write too much on *testimonio* and to maintain my focus on teacher formation across the continuum from teacher candidates to teacher educators. And still I share my *testimonio* with the hope that doing so might help mentor others by expanding their knowledge and understanding of politically urgent life stories or by feeling validated in their own experiences of work–life balance in academia and thus continue to excel and move forward.

NOTES

1. Wisdoms
2. A more detailed account of this experience appears in Prieto, L. (2015a).

REFERENCES

Higgins, M. (2013). *The night dad went to jail: What to expect when someone you love goes to jail.* Mankato, MN: Picture Window Books.

Prieto, L. (2015a). Shocked into silence no more. In J. Martin (Ed.), *Racial battle fatigue: Insights from the front lines of social justice advocacy* (pp. 45–54). Santa Barbara, CA: Praeger.

Prieto, L. (2015b). Inner conflicts between what I know and what I experience: Making invisible tensions visible. In G. Theoharis & S. Dotger (Eds.), *On the high wire: Education professors walk between work and parenting* (pp. 203–212). Charlotte, NC: Information Age.

Prieto, L., & Villenas, S.A. (2012). Pedagogies from Nepantla: Testimonio, Chicana/Latina feminisms and teacher education classrooms. *Equity & Excellence in Education, 45*(3), 411–429.

CHAPTER 13

BOUNCING BACK FROM A POOR THIRD YEAR REVIEW

Sylvia Martinez

I recently survived the tenure and promotion process at a Research Intensive (R1) institution. I say, "survived" because I know that many of my Latino/a peers in academia will not or have not. I felt compelled to share my story because after my third-year review, I did not think that achieving tenure and promotion was possible, but it is possible because I managed to recognize and acknowledge my psychological barriers regarding productivity, welcomed formal and informal mentorship from senior colleagues, and most importantly, I was not afraid to request resources and/or solutions to the challenges I was facing in the academy. Overall, I have learned to advocate for myself, but it has not been easy. As a newly minted Latina PhD in her very first tenure track job at a predominantly White institution, I could have easily fallen through the cracks. And almost did because I was suffering in silence my first few years on the job. I don't want other Latino/a graduate students and faculty to continue suffering silence. I write this to say, "You are not alone," and to share the moments of opportunity that presented themselves in my own journey towards tenure and promotion.

Abriendo Puertas, Cerrando Heridas (Opening Doors, Closing Wounds), pages 137–144
Copyright © 2015 by Information Age Publishing
All rights of reproduction in any form reserved.

MY FIRST YEARS AT AN R1 INSTITUTION

Overall, my first few years as a junior faculty member were a blur, keeping busy with extensive course development for a growing Latino Studies program, mentoring students, and various service obligations across campus. As I adjusted to a new environment where Latino/a students, staff, and faculty were highly underrepresented, I struggled to understand the publication game and converting the dissertation into several manuscripts ready for publication. I suspect that I appeared to be fine to those around me, but inside, I was beginning to struggle with feelings of inadequacy.

The imposter syndrome (Clance & Imes, 1978) has plagued my educational experiences since college. Downplaying my academic qualifications, I spent my first years in college and graduate school convinced admissions committees had made a mistake. Certainly, they meant to admit another Sylvia Martinez. The same insecurities came to light my first few years as a pretenured professor at Indiana University. Sometimes, faculty members afflicted by the imposter syndrome become overburdened with teaching, mentoring, and service obligations to overcome their perceived inadequacies; I found that the imposter syndrome had a paralyzing effect on my writing and research activities.

In all honesty, I was paralyzed by the fear that my work was not good enough to be published in peer-reviewed journals. I agonized over who might read my work and think it was of low quality. As such, I spent the better part of my first year at Indiana University reading more literature and rerunning my multivariate regression models because I worried about not having a "perfect" manuscript ready for submission. As my first year as a faculty member ended, I had not yet submitted anything for publication.

REALITY CHECK: THIRD YEAR REVIEW

Before I knew it, the spring semester of 2009 had arrived and I had to submit a third-year review dossier. Panic set in. As a result of my paralyzing fear in my first few years, my third-year review dossier was thin, very thin. In fact, I had absolutely zero publications (yes, zero!) when I submitted my third-year review. Sure, I had a few manuscripts under review or in the revision process, but I knew this would not sit well with the review committee. In all honesty, it was embarrassing to turn the dossier in to my department chair. Not surprisingly, the committee and department chair were gravely concerned about my ability to succeed at Indiana University after evaluating the merits of my dossier.

In many ways, the dossier accurately reflected my capabilities. I thought to myself, "I am an imposter. I am not qualified to undertake this job. Just look at this pathetic third-year review dossier!" I spent the next couple of weeks questioning whether this was the right job or institution for me. Deep down I felt that I enjoyed teaching and mentoring students, but I questioned whether I was cut out for making it at an R1 institution. On the other hand, I reminded myself that the reason I pursued a PhD was not only to open educational and occupational pathways for Latino/a students but also because I loved the research process. It was during this time of self-reflection that I received word that one of my manuscripts had been accepted for publication. I am not ashamed to admit that I cried (yes, an ugly cry) when I read that email. It truly was a pivotal moment. For me, it was an affirmation that I could do this job and do it well. It allowed me to recognize that I had been working on my research agenda and that I was a perfectly capable professor. The acceptance of this manuscript breathed new life in me.

FINDING THE RIGHT MENTOR

Aside from the affirmation that came with my first manuscript publication, I owe part of my success to the support and mentorship I received from a couple of colleagues in my department. Shortly after my third-year review, two senior colleagues (one Latina, one White male) invited me to collaborate on research projects with them. While shocked by their invitations (they were out of the blue), I did not hesitate to respond with an enthusiastic "yes!" Collaborating and writing with my colleagues taught me valuable information about the publication process. Through our extensive interactions and discussions about the publication process, I learned to research and find the right journal for manuscripts; balance the quality of journal vs. quantity of publications; lead a graduate student research team during the data collection and cleaning process; and, most importantly, to cope with rejection or multiple rejections of manuscripts. Recognizing that even well-established scholars also receive rejections was a liberating experience. The experience became one where I no longer took rejections so personally or as evidence of my poor qualifications as a scholar but rather as opportunities to improve my ideas and academic writing.

In the language of my disciplinary training in sociology, these colleagues helped me cultivate the cultural and social capital needed to succeed at an R1 institution. I truly believe that without their intervention I would not have survived the tenure and promotion process at IU. And for that, I am eternally grateful.

STOPPING THE CLOCK

Equipped with better skills to navigate the publication game, I started having some success. Manuscripts were accepted for publication, while others required revision. I was getting better at it, and my confidence as a teacher and scholar was building. Still, other factors such as family obligations affect progress in academia.

Per university guidelines, I was supposed to start the tenure and promotion review process during the 2010–2011 academic year. This meant that in January 2011, I would begin composing my personal statement, a statement summarizing my research, teaching, and service activities during my first 5.5 years at IU. While I had publications under my belt, I was once again gravely concerned about my ability to succeed during the process. I seriously considered the idea of not putting forth a tenure and promotion case and going on the job market instead. You might suspect that the imposter syndrome was rearing its ugly head again, but it actually was not. Contemplating going on the job market was based on an honest (and I think objective) reflection about my chances for tenure and promotion. At a research institution, number of publications is "king" and I certainly did not have the numbers to survive the process.

To make matters more complicated, life happened. During the same weekend in early January that I found out I was pregnant, my husband and I took in our 15-year-old troubled nephew from Chicago. We did not hesitate for two reasons. First, he was family and we were close to him since most of our regular visits to Chicago involved taking him out to eat or to the movies. Second, we truly believed that a change of scenery might do him some good. "He could use a fresh start," we thought.

Needless to say, our lives were turned upside down with a teen now living under our roof. We had a crash course in getting a teen to school on time, picking him up from school, preparing meals he would like, and getting him signed up for extracurricular activities around town. Furthermore, we had to account for all the emotional labor spent managing his feelings (and our own) about leaving his friends and family and adjusting to a new place.

Quickly overburdened by these new family demands and the fatigue that accompanies pregnancy, I sought out information about "stopping the clock." I soon found out that while "stopping the clock" is an option when you give birth or adopt a child, our circumstances did not technically fall under university guidelines. Without officially adopting our nephew, I could not stop the clock.

Disheartened but not defeated, at least not yet, I continued to search for options for my situation. Something that I have learned during my time at IU has been that you must ask for the resources that you need and or want in academia. The worst-case scenario is that the answer is "no" but sometimes the answer is "yes"! I once again turned to my faculty mentors for advice. While not officially ready to disclose my pregnancy to colleagues, I had to do so to find help. My mentors and I agreed that I was not ready to put forth a tenure and promotion case and that my situation might warrant a stop of the tenure clock. They contacted our department chair and advocated for me, which resulted in approval to stop my tenure clock from the vice provost of faculty and academic affairs.

Relieved by the news, I was able to dedicate one more intensive summer to advancing my research writing projects and to enjoy the birth of my son. Andres H. Barrera was born on September 2, 2011, three weeks earlier than expected.

SELLING THE "BALANCED CASE"

The extra year proved to be invaluable. Not only did I enjoy my maternity leave without the stress of putting together a tenure and promotion dossier, a few more manuscripts were also accepted for publication and others submitted for review. I felt more confident about the upcoming tenure and promotion process but I still did not feel like I had a "slam dunk" case. No one ever does, though. And so in January of 2012, I returned to work after maternity leave and started working on my research, teaching, and service statement for the dossier. Of all of my time at IU since 2006, the spring semester of 2012 had to be the most difficult one. I was beginning the tenure and promotion process, finishing up manuscripts, and trying to meet an infant's needs. I did not read many newborn or parenting books during pregnancy, but the few I read failed to mention how sick your little ones will get when you send them to daycare! Without help from a family network in town, my husband and I regularly had to take 1–2 days off of work each week because our son was ill or we were ill. Before long, we were both absolutely exhausted and stressed out about meeting our work obligations.

A few years before it was time to go up for tenure and promotion, my mentors and I had agreed that my work at IU and would be best represented by the balanced case. A balanced case requires "at least very good/highly satisfactory performance" in each of the three areas of teaching, research, and service (Indiana University-Bloomington, School of Education, 2010, p. 6). Furthermore, "very good/high satisfactory" is defined as better than satisfactory but less than excellent (2011). Most importantly, the balanced case demonstrates a thoughtful integration of the three areas of teaching, research, and service. My work certainly showed this integration because I often integrated teaching and research endeavors by publishing with my students (undergraduate and graduate) or integrated teaching and service activities by participating on diversity issue panels organized by undergraduate student groups on campus.

Many at research institutions think that putting forth a balanced case is a risky move because the institution values research above all else. The risk is that promotion and tenure committees still look for excellence in research, along with extensive teaching and service activities. Despite the risk, we felt that my work at IU was best represented by the balanced case because of my extensive course development in the Latino studies program, various service activities across schools and departments, and even my small but growing interest in the scholarship of teaching and learning. I knew that my statement had to serve as an educational tool for many colleagues at the School of Education. As the only person at the School of Education with a joint appointment outside of the professional school and in the College of Arts and Sciences, my statement had to accurately reflect the nature of my appointment and my interdisciplinary work, which straddles sociology of education, Latino/a studies, and higher education. The pressure to create a powerful and convincing tenure statement was high, to say the least.

I knew I had my work cut out for me because during my maternity leave, I received a disturbing call from the associate executive dean at the time. He apologized for calling me during my maternity leave but he needed to know the extent of my role in the Latino studies program. His questions implied that the School of Education understood my appointment in the program as one where I simply offered courses. I was appalled that after 6.5 years at IU, my tenure home school and department did not understand that I had a joint appointment in the ccollege that meant that I not only had teaching obligations in the college but also mentoring and service commitments. In fact, I recall the director of the program who hired me telling me that I would play an integral role in expanding the program. Years later, I have learned that there should have been a Memorandum of Understanding (MOU) between the School of Education and the College of Arts and Sciences, which houses the Latino studies program. This document would have outlined my research, teaching, and service expectations in each department. But one was never created, and I did not know that one should have been put in place.

In any case, my tenure statement, curriculum vitae, and publications were submitted in April of 2012 to solicit letters from external reviewers. The dossier was submitted in August of 2012. And the waiting game began. Waiting to hear about the decision was excruciating, but my department chair was great about keeping me informed throughout the process. The worst part is the months of November through March, when you don't hear anything as the university level committee reviews dossiers from campus-wide departments and professional schools. They say, however, that no news is good news. During spring break of 2013 I received the best news ever. My tenure and promotion case had received approval from the university committee. The last formality would be approval from the Board of Trustees. To this day, I am so happy that I was home when I received the news because like the time I cried when I received word of my first acceptance for publication, I cried tears of joy. My husband cried too. We followed the tears with dance and we frequently think about this joyous moment the two of us shared.

Not getting tenure at IU would have been a huge disappointment, I will not lie, but I always approached my work by doing the things that brought me the most satisfaction. I developed new courses for the School of Education and the Latino studies program, helped graduate students create minors in ethnic studies, mentored Latino/a undergraduate students, published with graduate students, and served on committees tackling issues of racial/ethnic diversity on campus. And I published, but certainly not at the rate of many of my colleagues. However, I feel that my life in academia has been balanced. I certainly love my work and I work hard, but at the end of the day, I value my family life most. Currently, as a mother of a 3-year-old, I find it difficult to work on weekends. My son is a ball of energy who requires a lot of attention, and I more than welcome the opportunities to provide creative and physical outlets for him. So at the end of the day, when I may have time to work, I am honestly too tired to think about work. Instead, my husband and I use the time to decompress and enjoy each other's company. As a result, I have become rather efficient with my time during the week. One of the most impactful activities on my research productivity this past academic year has been getting involved in writing groups. I have successfully protected my writing time with my involvement in both formal (sponsored by IU) and informal writing groups. In many ways, this new way of working allows me to thoroughly enjoy my time with my family. Still, had I not been granted tenure and promotion at IU, I would have found an institution that valued the work that I valued and one that would allow me to recreate the balance between work and family that I have worked hard to achieve.

NOW WHAT?

I still cannot believe that I am a tenured professor at an R1 institution. Many days, I still feel like that little Mexican American girl, a child of immigrants who dreamed of going to the closest postsecondary institution near her home (California State University, Northridge) to have an office job in the future. Other days I want to say that I'm "lucky," but women typically attribute their accomplishments to luck rather than hard work. So I will not do that. I feel that it is an injustice to do so—it downplays the hard work I have accomplished to get here. And it downplays the hard work of other Latino/a faculty who have paved the way for me. Other days I feel like a survivor of a tragedy and I am afflicted with "survivor's guilt." Every now and then I find myself wondering why I survived and not the minority faculty member from so-and-so department or university, or why talented, recent Latino/a PhDs are not finding success in the tenure-track job market.

Similar to the psychological torture of the imposter syndrome, entertaining these thoughts is a fruitless endeavor, and I force myself to focus. I focus on what I can do for the person who crosses my office door. I try to demystify the processes of the Ivory Tower in hopes of helping others in ways many have helped me.

And so I find myself struggling with this new identity as associate professor, which I hear is typical. Much of it stems from not knowing how (more psychological rather than logistical) to start new projects. What I know to be true, however, is that I am already thinking about how to approach the next level—promotion to full professor. Achieving rank of full professor is a personal ambition, but the goal is also wrought with a sense of obligation on my part. As a survivor of the tenure and promotion process, I want to see my fellow Latino/a peers succeed as well. Increasing representation at all ranks will require further adjustments to the tenure and promotion process and how academia understands the balanced case, joint appointments, and multidisciplinary/interdisciplinary work, which characterizes much of the work in which Latino/a faculty engage. Full professors are best equipped with the tools and power via governance committees to enact change. I want to enact change and truly feel it is my responsibility to do so. My first act towards that goal is to share my experience with others to highlight the unique challenges encountered by Latino/a faculty but most importantly, to say, "My door is always open."

REFERENCES

Clance, P. R., & Imes, S. (1978). The imposter phenomenon in high achieving women: Dynamics and therapeutic intervention. *Psychotherapy Theory, Research and Practice, 15,* 1–8.

Indiana University–Bloomington, School of Education. (2010). *Promotion and tenure criteria for the school of education.* Retrieved from http://education.indiana.edu/about/council/policies.html

CHAPTER 14

BETWEEN TWO WORLDS

María D. Avalos
The University of Texas of the Permian Basin

Between Two Worlds

Wind tugging at my sleeve
Feet sinking into the sand
I stand at the edge where
Earth touches ocean . . .
Where the two overlap
A gentle coming together
And at other places
A violent crash . . .

Gloria Anzaldua (2007)

I was poor, Latina, and a first-generation college student when I began college. Everything about me said I would not make it, including my college advisor who suggested I get married as soon as I could. Yet I remembered the story that my grandmother told me about her experience crossing the Rio Grande River. With a prayer to the Virgen De Guadalupe, she vowed to give her family the life that only America could give. The academic expectations and the commitment to my family told me that I not only had the right, but the responsibility to continue my education. Because of the sacrifices of my ancestors and my family, I am where I am today.

Abriendo Puertas, Cerrando Heridas (Opening Doors, Closing Wounds), pages 145–152
Copyright © 2015 by Information Age Publishing
All rights of reproduction in any form reserved.

Because of my family, I had a choice: the choice to enter the world by way of education and career. I completed college and earned my doctoral degree. I am happy that I had the opportunity to experience and achieve these things for myself and my family, but I was also completely unaware that I would have to leave, disengage, and often compromise my culture to achieve these things.

HIGHER EDUCATION

The majority of my career in higher education has been at a small, private, Lutheran-affiliated university located in my hometown. I thought that I had hit the jack pot when I began teaching as an adjunct faculty member, was offered an interim position in the provost's office, and then later became a full-time member and then an administrator at the university. I was blissfully ignorant of what would be expected of me. When I was offered an interim position in the provost's office, I was so excited about the offer that I did not ask about salary, insurance, or a job description. I had to go back and meet with the university provost the next day to ask him what a "provost" was and what it meant to work in his office. He said that my new job description would "include all things related to faculty and students." I used this explanation to describe my job to family and friends. They were so proud that I could not tell them that I had absolutely no idea what "all things related to faculty and students" meant.

I worked hard, and I learned quickly, but that was expected. What I did not expect was that this new world of work would be so different from my home culture. My work culture was competitive and individualistic, which is the opposite of my home culture that values family above the individual and humility above confidence and self-promotion. The more I learned, the more aware I became of how my worlds of work and home differed. I live in two worlds, and I use my time commuting to change and morph my identities in an effort to maintain my existence in both worlds.

Even with these efforts, I find myself negotiating more of myself to the point that I often feel like a foreigner in both worlds, not belonging to either. Because of my inexperience, lack of professional relationships with other minorities in higher education, and the lack of cultural support or awareness I received from my colleagues, I believed that I was desperately and utterly alone. Thus began my journey to pursue the goal of reconciling the differences between my home and work worlds. I continue to search for a balance between the competing value systems, cultures, and expectations of my worlds. I work hard to balance my vocation as a faculty member in higher education with that of my rich family upbringing, while remaining accessible to the traditions and discoveries that both of my worlds have to offer.

THE WORLD OF BIRTH AND HOME

I am one of three children. We were brought up in a humble, faith-filled home, where my parents led by example. My father worked the graveyard shift as a dockhand for a freight station. He was loyal to his company and hardworking, retiring after forty-two years. My mother worked at a grocery store and later in the school district. When my brother and I were in the last years of high school, my mother began her college career, and she would go on to become a teacher, counselor, and then principal in our hometown. My parents are the reason my siblings and I have been successful at school, at work, and in life. We were constantly challenged to do our best at work and school. My parents instilled a hard work ethic, and this has been critical to our success.

My parents made sure that my siblings and I knew that our education came first. We were expected to study immediately after we came home from school, and we were not allowed to play on the weekends until all of our homework for the following week was completed. Our days at school were a source of conversation around the dinner table, and we were rewarded when we brought home A's on our report cards. As children, we knew better not to ask for junk food or candy when we went to the grocery store because money was scarce, but our requests for books were never turned down. Our mother encouraged us to take care of our books and reminded us of how important it was to read well, encouraging us to read to each other. My parents held high expectations for our education, and I know that this foundation has been instrumental in forming my own beliefs about the power of education.

Although I was successful in college, I was not prepared for the cultural confusion and racism that I would experience. I did my best to assimilate by joining a sorority and the university soccer team, but around the corner there was always this undercurrent of racism. For example, an Anglo peer walked passed me on campus, asking, "How does it feel to be a token?" I had no idea what he was talking about, and I had to ask my friends what he meant. On another day, a classmate told me to "go back to Mexico." Comments such as these made me feel unworthy and unwelcomed. I often called home crying, begging my mother to let me come home, but she firmly told me I was going to stay until I finished college. I wanted to be with my family at home and safe from the awkwardness of college life. At that time, I could not recognize how difficult it was for my mother to make me stay on campus. Now I know that these experiences made me wiser and assisted in developing the strength necessary to brace myself and speak against racial ignorance.

After college, I became a high school teacher. I loved the classroom, students, and teaching. I learned more about graduate school and recognized that I had the opportunity to continue my education, which would foster my love of learning and open doors of opportunity that I had not yet discovered. I worked on my master's degree at a nearby university and later completed my doctoral program. Unfortunately, there were few minority students at the graduate level—I was one of two Hispanic students in my doctoral program—and although I looked for mentors, I was often ignored by Latino/a faculty because I did not speak Spanish fluently. I was not Anglo enough to feel connections with my peers, and I was not "Mexican enough" to be worthy of potential role models. I often felt like a cultural castaway, but I did not use this as an excuse to disengage. I listened and learned from my peers. I was able to understand the world as they each saw it, and I made an effort to contribute by providing my own perspective.

My family is extremely important to me. My cousins are my first and best friends, and they continue to be a source of support. Although I have 41 first cousins on both sides of my family, only nine of us obtained a bachelor's degree and five completed a master's degree. I am the only one in my family that has earned a doctoral degree. This is a great source of pride for my family, but because of my education and my job, I am different. My aunts scoff at the idea of my traveling across the globe for work, and my cousins have no interest in talking about inequity of education for marginalized populations. It is difficult for some of my family to understand why I would go to school for so long for the sake of learning. They are also confused as to how I could go to school for so long and not make more money. My aunts are continuously asking whether I want to get married. Educated or not, I am a failure in their eyes because I do not have a husband or children. When I changed jobs and moved to a new town, it was evident that my family was not so excited about the opportunity for me to begin teaching at the graduate level as they were thrilled at the prospect of me finding a husband in my new location. It can be difficult to explain to my family how some of my plans have changed not in magnitude but in appearance. I do not want to disappoint them, and it's a struggle to want to leave my family while achieve more than I had ever planned for myself.

I now find myself hundreds of miles away from my immediate family, pursing my own dream of teaching at the graduate level. Each time I return home to visit, I feel that another piece of me disappears among the walls of my home, and I wrestle with my own selfishness, wondering if I have abandoned my family. In my culture, selfishness is condemned; humility and selflessness are considered virtues (Anzaldúa, 2007), and I find myself feeling torn and lost in a world that does not have a place for me to fit in neatly. It is this stress of these competing values and identities that creates the disparities between me and my family. I live on the outskirts of my cultural home, but eagerly wait for the opportunity to celebrate traditions and serve as a resource to my younger cousins who are encouraged to call me when they do well in school and when they have questions about college and financial applications. My family replenishes my soul.

THE WORLD OF HIGHER EDUCATION

I was a high school teacher prior to beginning my work in higher education, and I assumed my position as a faculty member at a university would be similar. There was no one to prepare me for what I would experience. I found very few opportunities to meet cooperatively with fellow faculty members; it seems there would never be agreement among faculty members in any decisions that needed to be made, and I listened to conversations of faculty talking about unprepared students who needed to find their own way without support. I felt as if I was a new basketball player who got thrown out on the court with ten minutes left, but someone forgot to tell me the rules of the game. I was a foreigner in this new world.

Unfortunately, there were no mentoring programs for new faculty. I remember my department chair coming to my office the first week of classes. He kindly said, "Welcome, and let me know if you have any questions." If I did not know the rules of the game, then I surely did not know what questions to ask. It was trial by fire. I did my best to find fellow faculty members who genuinely wanted to be helpful and know me as a colleague and person. These individuals took the time to answer questions, to make helpful suggestions, and more importantly to call me "friend". Even with their unfaltering support, I knew that they would never know what it felt like to be a female, Mexican American faculty member. Beverly Daniel Tatum (2003, p. 18) writes, "How one's racial identity is experienced is mediated by the dimensions of the world around them: Who does this world say I am? Who do my peers say I am? How am I represented in the cultural images around me? Or am I missing from the picture all together?" What does it mean in the world of work when I walk into a room and find that I am the only one in the room who looks like me? Am I welcomed, lucky to be there, or appreciated for the differences I bring to our students, courses, and university? (Tatum, 2003; Turner & Myer, 2000).

If there was one place where I was confident that I would be welcomed, it was in the classroom. I knew how to work with students and took great pride in being an effective teacher. To my surprise, several students in my college courses would question my expectations and push back when I held them accountable to established rules. As a new professor, I expected a bit of this, but I did not expect it to the extent that I experienced, and I quickly became aware that I was going to have to try extra hard to earn my credibility. What did I do wrong? What did I say? The answers hit me in the middle of a faculty meeting. I realized that it was nothing that I did or said. It was the way that I looked. If being a faculty member in higher education meant that I had to be male and Anglo, and I am female and Mexican American, then I surely did not fit the expectation of a college faculty member (Martinez, 1995; Noguera, 2008). I was not dismayed. Instead, I used this as an opportunity to become a better teacher. I began to encourage my students to develop an appreciation for others' experiences. I encouraged students from various racial, socioeconomic, and educational backgrounds to share their histories and helped them understand how these histories influence their comprehension of the material being taught. Eventually, my students would feel free to ask others, "What do you think?"—recognizing that their perspective was not everyone's perspective.

As I spent more time at this university, my reputation as a favored professor and advisor spread, and I gained popularity among groups of marginalized students. Hearing about their experiences fueled my curiosity regarding access and support in higher education, and I began to conduct research in retention and the academic success of marginalized populations. There were colleagues who were not supportive of my research. Some of them indicated that talking about issues related to race or other marginalized populations made things worse: "If you would only stop talking about race, people wouldn't be racist" (Singleton & Linton, 2006). Some suggested that my research was self-serving and it was not viewed as viable. Although I did not allow unsupportive colleagues to affect my area of work, their arguments significantly fueled the feeling that I was misunderstood and created fear of my future experiences with the rank and tenure process (Berry, 1996; Turner & Myer, 2000). The best source of support regarding my research came from colleagues who held similar interests. While attending conferences or meetings at other institutions, I sought out others who not only shared research interests but also shared similar experiences as faculty of color. I met true trailblazers, found comfort in listening to others' experiences at their own institutions, and welcomed encouragement and advice from others who were more experienced and who helped remind me of why I chose to become a professor.

My own university was not designed to support faculty of color, so I sought out my own support systems where I worked. I found a significant amount of support and camaraderie with university cafeteria and maintenance staff members, which predominantly consisted of people of color. Because I worked in my hometown, I had grown up knowing many of these people and their families. They were tremendously proud of me. My success was theirs, but they served me at lunch, receptions, and banquets. When they were at work, they made little eye contact and definitely held no meaningful conversations during formal events. It would create unwanted barriers and walls neither of us could have predicted would materialize. Why could I talk freely with my friends after church or when we met at the store, but it was different while we were at work? Again, my worlds collided, and although I realized that many of these barriers were systemic, I continually make efforts to nurture my relationships that existed within both of my worlds.

BETWEEN TWO WORLDS

Sandwiched between worlds, I live and work within the borderland with one foot firmly planted in both worlds. It is a struggle of location, values, language, and transition, and it is only by remaining malleable that I can reap the blessings that both worlds have to offer (Anzaldua, 2007; Guzmán, 2002). I know that there will always be times when I find myself the odd one out: the only Latina in a meeting or the only one who is not married or has children, but I know that I am not alone. I now know that I must do my best to surround myself with others who see the beauty and value in our differences. I am blessed to work with several people who see my culture as valuable, and they honor the differences that we all bring. I continue to educate myself about the experiences of other female and minority faculty in higher education and welcome the opportunity to learn from mentors whom I trust. I also seek support from my members of my family, especially my mother. Although she may lack the contextual knowledge of being a professor, she keeps me grounded and continuously remind to return to who I know about myself, what I truly believe in, and where I come from. from. It is only because of this cultural understanding that I can thrive and better serve students, my academic program, and the university.

My family respects my work, and their support is something I could not live without. I speak to colleagues at other institutions on behalf of my family, culture, and community, which is something that only my education and experience could provide. My family also comes to me to discuss issues within their lives, and I recognize that this is a position of respect that is usually found among our elders. I honor my family, and I will do whatever is necessary to maintain and preserve the cultural traditions of my home, a place that my ancestors forged, where my family lives, and a place where I return to with pride and hope.

I have met some of the most amazing people, and I have visited almost half of the states in the United States. I have traveled to the other side of the globe attending conferences and learning from others who are different than me, and I have had the opportunity to work with some of the most amazing students. I am blessed to be a part of the most important part of their lives, as they search for their calling and place in this world. This is a precious opportunity to be a part of, and I welcome the opportunity to discuss issues of justice, equity, and the beauty that comes from the multiplicity of stories everyone brings to the classroom. I could not ask for more.

Finally, I have had the pleasure of meeting Latina/o faculty from other schools, and I have found that I am not alone in this voyage of balancing cultures and worlds. I have learned the importance of maintaining strong relationships with other Latinas who were raised to be strong, independent women. Having conversations with others who share my experience has been extremely powerful for me. I have learned that I must forge strong circles of Latina/o friendships, both personal and professional, for my survival and the survival of my own culture. These relationships have and continue to bring validation, support, and nourishment to all of my worlds.

REFERENCES

Anzaldúa, G. (2007). *Borderlands/La frontera: The new Mestiza* (3rd ed.). San Francisco, CA: Aunt Lute Books.

Berry, B. (1996). *I'm on my way but your foot is on my head.* New York, NY: Fireside Books.

Guzmán, S. (2002). *The Latina's Bible: The nueva latina's guide to love, spirituality, family, and la vida.* New York, NY: Three Rivers Press.

Martinez, M. A. (1995). Actuano. In R. V. Padilla & R. C. Chavez (Eds.), *The leaning ivory tower: Latino professors in American universities.* SUNY Series in Hispanic Studies (pp. 67–76). Albany: State University of New York Press.

Noguera, P. A. (2008). *The trouble with black boys: And other reflections on race, equity, and the future of public education.* San Francisco, CA: Jossey-Bass.

Singleton, G. E., & Linton, C. (2006). *Courageous conversations about race: A field guide for achieving equity in schools.* Thousand Oaks, CA: Corwin.

Tatum, B. T (2003). *Why are all the Black kids sitting together in the cafeteria: And other conversation about race.* New York, NY: Basic.

Turner, C. S. V., & Myers, S. L. (2000). *Faculty of color in academe.* Needham Heights, MA: Allyn & Bacon.

CHAPTER 15

NO SOY DE AQUÍ, NI SOY DE ALLÁ

Making My Way Through the Tenure Process

Margarita Jimenez-Silva

Throughout my professional career as a teacher and then a professor, I have struggled with fitting in and have often felt caught between two worlds—not being from here or there, *ni de aquí, ni de allá*. As a first-generation college student and the oldest child born to immigrant parents from Mexico, the balancing act actually began long before setting foot in my own classroom. Although my parents were very supportive of all of my educational endeavors, they often emphasized my role as a wife and then a mother above my professional accomplishments. Anyone familiar with the tenure process understands that the balancing of work and life is difficult regardless of one's background and circumstances, but the added pressure of living up to family responsibilities as a Latina daughter can make the tenure process even more stressful.

Abriendo Puertas, Cerrando Heridas (Opening Doors, Closing Wounds), pages 153–161
Copyright © 2015 by Information Age Publishing
All rights of reproduction in any form reserved.

I began my professional career as a bilingual elementary school teacher in Southern California. I soon realized that my college education had not adequately prepared me to work with English learners (ELs) to the degree that I felt was necessary. Therefore, I applied to graduate programs and although my parents were supportive of my decision to pursue a master's degree, my extended family strongly felt that I was cheating my parents and siblings out of the income I would be giving up to attend graduate school. When I announced that I would be studying at the Harvard Graduate School of Education on the opposite coast, there were many murmurs about the inappropriateness of moving so far away from home as a single woman. At Harvard, I felt very much caught between two worlds as one of only a few working-class Mexican-descent students. When I would return home, I felt very uncomfortable sharing any of my graduate student experiences with my extended family for fear of being perceived as arrogant.

ROUND 1: CONCORDIA UNIVERSITY

After teaching a few years and while still working on my doctorate, I was recruited by my alma mater, Concordia University Irvine, at an assistant professor position where I prepared teachers to work with ELs. I was one of only a handful of minority professors and the only Latina full-time faculty member at the time. Being a private, Missouri-Synod Lutheran university, the requirements for being promoted to associate professor included involvement in the Lutheran church as part of service requirements, along with the traditional requirements related to teaching and research. While the emphasis of the college was on teaching, there was still the expectation of engaging in research and a very strong emphasis on service within the Lutheran community, which presented a number of challenges as a Latina who was brought up in a Catholic home.

Although there are many similarities in terms of beliefs and traditions between the Catholic and Lutheran Missouri-Synod churches, there are a number of differences. My father had a very difficult time accepting that I had left Catholicism and converted to Lutheranism. In fact, having been married in a Lutheran Church, he often told me that he felt that my marriage was not valid. Attending Lutheran services, I always felt out of place not being completely comfortable with the differences between the Catholic services I had attended throughout my childhood and what I was now experiencing. I and a few other acquaintances who were also from Catholic backgrounds spoke frequently about the fact that we felt caught between two worlds. We called ourselves CaLus—a mix of Catholicism and Lutheranism. At many of the faculty and community events, other faculty and staff from Concordia often spoke about being "born and raised" Lutheran, which somehow made those of us not "born and raised" Lutheran feel like we were "less Lutheran." I did not have long-standing connections with Lutheran communities and had to seek out Lutheran communities that understood the issues of diversity that I advocated for in my research and were open to how I wanted to be involved—with ELs and Latino families.

On campus, many of the activities that I chose to attend as a faculty member were ones that supported Latino and African American students. I served as faculty sponsor for the multicultural student organization as well as the African American one. At the meetings and social events sponsored by these groups, I was often the only faculty member in attendance. Most other faculty members attended sporting events and social gatherings, and comments were often made about how I had been "missed" at the latest basketball game or happy hour. At this point in my life, I was married and had two very young sons. It was difficult to attend sporting or social events. Although Concordia did not grant tenure, it did have perpetual three-year contracts that were granted based on your annual reviews. As I looked towards moving from assistant to associate professor, I was very worried about my visibility on campus and being considered as an equal to others who had grown up within the Lutheran church.

One of my most uncomfortable experiences before I was promoted to associate professor occurred when I was approached by one of the national leaders of the Lutheran church to help with the production of a set of online modules that would prepare teachers, administrators, and others to become certified church workers. I had assumed that I would be teaching a module and was surprised when I was instead cast as a Catholic, Latina woman asking questions into a camera regarding the Lutheran faith. The questions were very stereotypical—for example, "Why does my family pray to saints?" I have very vivid memories of sitting in the make-up chair, feeling very disrespected yet knowing that if I wanted to reach the rank of associate professor, I should wait to address this issue after my promotion was approved. My first thoughts were to storm out of the session, utterly disgusted at the lack of respect for me or my Catholic upbringing, or to sabotage the video by properly enlightening my colleagues about the sacred role of saints in the Catholic faith. Instead, I decided to address my frustration, as many of us do in academia, through scholarship. I wrote a monograph for the Lutheran church, *Open Hearts, Open Minds: Diverse Learners in Lutheran Schools and Congregations* (2003), in which I called for our church leaders and congregants to move away from rigid stereotypes and view increasing diversity as an opportunity instead of as a problem. I also chose to focus my service obligations by visiting Lutheran schools and congregations with increasing Latino populations and provide professional development for teachers and church worker in those areas.

Concordia emphasized the importance of family and provided me with an extra office where my two very young sons could take naps and play. Fellow faculty members often offered to babysit while I taught if my regular sitter was not available. The cafeteria workers would fix special meals for my boys, and they were always welcome if they had to attend a meeting with me. I often taught five classes a semester and had student teachers to supervise and, thus, the challenge of balancing work and family was constant. I relied on my parents, my sisters, extended family, and friends to help me when needed. My grandmother-in-law attended many conferences with me where she attended to the boys while I presented my academic work.

I was successful in becoming an associate professor and after a few more years of teaching at Concordia, I wanted to pursue a position in a more culturally diverse setting and with a stronger emphasis on research. I left Concordia with the administration's promise that I could always "come back home," and I am grateful for the support that Concordia provided me as a working parent the first eight years of my career as a professor. However, I also have a number of wounds that have yet to heal, many related to my role as a Latina woman working in a very non-diverse setting.

ROUND 2: ARIZONA STATE UNIVERSITY

After eight years at Concordia University, I was looking for opportunities to grow as a researcher. At the time, my parents were living in Phoenix, Arizona, and since I had two young sons, moving closer to family was very appealing. Consequently, I applied to Arizona State University, which at the time had three different campuses with three distinct colleges of education. The College of Teacher Education and Leadership (CTEL) was the best fit for me since it was primarily a teaching college with what I considered reasonable expectations for teaching, research, and service. The fit between CTEL and what I was looking for in the next stage of my career was just right. I was hired as an assistant professor, my previous rank not having transferred. Along with me, two other professors were hired at the same time to work in the elementary education program with a bilingual/English as a second language endorsement. We were hired, in part, to create a center for teachers of English learners and hold an annual conference for teachers of ELs in Arizona, along with meeting our research, teaching, and other service obligations.

On one occasion early in the school year, a fellow new faculty member and I walked into the administrative assistant's office speaking Spanish. The administrative assistant turned to address my colleague, who is Caucasian and learned Spanish when studying abroad in Spain, and commented on how it was wonderful that she is bilingual. My colleague responded that I too am bilingual and without turning to look at me, the administrative assistant commented to my colleague, "She *had* to learn English since she chose to come to this country." I could not resist and did inform her that I was born in this country. My comment was not acknowledged. Unfortunately, that experience was a preview to a number of experiences where my colleague was definitely privileged over me in terms of resources, mentoring, and professional opportunities. For example, as part of a writer's group, any paper that my colleague wrote would receive extensive feedback while the head of the writer's group often commented there was nothing he could do for me and that there were special programs for minorities. On several occasions, my colleague offered to submit my papers as her own work after witnessing the inequity in how we were treated. She would then would pass on the revisions to me, never revealing to anyone our plan for supporting each as we moved towards tenure. I quickly learned that although there were more Latina faculty at CTEL than were at Concordia, I would still have to navigate an educational landscape where blatant inequities existed.

From the first day at ASU, balancing work and family became a lot more complicated than it had been at Concordia. My husband accepted a job in Sacramento, CA a few months before I accepted the position at ASU. We both agreed that he would spend weekends in Phoenix and we would make a decision regarding who would relocate after being at our respective jobs for two years. Although my parents lived in Phoenix and had offered to help, they were quite upset that we had chosen our careers over keeping the family together and felt that I was not being an ideal wife or mother since ideal wives and mothers *always* chose family first. Fortunately, my parents found a home for us to live in close to where they lived in a suburb of Phoenix. Unfortunately, it was a 98-mile round trip commute between my office and our home. I also was teaching at least one night class a week, and the expectation was that faculty be present in their offices as often as possible during the work week. In addition, I had taken over a $20,000 pay cut and so took on a second job to help make up the difference. I have significant school debt from my graduate degrees, and thus the extra income was necessary. This meant additional time away from the family, and my parents worried often about the effects my new position would have on my marriage and children. I had to make arrangements for before- and after-school care and for babysitting several evenings a week. The added expectations for research and service also meant that even when I was home, I was often at the computer working on manuscripts or having to travel to conduct research and attend national conferences.

During this time, there were many negative changes impacting English learners in Arizona. Teacher education was being impacted as state-mandated structured English immersion (SEI) courses were now required of all preservice and inservice teachers. Over the next few years, the political landscape in Arizona changed immensely. Tom Horne, superintendent of education at the time, was on a mission to carry out the mandates of Proposition 203 that placed severe limitations on any form of bilingual education. English-only and anti-immigrant (SB1070) policies were put in place and impacted large numbers of students, school communities, and teacher preparation. I was outspoken about the policies and was personally called out by Tom Horne. He and I went back and forth in the media and in a number of public forums over the course of several months. All the while, I felt very much at risk of not being supported for tenure by my administration or colleagues since we as a college had a reputation of "not rocking the boat" when it came to dealing with Arizona's department of education. I struggled with finding my voice as an advocate for ELs while not alienating the administration that would ultimately decide whether I could stay at ASU. Once again, I found myself balancing roles, this time as an activist in the Latino community and as an ASU faculty member.

A new dean was hired in my third year, and the expectations for my position and moving towards tenure changed. Whereas I had been hired in part to develop a statewide conference to bring together teachers of ELs with the goal of beginning a center and I had been working towards that objective, the new dean had new goals if I was to successfully advance towards tenure. My third-year review, provided at the end of my third year, reflected the changing expectations. The conference was now no longer to take place nor was a center focused on ELs part of the plan. My third-year review stated that I needed to focus on research and publications.

Some of the advice I received from trusted sources as I continued to advance towards tenure was that I needed to "toot my own horn" about my research, teaching, and service since nobody was going to "toot it for me." One of the values that my parents instilled in me was one of humility. Calling attention to my publications, student evaluations, and service commitments seemed contrary to the idea of being humble. I had hoped that I could be subtle about mentioning my latest research project or community award, but I soon learned that to be heard, you have to be pretty loud. I had to learn how to report my accomplishments to our college's newsletters and other electronic outlets, mention them at college social events, and definitely highlight them in my annual reviews. After three years at ASU, I felt that I had invested so much time and energy into moving towards tenure that my husband and I decided to keep our living arrangement for at least another two years.

Also during this same time period, the Arizona State University (ASU) underwent a number of major reorganizations. At the end, all three colleges of education were combined into one college, now named the Mary Lou Fulton Teachers College. Few faculty from the disestablished College of Education at ASU Tempe remained. That faculty had been the leaders in the state when it came to issues related to ELs. I now found myself with very little mentorship in navigating the political landscape in Arizona and at ASU. The newly established guidelines for tenure were aligned with those typical of a Research I institution, yet my teaching load and service requirements remained as they had been for the position for which I was hired in a teaching college. The rigor and number of required publications had more than doubled between the time I was hired and when I submitted my tenure package. I simply did not have enough time to fill the gap in expectations. I submitted my tenure file and was not recommended for tenure by the internal committee within my college.

During this very stressful time, my parents kept asking why I was spending such long hours in the office and traveling so extensively. Interestingly, my parents kept asking how I could be going for "ten year" when I had only been at ASU for six years. I repeatedly explained the tenure process, but other than a higher salary, my parents understood very little about the process. To be fair, other friends and family members outside of academia also had a difficult time understanding tenure procedures.

ROUND 3: ARIZONA STATE UNIVERSITY, AGAIN

After meeting with the dean and several conversations with others, it was recommended that I apply for and be granted a one-year extension and resubmit my tenure papers. In the meantime, I had learned how to tap into the Latino network of higher education faculty outside of my college for support and how to go about the process of submitting names for external reviewers of my file. I was approached by a number of attorneys regarding suing ASU regarding my tenure file. I knew a number of other Latino faculty across the country who were suing regarding tenure. In the cases where they were successful and were granted tenure, I often heard other faculty comment on how the tenure had been granted *only* because of the lawsuit. I decided that if I was not granted tenure at ASU in this second round, I would leave and return to California. I resubmitted my file and was granted tenure without any reservations. I had hoped to host a party to celebrate with my family having received tenure, but given that two of my siblings had recently lost their jobs, my parents requested that I not call attention to my "good luck."

POST-TENURE

I cannot count how many times I told my family that as soon as I was granted tenure, I would have more time for them. I have now had tenure for two years and instead of slowing down, balancing work and family life has become increasingly difficult. My two sons are now teenagers and no longer require babysitters. They can cook for themselves and drive wherever they need to go. Yet I still feel like I am neglecting my responsibilities as a mother and my husband and I have now spent more years living in different states than we have living together. My family has quite a collection of pictures they have taken of me working on syllabi, manuscripts, grant proposals, and other work documents while on vacation with them. The pictures include one of me on a stump in the middle of the California Redwoods where I took a conference call regarding a special journal issue, one sitting on a rock in the middle of the Truckee river while my family went tubing where I was finishing a manuscript, and one of me at Lego Land working on a grant proposal while waiting in line for a rollercoaster. My computer is always with me, and I seem to always be behind on work and on family responsibilities.

One of the reasons why I feel that I have not slowed down since being granted tenure is because I feel a great responsibility in making sure that issues of diversity are addressed throughout the university. There are simply not enough faculty who bring that voice to the table. Immediately after being granted tenure, I asked to become the program coordinator for the elementary education—bilingual/English as a second language endorsement program. Previously, the program had been led by non-tenure-track faculty. By having a tenured associate professor leading the program, the status of the program has been elevated, and I have been able to have a larger impact on programmatic decisions across the college. Being one of only a few Latina faculty at my college, I am often asked to sit on committees and attend events where they need minority representation. Even when not asked to sit on certain committees, I ask to have a voice on committees that deal with recruitment, admissions, policy, and supporting first-generation college students.

Throughout the past sixteen years since I entered academia, I have learned how to make myself visible in ways that are valued by the university and college while also pursuing my passions for social justice issues. I have learned how to reach out and form support networks in other colleges and avenues at ASU and in the national landscape. I have also formed support groups comprised of other faculty who are also balancing work and family and have the same values as I do. We help each other with everything from rides to the airport to checking on our kids when we are out of town.

SUPPORTING COLLEAGUES—PAYING IT FORWARD

In my current role as program coordinator and as a tenured associate professor, I have a voice in issues affecting many of our Latino/a students, power in providing political support for my colleagues who are preparing to go up for tenure in the next few years, and a say in hiring new faculty. I strongly believe in quality mentorship and am trying to provide that for many, but especially for Latino students and junior faculty. One of my major goals is to make the implicit rules explicit. Many of us Latino faculty as well as the Latino undergraduate and graduate students are first-generation college students. Although it was difficult for me to learn how to navigate the college experience, it was even more difficult to navigate the tenure experience given that I had to also consider balancing my role as a wife and a mother along with professional obligations.

Both of my sons will be attending college within the next year. As I look forward to the next stage of my career, I am now wondering how I can balance my responsibilities at work and my obligations as a daughter of aging parents. While my responsibilities regarding my own children are becoming less time intensive, my own parents are requiring more help from me. As the oldest daughter, it is expected that I will step up and take the lead in caring for them. I have thought about the possibility of pursuing a new faculty position in a setting that will allow my husband and me to live together again within the next couple of years. I have important decisions to make regarding whether I will pursue positions at other research-intensive institutions, perhaps return to a teaching college, or try a nonacademic position. Being mid-career, I would like to find a position in a place that values both my research interests and my teaching, and yet also understands my growing responsibilities with my parents. I have not found the secret of balancing work and family and do not believe that one exists. I do, however, believe that we must do the best we can each day and trust that our families will appreciate the work that we do and that our work will acknowledge the sacrifices our families make to help advance our causes. Instead of trying to fit the model of "good wife and mother" or "good researcher," it is important that we are at peace with how we fulfill our various roles. By sharing our stories and providing a place to have our voices heard, we can provide support for those coming up behind us and learn from those who are further along on the path.

REFERENCE

Jimenez-Silva, M. (2003). *Open hearts and minds: Diverse learners in Lutheran schools and congregations.* River Forest, IL: Lutheran Education Association.

CHAPTER 16

SCHOLARSHIP OF MIND AND SOUL

Claudia Cervantes-Soon and Juan F. Carrillo

All we knew about North Carolina was that it was really far and that they had good college basketball. For anyone outside of the dominant class, the image of the U.S. South is not necessarily inviting. As we prepared to take positions as assistant professors at the University of North Carolina at Chapel Hill, confederate flags came to mind, but we were also excited about the idea of new opportunities and possibilities as we learned about the recent boom of the Latino/a population. We were attracted to the idea of building something new, particularly in a place where Latino pioneers were paving new paths and new identities in the midst of hostile times and in contexts unaccustomed to their presence.

We were also motivated by a seemingly genuine desire on the part of the university to advance the educational goals of the growing Latino community. When the dean of the School of Education realized that in order to hire one of us, he would have to hire both, the school made great efforts to make this possible despite increasing state budget cuts. Hence, when we moved to Chapel Hill, North Carolina in 2011, we felt welcomed by the faculty, at least by those with whom we would be working more closely, and, excited about our research plans, we looked forward to hit the road running.

Abriendo Puertas, Cerrando Heridas (Opening Doors, Closing Wounds), pages 163–171
Copyright © 2015 by Information Age Publishing
All rights of reproduction in any form reserved.

However, we soon realized that the challenge that we had chosen to undertake meant more than contributing to scholarship and teaching that illuminated the Latino education experience. This challenge branched out in different directions permeating our personal lives in profound ways, challenging our ethics and identities as activist scholars, and affecting our ability to meet the expectations as junior faculty. Overcoming these difficulties would require new and creative approaches on our part.

One aspect of this challenge involved the isolation from our people and culture in both our personal and professional lives. Coming from the west and the U.S.–Mexico border area, we were accustomed to the contradictions but also to the jovial and soulful relationships in our Latino communities. The physical distance, the sanitized environment of a whitestream institution and professional life, coupled with the microagressions we experienced living in a small, mostly middle- to upper middle-class town became more draining to our spirits than we had anticipated.

Secondly, simply being some of the very few Latina/o faculty on campus brought with it its own challenges. On the one hand, we felt the responsibility to advocate for our community in various ways, ensuring our presence and contributions to any request to support the education of Latinas/os both inside and outside of the university. Needless to say, this soon became a problem, as this was time consuming and soon we were advised that we should focus on our scholarship rather than on so much service. On the other hand, this also created an ethical dilemma for us. Because we viewed our work as more than a simple job to get done in order to climb up the professional latter, but rather as part of our life project for social justice, refusing our support to community efforts felt like betraying our people and the previous generations that had selflessly fought for our civil and human rights.

In order to negotiate these challenges, we have each developed (and continue to develop) our own strategies, which, together with very specific institutional supports, have allowed us to *seguir adelante*. Below, we humbly share our individual *testimonios* and strategies for survival, healing, and growth, hoping that they may serve as a *granito de arena* for other junior faculty in similar positions looking for hope.

JUAN'S TESTIMONIO

I never, never, want to go home. Because I haven't got one.

—The Smiths, *There Is a Light that Never Goes Out*

There is a certain kind of homelessness that has always guided me for better or worse. Curiosity and pragmatic, intellectual, and romantic ideas of justice have taken me all over the U.S. and the world. My current experiences are rooted in some of this reality. Yet, while often embedded in incoherence and difficult demands, I do know that roots matter and they continue to pull me—this philosophical and spiritual umbilical cord is the source of much wisdom and strength in my journey. "Home" is deeply connected to origins, heritage, and the logic that stems from those early experiences. In that love for yesterday, there is a tragicomedic assessment of loss. Ultimately, I am but one ant in the long history that predates my notions of place, memory, and melancholy.

Moving to North Carolina is part of my fragmented journey. I used to sell shoes at the Paramount swap meet as a kid in the barrios of Los Angeles. I would go to the movies to watch *La India María* and *Cantinflas.* There was an intimacy in language, poverty, and large numbers. This world, in my Los Angeles (and later in Phoenix, Arizona), was embedded in immigrant and Chicano/a public space, without apology or savior narratives. In Texas, while in graduate school, I also lived in a working-class community, alongside many Latinas/os. When graduate school got too overwhelming, there were many decolonizing spaces.

In 2011, I was suddenly uprooted. I was immersed in a tree-cave of silence and privilege, surrounded by distance and invisibility: There were few poems that lyrically told me what to do next. The Chicano worlds of my graduate program—gone. The fast food joints full of *raza,* for the most part, gone. The bus stops with Latinos/as, the music coming out of cars, the Spanish language on the streets—gone. This is not to suggest that these places do not exist in the larger community, but in Chapel Hill, this was not very accessible. I complained about basic things that drew from a larger frustration: no lights on highways, the boredom, the limited Mexican food options, the public spaces that were too granola or too elitist. I had the barrio in my soul, or something semi-close to that, and I could not find it. I was instead surrounded by an endless amount of trees and ongoing reflexivity.

I remember wondering how I was going to survive the pressures of publications, teaching, and meetings in a context of silence and marginalization of what I represented. Moreover, I even heard a few Latinos/as mention that they hated being called Mexican since they were not from Mexico. I got that, I respected that, but it added to my sense of displacement and othering. Yet, in this ambivalence, I became a better listener, more active in the community and I found a few options for surviving these struggles.

In stories I found my way back home. When I started to conduct research on the life histories of Latino males who attend college in North Carolina, new pathways began to open. In these dialogues, I found visual, emotional, and story-driven community. I began to see my role in the new south as well as optimism related to forging larger networks that seek change. I could feel the energy in every interview. The stories outlined the desire of youth to be change agents, the desire to increase the Latino/a student pipeline to college, and the larger struggle to get out of the shadows and begin to nurture the next chapter of North Carolina history which includes: Latinas/os. It was clear to me that the second generation of Latinos/as in North Carolina want power and they want it *now.* I developed a network of mentees who were interested in social change.

In learning from these students, I was inspired to develop actionable projects. Two of the many projects were a high school mentoring program for Latino males in a low-income high school, and another project involved my participation in being part of the team that was pushing for a Latino/a center on the UNC–Chapel Hill campus. I started the Latino males program aiming to develop safe spaces where we could have critical dialogue and share our stories. Students would share with me the difficulties around their undocumented status, the role of gangs, and critical reflections on masculinities, and some students who lived in Mexico for a few years shared stories of joyful moments but also the horrors of drug-related violence. We talked and shared feedback, outlining our hopes for finding our way through life, and I leveraged whatever social and cultural capital I have. This program is in its infancy, but it already has provided much emotional and spiritual comfort as well as a clearer toolkit for how I can be part of emancipatory education projects in the larger community.

Similarly, with a few Latino/a colleagues on campus, I developed a tight bond, and we initiated a dialogue around building a Latina/o center at UNC–Chapel Hill. The process is still evolving, but dialogues with students and Latino/a alumni provided a sense of community and purpose and long-term commitment to making this happen. There have been encouraging signs along the way, and these kinds of exchanges, dialogues, and action projects have continued to build my evolving identity in a region that is new to me.

Outside of the job, I connected with students of color on the basketball court. Through "hoops," I had fun, got a good workout, but also found another way by which to build a brotherhood. Once again, stories were exchanged and we were able to grow together. I cannot emphasize enough how simple and yet influential these meetings have been. This is our "golf," where we get to convene and talk about life and expand our network as more students join us.

While I have been more connected to healing strategies, the struggle is still there. There are virtually no Chicano male faculty that come from a similar background to mine in the area. While Latinos/as continue to move into the state and populate our public schools, we are way behind in meeting this reality head on in higher education. I have to go to YouTube to remember those emotions, murals, and legacy. That is, until I have time to travel to conferences or visit family in the southwest. Ultimately, we are parties of one or two, having to do all the work and we have to embody all that is part of our "people" according to the way universities hire sometimes. We cannot do this alone. Nobody should be expected to do this.

CLAUDIA'S TESTIMONIO

"You will do great. Just don't get pregnant," was one of the first pieces of advice from Dr. May (pseudonym), a female full professor. Given that many senior faculty in the nation are women who have sacrificed their prospects of having a family during their reproductive years as they sought to succeed in the women-hostile environment of not too many decades ago (and even today), her statement was not surprising. Although now the UNC School of Education appeared quite family friendly, my colleague's statement was still relevant, even if politically incorrect, given the high expectations for scholarly productivity at a tier I research institution and the demands that this still entailed, particularly for women of color. This, I thought, would be my greatest challenge when I learned that I was pregnant less than one month into the job.

But as I continued my work, I became troubled about the state of affairs of the education for English language learners in the state and the marginal work that our institution was doing to address the issue, and I felt responsible for taking the lead to address this. When I expressed my concern to another senior colleague, he warned me about spending too much time and energy on service and on building programs, for these activities would divert me from my research: "What good will it do to start programs that you can't sustain if you don't get tenure? It may sound selfish, but I recommend that you focus on your research so that you may be in a better position to create long-term change."

My colleague's advice was not unreasonable. In fact, these were wise and helpful words coming from someone who had witnessed the dead-end path of too many junior faculty trapped in the snares of programmatic and administrative work. However, I had to deliberately train myself to say no to many requests for interviews, collaboration, meetings, and input from various students, program coordinators, and other stakeholders, all while suppressing my guilt. Initially, this was very difficult. While I felt some relief from having to accept the requests that bombarded me, I also had an internal battle, feeling that I was betraying my community in the process. This was the irony of academia: I had to be unhelpful until tenure, with the idea that it would all be worth it in the long run.

Meanwhile, I also began to experience intellectual exhaustion. Gone were the Chicana scholars with whom I used to deliberate for hours, who would challenge my thinking, nurture my consciousness, and make me laugh with the warmest and wittiest of humors. Instead, I was often positioned as a cultural worker for the well-intentioned White liberal, for whom the word "Chicana" sounded like the name of an exotic animal. In some cases I even experienced attempts to consume and appropriate my knowledge and expertise and infantilize of my brown female body and voice. Having to constantly fight white entitlement as well as the subservience expected of a Latina professor made me distrustful and isolated me further.

But soon, despite some caring gestures from colleagues and students during and after my pregnancy, the isolation that I felt being away from family and friends materialized in unexpected ways. The greatest challenge came in like a storm in the form of post-partum depression. After a very long and difficult labor that ended in a cesarean, I sat all day long in the same corner of my bedroom nursing and holding my baby, trying to recover my depleted and aching body and battling the most irrational and difficult thoughts. I mourned the mother I lost at age nine, pondering on how difficult it must have been for her to raise her three children as a single parent. And I worried every minute about the vulnerability of this new child that now I held in my arms, and about the fact that I was submitting him to grow up uprooted from the land of his grandparents, aunts, uncles, and cousins, and from the sounds, colors, and smells of his cultural heritage. These and other thoughts circulated in my mind all day and night, leaving me sleepless, exhausted, and emotionally drained.

True, I had been away from family for years before my move to North Carolina, but this time, lacking the cultural symbols and warmth of my culture, and without having built strong friendships yet, the separation from the southwest felt much more severe. How I wished for a sister, for a friend, for an aunt to be near me, to tell me everything would be OK in my own language, to cheer me up with the tunes of Mexican music, and to comfort me with the smells and tastes of family food. How I longed for *Aztlán*. Instead, here I was in this unknown land, driving my husband crazy and feeling disappointed at what I had chosen to do to myself and my family by going so far away. Why did I have to be alone, having so many people who loved me? Was it all for a job? Was it even worth it?

Thanks to medical treatment and a semester of maternity leave, I began to physically recover. As soon as I was able, I began to visit Mexico and the U.S. Southwest, which allowed me to dwell, albeit temporarily, in the caring of family and friendship. When I returned to work, Juan and I were also given the opportunity to take an academic leave to focus on our research. While this pre-tenure leave is offered to all junior faculty in the School of Education to support them with their scholarship, it was incredibly helpful to us, as we were able to live in Mexico for a semester and reconnect to our cultural roots in a substantial way. This time away also helped me realize that I needed to take active steps to nurture and sustain my personal relationships, even from afar, and develop my own sacred spaces. Needless to say, this aspect of my life was crucial for my own health and academic productivity.

The first thing that we did when we returned was to move away from the small college town of Chapel Hill to Raleigh, the state capital. While this move may appear insignificant, it brought a new perspective to us. On the one hand, this was a city, albeit small, but it offered us a life slightly more similar to our backgrounds. Being from Ciudad Juarez, Mexico and Juan from Los Angeles, we had been feeling suffocated by life in a small town. More importantly, having access to a more diverse community, where Latinos were not so severely silenced and pushed to the margins, but where they owned taco trucks and *panaderías* as well as upscale restaurants and schools and occupied public spaces with their families more liberally, all while speaking Spanish, Spanglish or English with an accent, had a surprisingly liberating effect.

Secondly, I looked within my own research activities for opportunities to explore new sources of connection. I became more strategic and began to use conferences and national meetings not only to present my research, but also to reconnect with close academic friends and colleagues who understood my work. I also began to conduct research with Latino parents at a bilingual school as part of a larger project investigating better ways to bridge Latino families and schools. I had done this kind of research before, but this was the first time I did it without the collaboration of other colleagues and with a new identity as a mother. Needless to say, the data collection was important for my scholarship, but as it is often the case, I benefited in more ways that I had anticipated. The focus groups and interviews turned into sacred spaces where particularly mothers expressed some sense of vulnerability, sharing their worries, stories, *consejos*, and hopes.

Although I was the researcher, as a new mother, I was also now able to identify with them in many ways. Listening to the mothers' experiences, both positive and negative, and learning about their many agentic strategies to support their children despite the many borders and challenges of a hostile environment gave me an uplifting sense of connection. Their stories reminded me of my privilege but also of both my human frailty and strength and the many sacrifices that my ancestors had done to lead me to where I was with the dream of a better life. I learned to recognize the importance of wholeness in order to be able to give, and that this did not come only from getting tenure. I also felt part of a collective that was eager to use its voice. In doing so, my research did not appear anymore as some task to complete in order to get tenure. On the contrary, I was able to recover the meaningfulness and sense of action as an activist scholar.

Today I still lack the type of social, family, and intellectual sources of nourishment that I was able to access in the Southwest, and the challenges persist. I don't know if I will ever get that where I am, but I am working toward a better adjustment that will not mean compromising my own humanization. The future will only tell what that will look like. For now, I still have to say "no" often in order to keep my sanity, but I am working toward a more holistic approach to "success," which includes acknowledging and working with my limitations, recognizing the importance of my feelings, and paying more serious attention to my health. At the same time, I have taken steps to merge my scholarship and community advocacy and have become more purposeful in my mentoring and service activities. This has allowed me to maintain my research productivity while remaining faithful to my purposes as an activist scholar and engaging with my community in more humanizing ways.

CONCLUSION

Cuando el jilguero no puede cantar
cuando el poeta es un peregrino
cuando de nada nos sirve rezar.
Caminante no hay camino, se hace camino al andar

—Joan Manuel Serrat, *Caminante*

We have shared our *testimonios* with the humble hope that others may find some insight for their own journeys. Taking care of our spiritual and cultural selves in a state with an emerging Latino/a population has been a process embedded in challenges and ongoing opportunities. We are still learning how to lean on each other, build a community for ourselves, cultivate our personal relationships from a distance, and juggle our responsibilities as new parents in attempting to balance our personal and professional lives. Given the many stories of unemployment for academics, we realize that we are in a privileged position as tenure-track faculty at a research institution. We also realize that as an academic couple we are able to support and understand each other in ways that perhaps other couples find difficult. But there is also the danger of becoming so involved in the pressures of academic life that we may allow our health, emotional well-being, and family and personal relationships to deteriorate without realizing it. For that reason, remaining committed to humanization and countering our isolation is a constant struggle in which we must deliberately engage. To this end, finding healing in the shared experiences that bring us together with the rest of the new Latino diaspora has been helpful as well as our ability to merge our scholarship with our community efforts.

There is also much to be said about how UNC–Chapel Hill has instituted policies and supports that have facilitated our ability to navigate the academy as faculty of color and respond to our personal needs. For example, as mentioned before, the opportunity to take a pre-tenure academic leave gave us the flexibility to work off campus for an entire semester. This opportunity allowed us to move to Guadalajara, Mexico for a few months where we were able to retool and reconnect to the rhythms that made sense to us while working on our scholarship. This time to find ourselves and grow with our questions and commitments was crucial for our development in a holistic sense. Also, the opportunity for Claudia to take a semester off on maternity leave and extend the tenure track clock for a year due to illness allowed us to provide much needed attention not only to our newborn son, but also to Claudia's recovery.

These policies, as well as a growing validation of engaged scholarship and the support of senior faculty mentors and the School of Education leadership who have been willing to challenge their own paradigms and expand the parameters of their thinking in order to understand not only our research but also our experiences as minority faculty, have been extremely instrumental. We realize that not all universities value engaged scholarship or provide maternity leave to their new mothers, much less pre-tenure leaves or ongoing mentorship, and we hope that our *testimonios* illuminate the importance of these institutional supports. Although these resources are not only offered to faculty of color, they can provide the flexibility necessary to meet individual needs.

Today the challenges remain. We are still too far away from our families, and sometimes our hearts get overwhelmed by the constraints of this distance, particularly when we worry about aging parents and growing children. But at least we have found healing, hope, and encouragement in the sacred spaces of stories and collective struggle. As Serrat's wise and lyrical words tell us, we must continue to trace our own path in this new space, in often unexpected ways.

CHAPTER 17

NUESTRAS RAÍCES GROUND US

Reflecting Comunidad and Cultura in Who We Are as Latin@ Faculty

Laura Cortez
University of Texas at Austin

Melissa A. Martinez
Texas State University

Danielle Alsandor
Louisiana State University

Aurora Chang
Loyola University (Chicago)

Anjalé D. Welton
University of Illinois at Urbana-Champaign

In 2012, we embarked on a journey to examine the experiences of junior faculty of color as they navigated the academy. As five novice female scholars of color (first author as a Latina postdoctoral fellow, second author as a Latina assistant professor, third and fifth authors as African American assistant

Abriendo Puertas, Cerrando Heridas (Opening Doors, Closing Wounds), pages 173–182
Copyright © 2015 by Information Age Publishing
All rights of reproduction in any form reserved.

professors, and fourth author as a multiracial assistant professor of Guatemalan, Chinese, and Italian descent), we captured the *testimonios*, or testimonies (Reyes & Curry Rodríguez, 2012) of our counterparts to give voice to their triumphs and struggles. In the process, many of our experiences in and with academia were validated as we heard participants share intimate details of how they balanced their personal and professional lives, identities, and values. Participants also served as sources of knowledge and inspiration, as they divulged strategies to stay true to their own cultural ways of being while making strides in the tenure-track game. While each of the 57 participants we interviewed had a compelling story, we dedicate this chapter to the testimonies of six Latino/a junior faculty members (3 females, 3 males) who work in various disciplines at four-year universities across the country.

The testimonies of Efrain, Carlos, Beto, Angelica, Lucia, and Rosa revealed how they embraced their *Latinidad* to navigate their professional roles. We found they purposefully engaged in work that was social justice oriented and used their research to address equity issues for Latinas/os. Their scholarship also served as a source of strength amidst difficult times in academia, reminding them of their greater role and responsibility as Latino/a scholars to pave the way for future generations as others had done for them. They also drew upon the familial nature of their culture to develop a network of allies within and outside their institutions. While we did not anticipate our lives would be so intertwined with the stories of our participants, it was hard to separate the profound similarities. We found their lives paralleled our own and became a reflection of what we had personally experienced or life lessons that would come as we followed in similar paths to theirs. We also discovered the degree to which we, like our faculty of color participants, continued to live partially in the shadows often never fully acknowledging the painful experiences we faced while making our own way in the academy. During this research project, we often looked to each other for support as we tearfully transcribed an interview or comforted a participant. Fortunately, we documented our experiences throughout this process; therefore, our stories are woven into this chapter as we acknowledge our own hybridity as researchers and scholars of color, sometimes straining and other times thriving on the margins of academia. For some of us, "it was comforting to hear some of the similar issues they were struggling with, and that I was not alone in my confusion about the politics of the tenure-track process." On the other hand, we also came to the stark realization that "[a]s so many things in academia, the personal is separated from the professional" and "objectivity is valued... as a removal from self, from biases, from prior experience, from the soul." Yet through our project we "redefined the research process as a collective by humanizing it, refusing to succumb to a false objectivity in resource." In "our recognition of one another's struggles and specifically our affirmations of the challenges in living and breathing academia in all of its imposing Whiteness, maleness, heterosexism, classism, and capitalistic notions of success, our work has given us the space to breathe."

WORKING FROM HYBRIDITY: EMBRACING NUESTRAS IDENTIDADES Y CULTURA

In the process of "becoming" there are two choices: to be completely stripped of all prior collection of experiences to become anew or to embrace a hybrid identity that acknowledges the future while never forgetting the past. The six Latina/o faculty members we honor here were acutely aware of their *Latinidad* and drew on their strong ethnic identities to navigate their professional roles in academia. *Latinidad* describes "a common pan-Latina/o solidarity that among Latinos is materialized in ways that invokes an understanding of identity, place, and belonging" (San Miguel, 2011, p. 4). While these six faculty faced varying degrees of racial microaggressions (Solórzano, 1998) within their institutions, and even in the larger communities in which their universities were situated, they embraced their hybridity as Latino/a faculty in a higher education system that remains structured to accommodate the values and norms of the middle-class White majority.

Efrain started his career at a predominately White institution and described the experiences he faced, arming himself with a "bulletproof vest" to tackle his first year:

> The racial conversations and the racist remarks... those microaggressions and those other areas that we talk about in the academy, I live them. I've had people make snide comments, kind of undertones and stuff and I know better than to ignore and a lot of folks told me, you're not going to like that area; it's a predominantly White institution and so is the community.... There are a lot of really powerful political struggles and fights in my program. I've put on my bulletproof vest and I stay out of it. The first year I didn't speak up very much. When I did it's because it was totally appropriate or something, but now I have a different relationship and dynamic. I've let my work speak for me, so now my colleagues approach me a little bit differently because I'm doing things that they didn't do.

Efrain was strategic in utilizing both his silence and his voice to survive, which provided him a level of protection letting him focus on his scholarship. At the same time, Efrain expressed how culturally, he was not used to working in isolation and recognized the need to build *comunidad* (community) in academia, "I think the community part that I was looking for has to be built and that's what I've been trying to do." He did this by seeking mentorship and building collegial relationships with other Latina/o scholars outside his own discipline and through professional organizations.

The powerful, political struggles Efrain highlighted validated some of our experiences, particularly Cortez's as she dealt with some unforeseen politics in her journey:

> I thought my experiences were isolated and that there was no one I could turn to about what was happening to me. I felt abandoned by the very people I trusted and I could not believe how quickly they found ways to discredit, humiliate, and mistreat me. When I began to hear this was commonplace among other Latin@ faculty I did not know whether to be shocked or disappointed that there is little place to discuss these issues for fear of disrupting the status quo or keeping things P.C.

Like Efrain, who built his own *comunidad* within academia, Cortez had us. We became her *comunidad* and we provided that culturally relevant, safe space of connection.

Unfortunately, the microaggressions participants described came not only from White peers, but at times from faculty of color. This was the case for Angelica, who ventured into her first year at a fairly isolated institution in a rural town with little to no social scene. Consequently, Angelica spent much of her time writing and committed to getting published. While she was focused on establishing a record of productivity, she faced some roadblocks because of petty politics with senior, tenured faculty of color:

> I've had challenges with colleagues. Specifically, colleagues of color—Here, unfortunately... I mean, [they] pretty much tried to pull the rug out from under me and get me in trouble and all this stuff. Because, I think they saw me, or see me as a threat. Which doesn't make any sense, but—because we're not competing for anything, right? They already have tenure. But it's, that's been really difficult for me. There are folks that really befriended me and took me in, pretty much, the first semester. Then, when they saw that I was pumping out publications and getting grants and doing study abroad, they didn't like that. They kind of set me up in a way where I would, they tried to make me look bad in front of my chair.... That's been really challenging, it's kind of the disappointment of working with people that you think are your mentors.

Angelica similarly drew on her *comunidad* at other institutions to deal with this situation. She also admitted how her own research, which focused heavily on issues of racial equity in education, helped ground her and provided her solace. "My writing has been a real source of strength for me. I use my writing to help me make it through and help me make sense of the situation here. Particularly doing work with Latinas and other students of color, that has been so wonderful."

The difficulty we experienced in capturing some of these stories was being witness to the lack of maturity or respect among grown adults. This was something that Alsandor reflected on during the course of the project: "You would think that these are excerpts you are hearing from high school students, but for some there clearly seems to be a loss of sensitivity, rationale, or humanity when you all of a sudden earn your PhD." However, what we found was the possibility of retaliation that could occur at a macro-level when Latino/a faculty spoke or wrote of injustices, as Carlos shared:

> At my University, you know, faculty [in other departments] have been sanctioned by their department heads for saying something, by putting out their official university title when writing an op-ed because it gets misinterpreted at the institution as a whole and it comes down hard.... [However,] I could not have landed at a better place, in terms of that kind of support [that I get in my department].

Working at an institution in Arizona provided for a very distinct, racially hostile environment for Carlos outside his institution. As a critical scholar studying Latino/a-focused educational issues, the political climate of Arizona could have curtailed Carlos' action-oriented research. Yet his commitment to the larger cause for Latina/o educational equity only kindled his *ganas*. Similar to Angelica, Carlos found strength through his Latino/a-centered scholarship. Carlos was also fortunate to have the support of his chair, who encouraged him to speak of his research on Latino/a issues through various outlets (news media, presentations, publications).

We found Latina/o pre-tenured faculty also tended to bear the burden of educating or tolerating the cultural incompetence of their peers, but once again, faculty relied on their cultural intuition and ways of being to navigate such instances. For example, Lucia was conscious and proud of her *Latinidad* but found her peers had different expectations of her as a Latina scholar.

> To be honest I think I surprise them. I'll totally be honest about that. I think generally as a faculty, I'm good, but I cannot disentangle the undercurrent of deficit thinking that goes hand in hand with me being a person of color. And I often, they don't say you're "articulate" but they say things like that. Like "Wow, it's really good to work with you on this committee because you speak so well." ... So, my success as a faculty member of color is no mistake for me, because I am always conscious, always, of how I represent, how I'm represented, and how I represent who we are.

Lucia was not rattled by the deficit thinking she often encountered on behalf of her colleagues, and instead recalled the guidance and *consejos* of some of her Latino/a mentors. She particularly heeded the advice of one mentor, a prominent Latino scholar in education:

> He taught me that, that I could be *me* in whatever I did. And he always taught me that what was most valuable about my research was how I approached it, how I thought about it, and that gave me a lot of confidence. On the flip side, I would also say that I was inspired to pursue the faculty because also I knew faculty who were jerks, who talked incessantly about themselves, and about social justice, and they really didn't do the work.... And I knew that I, you know, I'm not perfect, but I knew that I could do the job and I knew that I could do it well.

Beto echoed Lucia's philosophy of staying true to oneself as a means of traversing the academic terrain. His drive came from connecting his life experiences to his work with students. Raised by parents who were farmworkers and possessed only a 6th-grade education, Beto's journey to and in the professoriate was personal. His early memories of college began with his mom registering him for children's courses at the local community college, knowing that she always had an expectation of him to go to college. Being a mentor and guiding Latino/a students through the educational pipeline was a responsibility Beto did not take lightly. "Our work is always going to be there as advocates, as Latinos, as scholars, professors.... There's always going to be a need everywhere and that's something, one thing I did learn very well from my other mentors." More importantly, it's remembering that "at the end of the day if we can't make that connection, back to connecting the dots of the experience of children and the educational system to our role, then I find that it's problematic."

The *testimonios* of our six Latino/a faculty also revealed how living and working in a state of hybridity tested their boundaries and sense of worth. Efrain summed up this state of being when he described the moment he solidified his position. He recalled walking into the dean's office with a short letter of demands acknowledging that all he needed were the tools to work. Similar to his migrant parents who traveled across the country only knowing their lived experiences, he walked into the dean's office not as a seasoned professor, but as a novice Latino faculty member who, culturally and professionally as a former public school administrator, was not accustomed to negotiating his salary as was expected in the academy.

> The contract and negotiation, I was still a little intimidated being in public schools and in that type of role [to negotiate].... So I put some stuff in writing so I was prepared; I had my little letter of what I thought I would need and it was very minimal. I don't think I was brave enough or I had the confidence enough to really challenge the Dean or the college; I guess I just wanted the job, you know?... I reflect on that now how we [Latinos/as] don't determine

> our worth or our value as academics, but on the other hand it's kind of like I wanted to be respectful and part of my growing up and heritage and culture is like that, so it was an odd balance.

Ultimately, Latina/o faculty embraced their cultural identities, values, and ways of being to meet the academic demands of teaching, research, and service.

RESISTING AND NAVIGATING TOGETHER: BUILDING A FAMILIA OF ALLIES

The role *familia* played in the personal lives of Latino/a faculty was evident, but they drew upon the strength of their familial nature to develop a network of faculty of color and White allies within and outside their institutions. Latina/o faculty also recognized the vital nature of being true to themselves along the way. This was evident in some of the testimonies already shared. As we witnessed how these Latino/a faculty members found strength in the bonds they formed with other colleagues, mentors, and even students, we began to reflect on our ability to build *familia* within our own group. "What can I say about my team, my friends, *colegas, hermanas,* my sistas', deciding to befriend [all authors] has been one of the best decisions I ever made, ever. Period." We found the personal and professional benefits immeasurable, as Martinez admitted:

> First, I will say that we have definitely been productive in terms of the research project, conducting close to 60 interviews nationwide, and getting multiple conference papers and publications accepted so far with others in the process of being submitted and even other ideas yet to come. And while all of this productivity is definitely vital to our tenure and promotion, and/or to our research and publication record, I think the nontangibles are what have been the most beneficial.

While our support network first formed organically in graduate school, Rosa was intentional about creating a space for Latinos/as to connect. When she first attended a national research conference she felt isolated and decided it was important to build a network and *familia* for her and other Latina/o scholars:

> It was terrible; I was really upset and I'm like, I'm bringing my friend the next time because you know it was just interesting to observe what that conference was like. There was a lot of interesting posturing that was happening where people would pay attention to me if I said that I was—people always ask who is your advisor, right, and if it was someone that was like famous enough for

them then they would spend time talking to me, and if not it seemed to me like there was a pecking order, which really upset me. So I was like I've got to figure a way to make this conference more hospitable.

Rosa learned from this experience about the types of people she wanted to surround herself with, like-minded faculty who would provide the type of support and encouragement that only *familia* could.

I mean it's just interesting about who I surround myself with, so if it's going to be—obviously there is going to be some faculty of color but I have to say that it's not just obviously; like they have to be people who care about social justice and I cannot always assume; you can't always assume because you're a faculty of color that you're going to hear anything about that. I'd rather just kind of be with allies who kind of get it.... So in the fall I'll go to [conference] and I've started to do this—I got together with this group of Latino scholar collectives and basically all the Latinos that we know who attend [conference] will go to dinner and it's powerful; we have like twenty-five people who get to spend time together and we talk about whatever we want to talk about and have fun and have food, you know.

Rosa's testimony resonated with Martinez, as she recalled a time when she found strength in learning to be true to herself, despite the pressure of feeling everyone else was "selling their soul" to fit in within the academic world. She reflected on the "mental breakdown" she had experienced at a conference after witnessing her Latina peers take on a competitive, individualistic, and seemingly fake persona for the sake of networking. As difficult as the experience was, it shed light on the type of institution she wanted to work at and it made her realize that she would not compromise her own sense of being for a tenure-track faculty position:

At [conference] I felt like I was gonna have to sell my soul to be faculty and felt like I couldn't stay true to myself. [At current institution] I feel like I've been able to do that. I feel like I've, and I mean, I don't know if that speaks to the program I'm in, that they allow for that space and the fact that I came in, you know, even with my job interview, like, I came in with my research agenda, which was very Latino/a focused, and so, they knew upfront, you know. So I don't, I don't feel like I've had to compromise the soul of who I am, in being a Latina and that's very important to me and also doing research and working with students and families of color.

The concept of *familia* also bled into the ways Latina/o faculty connected with their communities and defined their work. As a Latino faculty member, Beto believed his personal and professional roles and values were undoubtedly interconnected and that it was important to build an "ethic of caring" for all the Latinos/as and communities of color coming along after him and all those who are in the profession:

> As a Latino faculty member you begin to really see how things are interrelated and interconnected. You begin to see why it is important to not only be a professor. You begin to see the connection as to why our service, our research, and our teaching and the alignment of all of that is important. And then moving up the ranks is even more important in the sense of advocating not only for our students, but our own colleagues. You begin to see the importance of being involved in [national conferences] and those circles because it is a network and there are politics. When it comes to supporting other faculty of color, reviewing tenure packages, getting letters of support from other colleagues, when you see the importance of supporting other colleagues in their publication and research, those networks, [you] begin to realize that's why. It's not just moving up for the sake of having this ego and saying I'm tenured and that's it. I kind of feel like right now what's driving my ambition is the greater responsibility to others. And really that's that ethic of caring for others that has driven me since the get go.

More importantly, Beto saw that the bond of community transcended all other things and that in the end "we are doing this for our families":

> That idea that we are doing this for our families, for our communities, it's that connection. We understand that there is [sic] some real systemic challenges that we face and most of our work is about social justice and changing, when you look at demographics and where Latinos or black scholars or advocates are working, even the degrees we generally seek out, we tend to be attracted more to service type of roles and careers, and I don't think that's a coincidence. I think that has to do with wanting to improve the conditions of our own families, our own communities and that's that connection I do see with my colleagues.

CLOSING THOUGHTS

As the five of us worked on this chapter, we considered the significance of sharing the *testimonios* of Efrain, Carlos, Beto, Angelica, Lucia, and Rosa along with aspects of our own journeys in the academy. We recognized their/our stories were likely not new, but we felt compelled to share them as a means of advocacy and resistance and to guide others on the same path. We believe that while we live in a hybrid space where conflicting cultures and uncertainty can be painful, it can also provide for the development of "tolerance for contradictions, a tolerance for ambiguity," as renowned poet, scholar, and Chicana feminist activist Gloria Anzaldúa described (p. 1987,

p. 379). To that end, we proudly embrace our struggles so we can fully appreciate how far we have come and how far we will continue to go.

REFERENCES

Anzaldúa, G. (1987). *Borderlands/la frontera: The new Mestiza.* San Francisco, CA: Aunt Lute Books.

Reyes, K. B., & Curry Rodríguez, J. E. (2012). Testimonio: Origins, terms, and resources. *Equity & Excellence in Education, 45*(3), 525–538.

San Miguel Jr., G. (2011). Embracing "Latinidad": Beyond nationalism in the history of education. *Journal of Latinos and Education, 10*(1), 3–22.

Solórzano, D. G. (1998). Critical race theory, race and gender microaggressions, and the experience of Chicana and Chicano scholars. *Qualitative Studies in Education, 11*(1), 121–136.

PART III

BUILDING PEDAGOGY AND ACADEMIC/SOCIAL CAPITAL FOR LATINA/O STUDENTS

CHAPTER 18

INTRODUCTION TO PART III

Higher Education and the Void of Culturally Relevant Spaces

Elizabeth T. Murakami

The symbolism behind the act of *abrir puertas* is powerful, especially when referring to Latinas/os entering academia. Since Latinas/os have not been largely represented among academics, in the third part of this volume, we focus on postsecondary spaces as important places where Latina/o faculty and students feel welcome and where culturally relevant practices can be developed. The void of culturally relevant spaces in higher education is of significance, especially after understanding in previous sections that Latinas/o scholars often work in isolation and struggle to create balance. This section's *testimonios* reveal a need for higher education institutions to improve their institutional culture in order to legitimize, retain, and enhance the experiences of Latinas/os and other people of color, in administration, or among faculty or students. The void of culturally relevant spaces can be identified, not only among undergraduates, graduates, or doctoral students alone, but among those *después* or *detrás de las puertas* of academia—in the professoriate or in higher education administration.

Abriendo Puertas, Cerrando Heridas (Opening Doors, Closing Wounds), pages 185–190
Copyright © 2015 by Information Age Publishing
All rights of reproduction in any form reserved.

Hilario Lomeli, one of the authors in this section, brings a remarkable reflection related to the balance between work and life. He noticed how academia pervades the home and life of a doctoral student, but there is a void the other way around—why aren't the life and home experiences of Latinas/os permeating postsecondary institutions?

I relate to Hilario when reflecting on my early experience as a doctoral student in a predominantly White institution (PWI). There were no Latina/o professors in the program and very few doctoral students of color. I was recruited into one of the best education programs in the U.S. via an outreach effort to attract educators working in American schools overseas. At the time, I was working at an American school in Brazil. However, upon my arrival into the doctoral program, I was surprised to find no other educators from the international schools sphere. In a cohort of about 21 doctoral students, there was only one other educator of color who was African American (a local assistant superintendent in a nearby city). There were also two international students of Muslim faith who came to the university via their ministries of education, noticeable because they wore beautiful hijabs: a Malay and a Jordanian government official.

One of the first activities in our introductory class was to build working groups. The professor handed a sheet of paper to the first student sitting in a big semicircle. We were to pass the sheet around, indicating our preference of whom we would like to work with during the semester. Since very few of us knew each other, it seemed a bit awkward to choose whom to work with. The list finally reached me, as I was sitting at the opposite end of the semicircle. The students left the only space available for me to join—somehow all the names filled the slots of three or four student groups, with one slot left for the group with the international students and the African American. I returned the list to the professor without my name in it. I discretely shared with the professor that I felt uncomfortable with that division of groups. In my view, there should not be a line between international or local education—on the contrary, the international students were there to learn about best educational practices in the U.S. and should not be left talking among themselves. Also, the only other person of color was grouped with the internationals.

Sometimes, in the best interest of students, our view as faculty of what is best ends up being exclusionary or discriminatory. I still wonder if the groups would not have been rearranged if I had not questioned the process. Microaggressions attest Solorzano, Ceja, and Yosso (2000), often happen accidentally and unintentionally. However, most troublesome is the preparedness of faculty (or lack thereof) to understand culturally relevant pedagogies that would prevent such incidents from occurring or running the risk of being perpetuated. If the group of international students and people of color acquiesced without the professor's interference, the professor would be validating such discriminatory practices as acceptable, or worse, he or she would add that students voluntarily assigned themselves, freeing him- or herself from any responsibility. At the end of class, the professor collected the list and revised it, bringing it back the next class—with her own distribution of groups. She also talked about the importance of supporting the introduction of local schools to all those unfamiliar with education in the area.

Once in academia, Latinas/os and other instructors/scholars of color may be aware of roadblocks that can prevent students from engaging in the best experience colleges and universities can provide. *En las puertas de la academia*, however, faculty still encounter roadblocks that prevent them from helping students succeed. These are the *testimonios* included in this section—reflecting a struggle for balance between life and work and the negotiation of work and life in academia.

When examining the experiences of Latinos in the educational pipeline, much effort has been invested in the recruitment of students. With a governmental focus on developing a college-going culture (U.S. White House, 2014), K–12 schools and classrooms can be seen with beautiful pennants and flags, with teachers asking students what college these students will choose once graduating from their senior year. Similarly, higher education has gone through a transformative process where a college degree is no longer seen as a path for a selected few, but as a prerequisite to entering the job market (U.S. White House, 2014). In addition, although controversial, quotas have been in place—examining whether universities and colleges are mindful in the inclusion of people of color in postsecondary degrees.

The recent National Center for Education Statistics (2014) report showed that 17.7 million undergraduate students were enrolled in degree-granting postsecondary institutions. Of these, 11.1 million were full-time and 6.6 million were part-time students. Forty percent of these students enrolled in two-year institutions. The majority were enrolled in public institutions (13.5 million in 2012). Latinos composed 14% of students enrolling in public institutions, 10% in private nonprofit, and 15% in private for-profit institutions. Seven in ten Latino high school graduates (69%) enrolled in college in 2012, when compared to their White counterparts (67%) (Fry & Taylor, 2013). Twenty percent of Latinos were enrolled in public two-year institutions, 14% were enrolled in public four-year institutions, 10% in private nonprofit, and 15% in private for-profit institutions (NCES, 2014).

The number of Latinos has increased in higher education. However, with all these efforts, why do students still feel isolated, discriminated, and marginalized? Especially in educational leadership, a safe space for the development of a supportive environment is needed (Murakami-Ramalho, Militello, & Piert, 2010). Despite their attainment in enrolling in higher numbers, the Pew Hispanic Center reports that Latinos are less likely than their White counterparts (56%, as opposed to 72%) to enroll in a four-year college; they are less likely to attend a selective college, less likely to be enrolled full-time, and less likely to complete a bachelor's degree (Fry & Taylor, 2013). Latinas/os are also more likely to be the first in their families to go to college. Even in academia, they are still trailblazers, with few representatives coming before them to be role models and mentors.

THE IMPORTANCE OF COUNTERSTORIES AND TESTIMONIOS

Counterstories and testimonies throughout the book demonstrate a need for culturally relevant spaces in academia. In this section, Antonio Estudillo and Amanda Flores talk about the importance of advocating for intergenerational leadership among Latina/o faculty, staff, and students. They indicate how important it is to include culturally centered approaches in order to advocate for and empower Latina/o faculty and staff—who can in turn mobilize efforts to advocate for and impact students' success. Estudillo and Flores realized that while working at a large regional PWI located in East Texas—they were the only Latino and Latina identified professionals within each of their respective spaces (a university department and a student services division). The total student of color population at that university was of approximately 40%, while the Latina/o student population is roughly 10%. In contrast, the authors recognized that tenure-track, lecturer, and adjunct faculty were mostly comprised of White/European-American at 78% with only 2% of all faculty on campus identified as Latina/o. In finding balance between work and life as the few Latinas/os in their respective institutions, the authors show the importance of Latinas/os to feel safe in academia—safe to develop research, safe to advocate for students, and safe to adopt innovative pedagogies or to participate in committees and institutional leadership efforts.

In a chapter focused on the retention of Latina STEM students in Texas, Elsa Gonzales, Maria Valentin, Detra Johnson, Celestino Valentin Jr, Beatriz Lopez, Ariana Gonzalez, Yvonna Lincoln, and Christine Stanley argue about the importance of role models. The importance of having people to look up to, as well as to have people that *look like you*, is of utmost concern, in order to engage Latinas/os in college studies, especially in the sciences, in order to persevere and complete their degrees.

Both Hilario Lomeli and Margarita Berta Avila reflect on the adaptation to graduate school. Through vignettes, Lomeli exemplifies what it is like to move away from home in Texas and join a predominantly White institution (PWI), an institution Lomeli recounts as "so far removed both physically and psychically from his home, family, and people—from his familiar faces and cowboy getups." He describes the struggles and the resilience necessary to survive and navigate through graduate school.

Berta Avila's *testimonio* shows that there is a Latina/o consciousness in the development of a scholar, from one's development of research in graduate school to the transition to a faculty position. She states: "It takes all the strength I have inside of me to not be afraid, to not stay silent, and advocate for our Raza students on our campus. Not a day goes by that I do not reflect on what I teach, what I write, a statement I might have made in a committee meeting, a reaction I might have had, a decision I might have made, and what effect it might have." The responsibility of developing the representation of Latinas/os in education is significant. It includes the responsibility of Latina/o faculty, as scholars and researchers, to reflect on their own stories to accurately reflect the stories of others through research, teaching, and service.

Even in fields providing social and academic services, like counseling, the lack of Latina/o representation is noted. Angelica Tello reflected on the disconcerting lack of Latina/o faculty members and leaders in the profession to whom she can relate through networks and mentoring opportunities. In her chapter, she contends that even though there is a current focus from accredited organizations such as the Council for Accreditation of Counseling and Related Educational Programs (CACREP) on diversity and multicultural counseling counselor education, "there is a lack of faculty members and leaders in the profession who come from diverse ethnic backgrounds."

Finally, Fernando Valle, Sylvia Mendéz-Morse, and Irma Almager defined Latinas/os in academia as the "only lonely"—and point to the need to develop *espacios de confianza.* These safe spaces can enhance and encourage persistence and retention of Latina students, not only in the STEM fields, as Gonzales and her colleagues recognized, but among faculty members, who can generate trusting spaces to share experiences, and *consejos.* Artfully, Valle and colleagues developed a space where they could laugh, enjoy each other's knowledge and expertise, and share *dichos* and "examples of *amor, cultura, trabajo, música, éxito, comida, y familia*" as connecting life with their scholarship space.

REFERENCES

Fry, R., & Taylor, P. (2013). Hispanic high school graduates pass whites in rate of college enrollment. *Pew Research Hispanic Trends Project.* Retrieved from http://www.pewhispanic.org/2013/05/09/hispanic-high-school-graduates-pass-whites-in-rate-of-college-enrollment/

Murakami-Ramalho, E., Militello, M., & Piert, J. (2013). A view from within: How doctoral students in educational administration develop research knowledge and identity. *Journal of Studies in Higher Education, 38*(2), 256–271. DOI: 10.1080/03075079.2011.578738.

National Center for Education Statistics. (2014). The condition of education 2014. Retrieved from http://nces.ed.gov/pubs2014/2014083.pdf

Solorzano, D., Ceja, M., & Yosso, T. (2000). Critical race theory, racial microaggressions, and campus racial climate: The experiences of African American college students. *The Journal of Negro education 69*(1/2), 60–73.

U.S. White House. (2014). Higher education. Retrieved from http://www.whitehouse.gov/issues/education/higher-education

CHAPTER 19

ADVOCATING FOR INTERGENERATIONAL LEADERSHIP AMONG LATINA/O FACULTY, STAFF, AND STUDENTS

Antonio G. Estudillo and Amanda Flores
Stephen F. Austin State University

An underlying force behind writing this chapter is the opportunity to share with you, the reader, distinct personal, social, and academic perspectives from the vantage points of a Latino male faculty member and a Latina university staff member. The timing is critical as our positions reflect early career aspirations and continued progression through our respective personal and professional lives. From humble beginnings to the professoriate as well as university rankings, we first each take a moment to center in on our individual backgrounds and then lead into the remainder of the chapter focusing on a range of formulating aspects that speak to the advocating for intergenerational leadership among Latina/o faculty, staff, and students.

Abriendo Puertas, Cerrando Heridas (Opening Doors, Closing Wounds), pages 191–203
Copyright © 2015 by Information Age Publishing
All rights of reproduction in any form reserved.

NUESTRAS HISTORIAS

Antonio

Having been born and raised in a predominantly Latino community in the state of Washington, the Yakima Valley, my entire schooling from P–12 consisted of being in classrooms where the majority of students were of Mexican descent. In fact, it would not be until I began attending a four-year university, a predominantly White institution (PWI), that I actually experienced being *in the minority* as far as ethnic-racial heritage and background. This experience alone—a genuine culture shock—has undoubtedly had a profound impact on my viewpoints associated with access to, engagement with, and ultimately opportunities present for students to develop positive perspectives on experiences in higher education. Having experienced a culture shock was both challenging and at the same time compelling enough to propel me to seek out support within the established Chicana/o/Latina/o student presence in my undergraduate campus.

In order for me to have successfully navigated through the university system, I had to ultimately leverage and accommodate the university learning environment that from my perspective had little to practically no alignment with the quality of schooling that I had received prior to attending college. Whether it was the expectations of reading material from one class lecture to the next or to simply having a clear understanding for the sort of social interaction among current college students versus any normalcy that I had previously experienced associated with day-to-day interactions with a Chicana/o/Latina/o community—one that I not only self-identified with, but one that I had experienced my entire pre-college career—my undergraduate years challenged how enculturated I was.

As an undergraduate, I found it difficult at times to make connections with faculty—moving beyond simple conventional thinking of interacting with faculty during office hours to a belief that maybe many faculty frankly did not share the same types of sociocultural experiences that I had (i.e., as a son of Mexican Immigrants, a first-generation college student, a Latino male) and so relating to faculty and lectures or vice-versa from a culturally relevant perspective was more often than not a rare occasion. Steadily progressing through my undergraduate education and on into graduate studies, I continued to reflect on these personal encounters with faculty and student peers alike. Not surprisingly, these same types of themes of having a clear sense of belonging, reflections on previous culturally relevant experiences, and the overall development of changing positions from a student's perspective to now that of a working professional, in academia, seem to present themselves in a recurring manner.

A significant lesson I learned is that the very sociocultural reflection that I would have liked to have encountered early on in my academic career in higher education is the very same form of opportunity I now have in front of me to potentially serve as a positive role model to students and colleagues whom I now work with. This self-awareness is a motivating and empowering factor that I foresee and will continue to develop, shape, and impact my understanding for supporting the necessary conditions to promote advocacy among the Latina/o community in higher education.

Amanda

Similarly, I was born and raised in the Rio Grande Valley in south Texas where I grew up in a community rich in Latino culture. I was a part of an educational system that fostered the appreciation of the richness of my culture's values. My teachers looked like me, I was in the majority, and the interweaving of Spanish and English in our vocabulary was the norm. Life as a Latina was *normal* in the Rio Grande Valley. It was not until we would migrate to Minnesota and North Dakota that race began to play a prevalent role in shaping my experiences.

I grew up in a migrant family where working the fields in the summer and fall seasons was our family's lifestyle. For 15 years, I straddled two polarizing communities and environments. As migrant children, my sisters and I were forced to manage our education in unstable learning environments (Zalaquett, McHatton, & Cranson-Gingras, 2007). This relentless cross-country travel between states resulted in different educational settings and a constant code-switching between states resulting in playing catch-up (Martinez & Cranson-Gingras, 1996). Code-switching is the maneuvering of two or more languages, and in this sense, the educational languages and cultures.

The lack of institutional alignment among states exacerbated the already difficult transition from one school to another. This factor most profoundly affected our academic success because aside from grounding my academic learning in two different systems, I failed to establish significant relationships with teachers and mentors. Upon my college acceptance into a PWI in East Texas, I was determined to remain in college and establish significant relationships with mentors. However, not having access to Latino/a faculty and staff on campus made it difficult to share intimate and vulnerable experiences that would essentially provide a foundation for success. Thus, my mentors consisted of mostly White women who helped me in the process of identifying and clarifying my career goals, but in doing so, I struggled in bridging my past with my present, my identity as a college student and closeted migrant farmworker.

I grew ashamed of my identity as a migrant farmworker because as a *migrante* I was constantly exposed to messages defining me as "dysfunctional," "at-risk," "developmentally challenged," "uneducable," and "an endangered species"; I came to internalize these negative messages and became "self-threatening" and "self-defeating" (Strayhorn, 2010, p. 307). I struggled to share my story, and with a lack of Latina/o faculty and staff mentors, I found it challenging to trust others with the process of confronting my past.

I went on to attend graduate school in New England where I quickly became enveloped by multiple women and men of color who purposefully assisted me in making meaning out of my experiences and the shame I felt from identifying as a migrant farmworker. Through careful mentoring and guidance, they motivated me to relearn my history and understand the significant contributions my community had on our American past. This empowering chapter in my life provided me with the life skills to identify and assist students in their own process of self-awareness and understanding.

Crossing Paths

Antonio and Amanda crossed paths when they both took up positions at a relatively large regional PWI located in East Texas. We are the sole identified Latino and Latina professionals within each of our respective university spaces (e.g., university department and student services). Our institution's total student of color population stands at approximately 40%, while the identified Latina/o student population is roughly 10%. As of fall 2013, our faculty, including tenure-track, lecturer, and adjunct, are mostly comprised of White/European American at 78% with only 2% of all faculty on campus identified as Latina/o. With about one third of the student population identified as students of color and over three fourths of the faculty identified as White/European American, these ratios put forward an institutional environment likely beneficial for reinforcing attitudes and values of the latter, not the former. Additionally, our institution serves a very large first-generation college student population; it is estimated that 50% of all students at our institution identify as being first generation, meaning that neither parent of a given student has attained a four-year college degree. In our respective positions, we have each worked to find our niches, and yet as early career Latina/o professionals in higher education, we are not without having to face both perceived and real challenges—including issues at our institution, revolving around the following contexts:

- historical and present lack of institutional infrastructure to support faculty and staff of color (e.g., both Latina/o and Black/African American: currently not a single faculty/staff representative organization serves the needs and concerns of faculty/staff of color)

- concentrated university-sponsored programming that outreaches to Latina/o students, faculty, and staff (e.g., student demographics, including outreach to students in the surrounding schools regions of East Texas, an area of increasing Latina/o demographics, warrants strategic planning to both promote and enhance the quality of education and opportunities for Latina/o students, in particular those students who may also identify as being first generation in addition to Latina/o)
- university recruitment and retention policies as well as recognition and advocacy means to foster best practices in relation to the hiring of diverse faculty and staff and not only efforts to encourage the increase in Latina/o faculty and staff applicant pool—but actual targeting of qualified Latina/o faculty and staff for job offerings (e.g., concentrated recruitment efforts in already established Latino academic spaces such as Hispanic-serving institutions, special interest groups within multiple professional organizations, and targeted Latino research conferences).

To be clear, we do not wish to overshadow the potential number of opportunities for personal community and career advancements that can be found at our institution—but on the contrary, we want to bring to light the implications for nurturing a greater sense of awareness regarding the presence of Latina/o faculty, staff, and students in higher education. In this chapter, we (1) explore and emphasize intergenerational leadership among Latina/o faculty, staff, and students to better conceptualize capacity building among our community; (2) offer an example of a conceptual framework for advocating stronger links between identified Latina/o university members to provide a space for critical conversations as well as opportunities to bring together our histories, cultures, knowledge, and experiences, to move forward in promoting and advancing careers and degree attainment; and lastly, (3) present a plan of action for modeling intergenerational leadership between Latina/o faculty, staff, and students.

A SNAPSHOT OF LATINAS/OS IN HIGHER EDUCATION

There are institutions of higher education that specifically recognize the increases of college-going Latina/o students, and in an effort to increase retention and college persistence among these students, many of these same colleges and universities seek to create an academic community reflective of the changing student body by hiring Latina/o staff and faculty. These changing conditions and priorities have led to the classification of many institutions as Hispanic-serving institutions (Gasman, Baez, & Turner,

2008). These continuously unfolding developments—shifting demographics and institutional practices—have leveraged the formation of initiatives to assist in the creation of an inclusive multicultural campus environment. For example, some institutions have created a role or a department aimed at recruiting and supporting Latina/o students on campus. We have seen a development of coordinator positions emphasizing experience and direct connection to Latino communities and, most importantly, the ability to communicate effectively in Spanish. However, despite these attempts to meet the changes in student bodies within institutions of higher education, there continues to be a lack of attention placed on actually implementing best practices for the retaining of Latina/o staff and faculty. Existing research has notably highlighted the lack of visibility among faculty and staff of color, particularly in higher ranking leadership and administrative roles (Leon & Nevarez, 2007) on college and university campuses.

Changing demographics in higher education enrollments alone among United States Latina/o students, as of 2012, suggest the largest gains in terms of enrollments than ever before (Fry & Taylor, 2013). However, how colleges and universities respond to these contexts ought to call attention to recruiting and retention practices that target Latina/o faculty-staff-students, specifically in light of supporting prospective career advancement, job security, and individual degree attainment. Although higher education enrollments are currently up among U.S. Latina/o students, actual degree completion continues to fall short for Latinas/os in comparison to the majority of other large ethnic-racial segments of students (Fry, 2004). In addition, U.S. Latina/o students reflect the largest proportion of first-generation college students attending an institution of higher education (Contreras, 2005). In terms of faculty and administrative representation, approximately 4% of all faculty and 5% of all administrators identify as Latina/o on U.S. college campuses and universities (NCES, 2011). Taken together, these trends reflect the current state of affairs for U.S. Latina/o faculty-staff-students in higher education.

We call attention to the involvement of Latinas/os in higher education: for example, anticipating, pursuing, and actively fulfilling expectations to institutional hiring practices that may lead to successful recruitment and retention strategies. The retention of Latina/o professionals in higher education has some relation to the general recruitment of and higher education job opportunities for qualified Latinas/os. An area of concern may be in increasing the applicant pool for respective faculty and staff positions on college campuses, in which specifically more qualified Latina/o applicants are reviewed, interviewed, and offered the opportunity for employment. Although it may be clear that few Latinas/os are reflected in graduate study programs, including PhD programs, what may not be so clear is how much effort is dedicated to targeting upcoming and recent Latina/o graduates.

For example, targeted recruitment starts with first identifying the need to hire more Latina/o faculty and staff followed by concentrated efforts to offer the leveraging of institutional policies to create both advocacy and space for developing careers. The retention of Latinas/os in higher education should be seen as adding significant social and cultural capital to an institution. Until this is made clear, institutions in question will have a hard time seeking to secure faculty and staff positions held by Latinas/os.

CRITICAL CONVERSATIONS

Student self-perception is a growing and developing awareness among Latina/o students when they arrive on college campuses, especially when they attend a PWI (Jones, Castellanos, & Cole, 2002). In efforts to mobilize the Latina/o students on campus, as a key staff member, I (Amanda) brought together a few students who have shared with me their own personal journeys in college, and having found a common theme of perseverance, it was only fitting to bring them together under the same roof. The students ranged from first- to fourth-year students, from historically based Latina/o fraternity and sorority members to non-fraternity/sorority members, and from both respected leaders to members of related student organizations. Our meeting centered around one main objective: to help students make meaning out of their current college experience in relation to their Latina/o identities. I asked them for their thoughts and experiences around the word "*raza*," a term often used to express ethnic pride and solidarity among Latinos. Out of this conversation a common theme emerged as students began to see one another as one representative, collective community. They echoed similar observations about the lack of Latina/o representation among faculty and staff, programming initiatives, and overall Latina/o student presence. Childhood experiences were shared, and authentic relationships began to form. I presented a programming framework to them for National Hispanic Heritage Month as a start to bringing the conversation about understanding, servicing, and recognizing our Latina/o student population on campus. It was also noted that the changes they wanted to see and experience would only happen with their participation. In all, these conversations clearly speak to a tremendous need for stronger emphasis on organizing and engagement in Latina/o leadership—whether from students to students, faculty-staff to students and vice-versa, as well as among faculty and staff. Thus, there is a great need to establish and develop personal, social—even academic relationships; identify important individual and community roles; create team building practices; and have a clear set of shared goals among the Latina/o faculty, staff, and students within the university setting. This is when intergenerational leadership came into the conversation. We began to notice the creation of intergenerational mentoring, guiding, and leading within our community.

INTERGENERATIONAL LEADERSHIP

Intergenerational leadership focuses on a familial perspective that brings together shared responsibilities of a given community for the purpose of bridging together varying perspectives between older and younger generations (Bordas, 2013). The overarching premise behind intergenerational leadership is essentially to bridge any knowledge gaps across more than one generation so that information shared between the more experienced and less experienced provides a meeting space for combined shared knowledge exploration and formation. Although relatively simple in concept, the application of intergenerational leadership among Latina/os in higher education speaks to the potential of learning from past experience to promote present and future endeavors—a linking of key insights and perspectives, if you will, offering a sounding board for multiple engaged Latina/o community members. For example, whereas identification of issues impacting our community can generally serve as a springboard for extending important community platforms and the identification of Latina/o leaders within our community is important to generate ideas for comprehensive reviews (e.g., strengths and areas in need of development within the community), intergenerational leadership, at a minimum, can offer guidance and reciprocal perspective taking needed to inform, inspire, and co-produce solutions.

Although small in physical numbers, one can argue that there are some identified Latina/o leaders within higher education—this entire book is reflective of this—where challenges must be met in bringing together identified Latina/o leaders herein, presenting a critical mass and opportunity for intergenerational leadership to unravel and take place. In thinking about past, present, and potential future trends associated with U.S. Latina/o education as a whole, much work is left to be completed, and pursuing solutions through a comprehensive lens such as leaning on intergenerational leadership to provide a special set of dynamics will allow positive change to emerge. Specifically, intergenerational leadership can serve as a pathway to integrate pedagogic components that support and reflect strategies that advance Latinas/os in higher education.

We need look no further than events such as the 5th annual Latino Education and Advocacy Days Summit (e.g., LEAD Summit) that took place recently in southern California and its successor to be taken place in San Antonio, TX in 2015. This example, unique in some ways as it is understood as the first (inter)nationally live-streamed interactive conference dedicated to informing stakeholders on the US Latino education crisis, not only serves as an inspiration for bringing about positive change to Latinas/os in education, but it is also a direct reflection of what intergenerational leadership among Latinas/os is and how it can influence and inspire. Appreciating and looking back at past community endeavors with an intention of moving forward fits exactly with reasoning behind pursuing intergenerational leadership.

At a local level, we are applying this dynamic of intergenerational leadership to strengthen unity among identified Latina/o faculty, staff, and students. In the immediate, we are focusing on bringing community together to exchange perspectives to expand programming for the upcoming National Hispanic Heritage Month in the fall while also revisiting ongoing programming during the academic year. We will continue to intentionally explore themes of identity formation, discussions on Latina/o student perspectives, implications for what it means to be Latina/o in the Southwest, and the continued expression of personal stories that, when combined, support the raising of our collective social consciousness, spirits, and means for positive change.

ORGANIZING: A LATINA/O SCHOLAR COLLECTIVE

With an increase in Latino/a student enrollment, there is a need for Latino/a faculty and staff to mobilize in efforts to maximize the depth of support we can provide students as a community. Upon my arrival as a staff member (Amanda), like many other individuals, I sought out professionals who shared similar interests and who I could count on as allies. As a woman of color, initially my outreach consisted of identifying women whom I saw as potential mentors. Having experienced my undergraduate years with no people of color as mentors and having navigated my graduate studies with women and men of color as mentors, I immediately knew what I needed in order to make it through my first year as a professional. Through connecting with others and sharing stories, I quickly learned I was one of only about four or five Latinas at our institution. Initially, this group consisted of just three Latinas, and we would share our lessons learned over *comida* and laughter with the hopes of finding humor in the pains in our individual stories. After a year of understanding and learning the campus climate, I knew our only way to survive was to keep this group moving forward and to continue to grow. Over the span of three years, I have met with and broken bread with a couple of other Latina/os and have found a common thread between all of our interests: *a need for the retention of Latina/o students and a clearer emphasis on ensuring that students gain awareness of her or his own Latina/o identity development.* Today, our group consists of Latinos/as working on similar research, helping each other navigate through the tenure process, and working together to bring critical consciousness raising programs and lectures to the university community. We now refer to ourselves as the Latina/o Scholar Collective.

The objectives of the Latina/o Scholar Collective are important to distinguish, noting both direct and indirect contexts that impact our organizing and perspectives. We understand that at the micro level we have to identify our values and our guiding principles, and we need to make meaning out of our lived experiences in order to create authentic dialogue and relationships between us—despite our backgrounds. Through these interactions we have found overlapping stories and experiences of heartache, triumph, and resilience. But the most powerful tools that we have found are multiple aspects of critical mentoring. A form of critical mentoring that we have engaged in is *mujer-a-mujer* mentoring, which aims to empower one another as Latinas in a field dominated by men. For example, speaking from a Latina perspective, I have leaned on other Latinas to find solace in our stories characterized by defying stereotypes and compromising cultural norms, such as the experience of leaving home as a single woman living independently from our families and pursuing a career as opposed to a family. The second form of critical mentoring we engage in is *colega-a-colega* mentoring, which mostly targets the areas of scholarly work, research, and assessment.

As authors of this chapter, we were both drawn to the opportunity of writing together, publishing together, and using our roles to facilitate the creation of research in relation to our experiences. Combined, these efforts have led to further development of a foundational *comunidad* where we are maximizing our strengths and reinforcing our own roles as individuals and as a collective. As a means of modeling critical mentoring, a presentation on intergenerational mentoring and leadership was presented to a group of undergraduate Latina/o students (e.g., Latina/o students from varying majors and multiple years at our institution) in order to help students visualize and recognize their own efforts in mentoring one another and building their own capacity while attending a PWI. At a macro level, we have begun to establish indirect relationships with colleagues, identifying key university personnel and stakeholders who can serve as a vehicle to institutional reform with regards to supporting the Latino/a community. An example of organizational impact being made is identification of key Latino/a student leaders who share an interest in mobilizing others to increase visibility and presence on campus. One student organization has been identified as a model in leading these student efforts because of its heightened awareness of Latina/o issues. The potential benefits in building community were shared with these students, who have now expressed interest in developing critical dialogues centered on the Latina/o experience.

As individual members of the university community, we have made considerable efforts to organize and build upon our working relationships with colleagues—particularly in light of bringing together members of the university Latina/o community. Institutionally as a whole, more work is needed to build a coalition with the inclusion of non-Latina/o faculty, staff, and students. Considering the impact of building from within, at the grassroots, the next step is strategically targeting institutional change. The Latina/o Scholar Collective cultivates an initial pathway available to one another allowing room for opportunity to progress forward together.

ACTION PLAN: RECOMMENDATIONS AND BEST PRACTICES

This chapter has served as a means for thinking about best practices for identifying key issues relevant to Latinas/os in higher education and consideration for what steps can be done to (re)evaluate, discuss, and proceed with an action plan. We began the chapter by providing a bit of personal background to engage the reader in our experiences and then shifted towards introducing themes of the current state of affairs for Latinas/os in higher education, including perspectives on intergenerational leadership and relevant contexts associated in organizing. There are multiple levels associated with change. Case in point: We suggest the consideration of organizing a group of faculty and staff of color to support one another with the possibility of additional conversations emerging, such as the following:

- support for the increase of appointment of women of color in leadership roles
- support for individuals who may not be native to the given institution (i.e., the environment where she or he now lives and works; new faculty and staff of color to a particular new region)
- support for services addressing the inclusion of LGBT/queer allies of color (e.g., faculty, staff, and students)

As a result of this chapter, a set of recommendations for best practices is suggested with a plan of action alluding to advocacy in the following areas:

1. The creation and implementation of consistent professional development for faculty and staff in relation to meeting the needs of the Latina/o community in academia
2. Supporting and embracing cultural preservation of Latina/o voices from *la frontera* (e.g., historical significance of Latina/o contributions to American society in relation to the political and educational climate)
3. A conscious effort by departments to connect marginalized faculty and staff to one another (e.g., linking to university Latina/o based interest groups)

In summary, these aforementioned areas express steps that institutions of higher education can further conceptualize and develop. In particular, when considering professional development needs of faculty and staff alike, why not pursue conversations around meeting the needs of a rapidly growing underrepresented community, such as Latinas/os in education? Additionally, this embrace of culturally centered approaches to advocacy has the potential to empower Latina/o faculty and staff to continue mobilizing in efforts to reinforce support and overall impacts on student success. When faculty and staff in colleges and universities work to become more in sync (e.g., the sharing of common visions for faculty/staff/student advancement, intentionally placing the needs of students first while simultaneously aligning university policies with current trends and directions), educators are attempting to realize the achievement behind closing gaps, whether institutional or among colleagues. Therefore, a strong community of leaders, university faculty and staff, must be reflected or unfortunately we fail to offer sufficient support to students.

REFERENCES

Bordas, J. (2013). *The power of Latino leadership: Culture, inclusion, and contribution.* San Francisco, CA: Berrett-Koehler Publishers.

Contreras, F. E. (2005). Access, achievement, and social capital: Standardized exams and the Latino college-bound population. *Journal of Higher Education, 4*(3), 197–214.

Fry, R. (2004). *Latino youth finishing college: The role of selective pathways.* Washington, DC: Pew Research Hispanic Center.

Fry, R., & Taylor, P. (2013). *Hispanic high school graduates pass whites in rate of college enrollment.* Washington, DC: Pew Research Hispanic Center.

Gasman, M., Baez, B., & Turner, C. S. V. (Eds.). (2008). *Understanding minority-serving institutions.* Albany, NY: State University of New York Press.

Jones, L., Castellanos, J., & Cole, D. (2002). Examining the ethnic minority student experience at predominantly White institutions: A case study. *Journal of Hispanic Higher Education, 1*(1), 19–39.

Leon, D., & Nevarez, C. (2007). Models of leadership institutes for increasing the number of top Latino administrators in higher education. *Journal of Hispanics in Higher Education, 6*(4), 356–377.

Martinez, Y., & Cranson-Gingras, A. (1996). Migrant farmworker students and the educational process: Barriers to high school completion. *The High School Journal, 80*(1), 28–38.

Strayhorn, T. (2010). When race and gender collide: Social and cultural capital's influence on the academic achievement of African American and Latino males. *The Review of Higher Education, 33*(3), 307–332.

U.S. Department of Education, National Center for Education Statistics. (2011). *Digest of Education Statistics, 2010* (NCES 2011-015). Washington, DE: Author.

Zalaquett, C., McHatton, P., & Cranson-Gingras, A. (2007). Characteristics of Latina/o migrant farmworker students attending a large metropolitan university. *Journal of Hispanic Higher Education, 6*(2), 135–156.

CHAPTER 20

RETENTION OF LATINA STEM STUDENTS IN TEXAS

Exploring the Experiences That Should Be Considered

Elsa Gonzalez, Marie Valentin, Detra Johnson, Celestino Valentin Jr., Beatriz Lopez, Ariana Gonzalez, Yvonna Lincoln, and Christine Stanley
Texas A&M University

As we became engaged on this project, as a principal investigator of this project, I started questioning myself, how I started this journey.

[E. Gonzalez]

My journey as a scholar in the United States, started 16 years ago, when I started my doctoral degree; since then the idea of work–life balance has become so natural for me.... Through the years, I have become a wife, a mother, and a faculty member... all of those roles intertwined to become who I am, and who I am interested in personally, and as scholar.

A couple of years ago, as I was recruiting undergraduate students for the purpose of mentoring them in conducting research activities. I became aware of

Abriendo Puertas, Cerrando Heridas (Opening Doors, Closing Wounds), pages 205–215
Copyright © 2015 by Information Age Publishing
All rights of reproduction in any form reserved.

how Latina students face specific challenges that perhaps other students do not face. These students had challenges because they were women and Latinas; in addition, the students that I became familiar with were pursuing their degrees in the STEM fields.

My role as a Latina faculty was to become a facilitator for these students—who opened their feelings, their lives, and their realities to me, seeing in me one of the few [Latinas] in a predominantly White institution. So my role as mentor was added to those roles that are part of this work–life balance that I live with. As a mother, I couldn't help but to be consciously aware of the surprises that a Latina student with inclinations to STEM fields can provoke as a broken link in the stereotype that a women and Latina should be interested in.

So all the pieces fell into place in this natural work–life balance where personal experiences can become research passions and then the balance that you are trying to keep between your work and your life becomes a similar interest that these girls, these students expressed, when they came to my office and opened their life experiences to us. We, the authors, are a research team conducting a project that looks to identify strategies for the retention of Latina higher education students in the STEM fields. Particular experiences of the Latina authors enlighten the cultural perspectives of Latina scholars that parallel with our participants.

BACKGROUND

Upon exploring the experiences of Latina students around college retention and persistence in the STEM fields in Texas, a preliminary hypothesis was formulated by this research group regarding the cultural reasons for these students' retention and graduation. This chapter reviews the experiences of Latina students in the complex issues of college retention and persistence in STEM fields in a Tier 1 research institution in Texas and ultimately contributes to the limited literature in the particular area of Latinas in STEM programs in higher education in Texas as their strategies are based in a strong cultural component. Additionally, this research provides understanding of the crucial support that family culture of Latina students from STEM programs provide during college years. The lack of consideration of this female population, intentional or unintentional, has since been analyzed to understand that their male counterparts' reality is totally different than their reality, particularly, in the STEM fields.

Currently, there is little information about how culture, background, family support, and so on shape the experiences and strategies of Latina students specifically to make them pursue and complete a college degree in the STEM fields. Special emphasis is placed on the reasons for the ongoing underrepresentation of Latinas in general in higher education institutions in the U.S. and the parallels that these situations have with the challenges that Latina scholars (such as some of the authors) face in keeping work—life balance. With an increasing number of Latina/o/Hispanic college students in states like Texas (with higher female representation than the rest of the nation) and the decreasing number of students interested in the STEM field, it is important to understand and find out if there are particular cultural reasons that might support a Latina student to complete her college degree.

The crux of the literature exploration will be informed by Gottfredson's (2002) theory of Circumscription, Compromise, and Self-Creation, which describes the process of delineation in career (educational) choices based on one's self-concepts. Gottfredson's theory emphasizes the barriers that individuals face in career development, specifically considering gender and class differences.

UNDERSTANDING LATINAS IN COLLEGE: WHAT DOES RESEARCH TELL US?

The extension of Gottfredson's (2002) theory can be supportive in understanding the optimal achievement of Latinas in any college field. The climate of engineering, science, math, and technology has been raised as one important aspect for women's experiences. Anderson's (2002) study explored gender and achievement-related beliefs and argued that female engineering students face a social climate that contains negative stereotypes about women in technical fields. When female students know they are being judged in terms of stereotypes, this can cause them to question whether they belong in the field of engineering (Heyman, Martyna, & Bhatia, 2002). This fixed stereotype of "who does well in science and math" also adds to the self-consciousness of minority girls in classrooms, making teachers simply give up on them since they are not expected to do as well as non-Hispanics and male counterparts (Rosenthal, Tang, & Semple, 2013).

Cox, Joyner, and Slate (2011) claimed that

> with minimal gains in even associate degree completion by Hispanics in Texas, it follows that the largest group in the state will not be contributing to or benefitting from an economy that can provide better paying jobs, health insurance, social programs, and a standard of living associated with a healthy society. (p. 72)

Therefore, the authors have claimed that the lack of education could have "strong negative economic implications" especially in the STEM fields, when "Latina/o students earned only 7.7% of the science and engineering bachelor's degrees compared to white students who earned 64.7%" (Cox et al., 2011, p. 64).

LATINA HE STUDENT RETENTION, OUR STUDY

According to Cole and Espinoza (2008), "in 2005 Latinas received 60% of the bachelor's degrees awarded to the Latino population, but Latinas only earned 37% of the degrees awarded to this population in STEM fields" (p. 285). Research (Bean, 2005; Berger & Lyon, 2005; Tinto, 1975, 1993; Villa, 2008) has shown that social integration is a pillar in the retention process for college students. Astin and Oseguera (2005) proposed that students who show a propensity to become involved in the social and academic life of the institution have better chances of finishing college. If students do not feel connected and involved within their environment, it is likely they will not be retained (Johnson & Johnson, 1993). If students, especially those from different cultural and social backgrounds, believe they are discriminated against because of race, ethnicity, gender, or socioeconomic status, they are less likely to feel they fit into an institution and are therefore more likely to leave college (Garcia & Hurtado, 2011).

Who Were Our Participants?

Our participants were first generation college students, most of them were the oldest child in the family, and had strong connection to their families as most Latina students. As we advanced with this study, we kept finding common experiences among our participants and our experience as Latina scholars; their words, their feelings, their reactions were so natural and familiar to me; it was so easy to understand them and their own families. Some studies address female engineering students' experiences in college; however, little attention has been focused on determining the elements that facilitate success in this environment. Most of the studies that do exist are based on surveys and interviews about the negative experiences of women in engineering program environments. Few studies have asked students to share their experiences and study the dimensions that help them stay in programs.

In this study, we propose to answer the question: *How do culture, background, and family support among other factors shape the experiences of Latina students to make them pursue and complete a college degree in the STEM fields in Texas?* Special emphasis is placed on the reasons for the current underrepresentation of Latinas in higher education institutions in the United States as we have mentioned. We look through an exploratory descriptive and qualitative study to generate a clear and accurate portrayal of the perceptions of one group of Latina STEM students in higher education institutions in Texas in a particular context—as a parallel context that authors have identified in their own personal experiences and challenges maintaining a work–life balance. Data were collected from interviews with Latina STEM college students; observation of participants during the interview sessions, as well as prior to and after the meetings; and analysis of records.

The researchers used an open-ended interview protocol (Banda, 2012), which has been expanded upon and revised as the research progressed. In addition to the interview guide, additional data are being collected regarding demographic information for the interviewees. These data constitute an important analytic source to understand the context and reality of each participant and her responses. Observation of our participants, nonverbal communications, document reviews, broad consultation on the topic, as well as our personal insights and experiences are all activities that are assisting the researchers in exploring and assembling a contextual foundation sufficient for accurate interpretation.

Students were referred by faculty and student organizations; we contacted them by email to request their voluntary participation. Participants are students from a Tier 1 HE institution in Texas in the STEM fields.

FINDINGS

The Responses: Latinas' Experiences, Cultural Background and Family Support Related to Their Life in STEM Fields

First, the *challenges* that they described are strongly related with the higher education institution. Due to the growing number of Latino/a college students, research is needed on factors understanding the adjustment, retention, and academic achievement of these students (Crockett, Iturbide, Torres-Stone, McGinley, & Raffaelli, 2007). Rosie explained in her words how she felt about her parents and her attendance at the university:

> It got really hard around my second semester, they didn't really come to visit me as much and I kinda started having the whole . . . like the conflict that they didn't want me to go to school here at the university. But I continued to go to school here. It got pretty hard . . . aah. . . . So, I started my bach [bachelors] classes really soon and I was out of my league.

Reason (2009) confirmed that there is an array of pre-college background characteristics, academic preparation and experiences, and social and personal dispositions and experiences that can impact Latina students' adjustment, retention, and academic achievement. He further states that students' gender, race/ethnicity, age, and parents' education and family income as well as their persona and academic and occupational goals can affect their motivation and choices when persisting in and completing college. We identified one potential factor that might contribute to Latinas' retention, persistence and academic achievement in college as psychological stress, specifically, acculturative stress (Crockett et al., 2007).

We identified substantial *levels of stress related to financial problems* as an antecedent to various academic problems. However, additional stressors can be related to acculturative process stress that can stem from incongruent cultural values, discrimination (stereotyping), and language difficulties that may force second-generation children/first-generation college students to feel "caught" between opposing values of their own, their families, and peers (Cole & Espinoza, 2008; Crockett et al., 2007). Social support and coping strategies that involve provisions and buffers against stress, including stress-adjustment regulations, can be essential in reducing acculturative stress. This support and strategies can come from multiple sources and can be presented at various levels and types, accommodated through the Latin culture that emphasizes *familismo,* which involves strong feelings of attachment, loyalty among family, and shared identity (Crockett et al., 2007). Jessica explained:

> After the year ended, my parents really didn't want me to come back to college. So I decided against their will that I was going to come back. They said that if you did, you're on your own and you're going to have to pay for everything yourself. So, I worked my butt off over the summer. I worked three jobs. I came back and I was working one job about 40 hours a week doing my whole first semester just trying to pay... for tuition. I paid everything with loans. I was just trying to pay for my apartment and my bills and everything.... My dad started sneaking me money behind my mother's back (laughing). I was trying to be a full-time student [with a] full-time job and it was mentally, physically breaking down.

However, there are several *motivations* as to why minorities stay in the classes, including the desire to make a better living than what their parents could provide for them (Cox et al., 2011). For minority women some of the main influential factors to completing their STEM degree come through the *support of their family and their communities.*

Maria mentioned,

> So, everybody else has kinda been looking to me. They're like, "mija is going to college and mija going, and she's going to do good things."... My parents were especially... My grandparents, they liked the idea. They were happy for me.

Jessica described a very difficult situation and how she overcame it:

> So, I started asking around for help and then I went to a meeting for organization in Latinos in science and engineering and I asked if anyone could

> help me. And one of the kids said, 'yeah, I will help you.' So, then we kinda became best friends and he introduced me to everybody else. And we realized that everybody sort of came from the same background, the same situation. They were the first in their family to go to college, they're Latinos and it was nice.... It was kinda like a taste of home. So, when my family stopped supporting me, it was kinda like they stepped in, kept me, pushing me to keep going.

Jessica, continues, with tears in her eyes,

> I guess that they saw like how hard I was actually working and it kinda reminded them of the stuff they [parents] have gone through. And they realized that if they had the means to help me that they would help me. So now, I'm sort of getting back on better terms with my family.

In Hispanic cultures, the most important thing in life is family, and continuing to maintain the family name, which places great pressure on females, since it is their responsibility to marry and bear children. Therefore, it is found that for most Latinas, the anticipation of future family responsibilities is a huge discouragement from seeking education in STEM disciplines, especially when looking at medicine or doctoral programs, since they are perceived as long academic careers. However, if raised in a patriarchal family structure, Latina women can be much more likely to consider STEM degrees, since they might even be encouraged by their father to seek these male dominated careers (Crisp & Nora, 2012).

Our results show that participants from this study learned from obstacles, which served to allow them to transform challenges into successful experiences, through the use of *specific strategies* that many times were learned from cultural contexts and familial background and support. These specific strategies serve to provide *consejos*, which will enhance and encourage persistence and retention of Latina students in the STEM fields. Jessica, a first-generation college student, said:

> I started researching just based on engineering and I thought that this is what I wanted to do. I like being innovative. I took the aptitude test for your career and stuff like that. So, the one [engineering] always popped up.

Starting early searching on their academic interest, as their White counterparts, makes these students start locating themselves in a similar condition to compete. We couldn't stop thinking how setting our minds, as the students did, in order to be in the position to complete and overcome many barrier; indeed, that should start inside us, as Latinas. Certainly, there are major barriers that are totally real, but along with those we need to face the ones that might exist based on our particular experiences.

Peralta, Caspary, and Boothe (2013) mention that besides race, class, and gender, immigration and language played a huge role on how Latina students saw their ability to persist in school. With the lack of support or guidance from teachers, there was very little motivation to enroll in science classes. While for those who did take on the challenge of these courses, they felt they could not seek assistance at home because of the educational and linguistic barriers, "they [parents] do not have an idea of how hard it is to reach a higher education" (p. 193).

A *supportive environment* is important for optimal achievement in any college field. The climate of engineering for women has been raised as one important aspect of women's experiences. Several studies (Anderson, 2002; Clark, Revuelto, Kraft, & Beatty, 2003; Romkey, 2007) have explored how women's educational experiences differ significantly from their male peers. One study that explored gender and achievement-related beliefs argued that female engineering students face a social climate that contains negative stereotypes about women in technical fields. When female students know they are being judged in terms of stereotypes, this can cause them to question whether they belong to the field of engineering (Heyman et al., 2002). Maria described the environment in her department:

> We are a really small department...before this year. I had never met any girls in my major before this year, (sophomore year). Yeah, I was very astonished... my friend, she's Hispanic and now maybe there are very few and now that I'm introducing her to people, she never knew that there were so many Hispanics in the STEM field. I like it. I don't know if it's because I am Latina or I'm a woman or maybe it is just because who I am. I do get a lot of respect from the professors.

Women as minorities often feel isolated in engineering. If students do not feel connected and involved within their environment, it is likely they will not be retained (Johnson & Johnson, 1993).

Participants from this study recognize that it is important to have people to look up to and people who look like you; Latina students in STEM fields consider the presence of *role models in the academy and the profession* of utmost importance. Students look at the role models in order to "reach out" to their personal goals, as they themselves become role models for other students.

Jessica explained:

> It's nice when people come up to me and be like "I can't believe you do it because sometimes I get down on my luck and think she is working two jobs and going to school, I can do it'. It's kinda nice knowing that you can be an inspiration to someone and I kinda help them when they're going through tough times.

DISCUSSION: WHY WAS THIS STUDY IMPORTANT TO US? WHY DID THIS BECOME A TESTIMONIO?

The participants expressed their clear conviction that in their minds and in the minds of some of their families exists the idea of, "*Why not?*" and it was present most of the time—the importance of not limiting themselves, stereotyping themselves, and framing themselves in a group that has extreme difficulties in order to pursue their dreams has been an important factor in their success. "While I am here, I want to help so that I can increase the retention and help other people who are going through what I am going through and tell them that it is possible," as Maria emphasized.

Because of the challenges that these students live with, they have shaken our reality, and their intense wish is to become a motivation to future Latinas to pursue these fields. They expressed their wish to become change agents and an example for future students; at the same time, they support research like this in order to identify students and support their interest. Their answers, their reflections, and their problems illuminated those experiences that we have faced as Latina scholar; their solutions found parallels in the ones that many Latinas scholars have found to achieve what we want.

Gottfredson's (2002) theory of circumscription, compromise, and self-creation lends itself very well to the issues and findings presented; this theory also speaks of a "zone of acceptable alternatives," in that selections are weighed against the accomplishments of the parents and family members, which is very similar to what happens in Latino families. Children aspire to do better than their parents and in turn expect more from their children. Strategies of *familismo*, a supportive environment, student involvement, and a positive role model, all lend themselves for the Latina to recreating herself in her new educational endeavor. This recreation of self has implications of more (educational and career) alternatives for Latinas and more satisfaction with choices made. Restricting alternatives is no longer necessary, and Latinas will be more aware of opportunities and the requirements necessary to obtain those opportunities.

It is imperative that stakeholders, family members, and Latinas themselves understand the process of circumscription, compromise, and self-creation to avoid the delineation of a STEM education and the unexplored possibilities for Latinas to be able to ask themselves the question, *Why not?* As the largest minority population in our country and as the fastest growing youth population in the nation, it is vital for us to pay attention to the future of young Latinas in STEM fields. Their strategies become our strategies, as their experiences and the experiences of most Latina scholars are shaped by our culture.

REFERENCES

Anderson, I. J. T. (2002). *The social construction of female engineers: A qualitative case study of engineering education.* Unpublished doctoral dissertation, University of Saskatchewan, Saskatoon, SK, Canada

Astin, A., & Oseguera, L. (2005). Pre-college and institutional influences on degree attainment. In A. Seidman (Ed.), *College student retention. Formula for student success* (pp. 245–276). Westport, CT: American Council on Education/Praeger.

Banda, R. (2012). *Perceptions of social support networks and climate in the persistence of Latinas pursuing an undergraduate Engineering degree.* Unpublished doctoral dissertation, Texas A&M University. Retrieved from http://hdl.handle.net/1969.1/148272

Bean, J. P. (2005). Nine themes of college student retention. In A. Seidman (Ed.), *College student retention. Formula for student success* (pp. 215–244). Westport, CT: American Council on Education/Praeger.

Berger, J., & Lyon, S. (2005). Past to present: A historical look at retention. In A. Seidman (Ed.), *College student retention. Formula for student success* (pp. 1–30). Westport, CT: American Council on Education/Praeger.

Cervantes-Soon, C. G. (2012). Testimonios of life and learning in the borderlands: Subaltern Juárez girls speak. *Equity & Excellence in Education, 45*(3), 373–391.

Clark, M. C., Revuelto, J., Kraft, D., & Beatty, P. (2003). Learning to work in teams. *Journal of Student-Centered Learning, 1(3)*, 171–178.

Cole, D., & Espinoza, A. (2008). Examining the academic success of Latino students in science, technology, engineering, and mathematics (STEM) majors. *Journal of College Student Development, 49(4)*, 285–300.

Cox, S., Joyner, S., & Slate, J. (2011). Differences in Hispanic graduation rates at Texas community colleges over time. *Community College Enterprise, 17*(2), 62–76.

Crisp, G., & Nora, A. (2012). *Overview of Hispanics in science, mathematics, engineering and technology (STEM): K–16 representation, preparation and participation.* White paper for the Hispanic Association of Colleges and Universities. July.

Crockett, L. J., Iturbide, M. I., Torres-Stone, R. A., McGinley, M., & Raffaelli, M. (2007). Acculturative stress, social support, and coping: Relations to psychological adjustments among Mexican American college students. *Faculty Publications, Department of Psychology, 299,* 347–355.

Garcia, A. G., & Hurtado S. (2011, February). Predicting Latina/o STEM Persistence at HSI's and non-HSI's. Paper presented at the American Educational Research Association Annual Meeting, New Orleans, Louisiana.

Gottfredson, L. S. (2002). Gottfredson's theory of circumscription, compromise, and self-creation. In D. Brown (Ed.), *Career choice and development* (pp. 85–148). San Francisco, CA: Jossey-Bass.

Heyman, G., Martyna, B., & Bhatia, S. (2002). Gender and achievement-related beliefs among engineering students. *Journal of Women and Minorities in Science and Engineering, 8*(1), 41–53.

Johnson, D. W., & Johnson, R. T. (1993). Implementing cooperative learning. *Education Digest, 58*(8), 62–66.

Peralta C., Caspary M., & Boothe D. (2013). *Success factors impacting Latina/o persistence in higher education leading to STEM opportunities.* New York, NY: Springer.

Reason, R. D. (2009). An examination of persistence research through the lens of a comprehensive conceptual framework. *Journal of College Student Development, 50*(6), 659–682.

Romkey, L. (2007). *Attracting and retaining females in engineering programs: Using an STSE approach.* Retrieved from http://www.asee.org/conferences/paper-view.cfm?id=5518

Rosenthal A., Tang T., & Semple R. B. (2013). Missing from science class: Too few girls and minorities study tech subjects. *The New York Times.* Retrieved December 10, 2013 from http://www.nytimes.com/2013/12/11/opinion/too-few-girls-and-minorities-study-tech-subjects.html?hp&rref=opinion

Tinto, V. (1975). Dropout from higher education. A theoretical synthesis of recent research. *Review of Educational Research 45*(*1*), 89–125.

Tinto, V. (1993). *Leaving college: Rethinking the causes and cures of student attrition* (2nd ed.). Chicago, IL: University of Chicago Press.

Villa, C. G. (2008). *The impact of students' life experiences on program retention. A study of female engineering students in Mexico.* Unpublished doctoral dissertation, Texas A&M University, College Station, TX.

CHAPTER 21

MEMORY AND HUNGER

Feeding on Remnants of the Past in a PWI

Hilario Lomeli
Penn State University

I came to graduate school at Pennsylvania State University from East Texas searching, like many others, for a sense of home, safety, and belonging in both my work and life. Although I was invited to tour the campus and the surrounding town of State College, located in rural, central Pennsylvania prior to arriving, I did not have the means or resources to visit. I arrived with very few ideas of what central Pennsylvania and Penn State were like outside the high national rankings for its college of education. Despite these unknowns, I ventured forward with a heavy heart, from the home I had only recently learned to love again. Driving through the night from Texas to Pennsylvania, I conjured up all kinds of fantasies about this new place I was going to call home.

When I first arrived in State College, I stopped at a diner for breakfast. I kept searching for someone who looked like me, but much to my disappointment there were only white faces around. Not a single white face wore the familiar cowboy hats or boots that were so present in my hometown. My

Abriendo Puertas, Cerrando Heridas (Opening Doors, Closing Wounds), pages 217–224
Copyright © 2015 by Information Age Publishing
All rights of reproduction in any form reserved.

search, now I realize somewhat silly in retrospect, for familiar faces and cowboy getups continued. I wandered around the main drag of State College aimlessly and endlessly searching for cowboys and Latinos/as.

Excuse me, miss? Are you Latina? Oh. Sorry.

The first week of classes I asked those in class, my cohort, and my professors: *Do you know any Latinos/as on campus? Is there a Mexican American studies program here?* At the University of Texas, I was privileged enough to be surrounded by a formidable band of Latino/a peers and mentors as a Mexican American studies student. It reminded me of my family, of home. But those memories of UT were just absent spirits here at Penn State. In stores, hallways, and classrooms I looked for the faces of those peers and mentors, but as I rounded every corner in the halls of this institution their apparitions quickly darted behind doors, walls, or into thin air. Faces I encountered were recognizable from afar, but up close their faces morphed—surely, I told myself, a result of trying too hard to make the unfamiliar look a little familiar.

Through connections with other Latinos/as, I found a Latina doctoral student from Texas. Her deep soul and fierce Chicananess kept me from leaving the academy. Whenever we had free time, we broke bread, drank Corona, and lamented. We saw in each other the desire for home and the utter whiteness that surrounded us at work and at "home" in State College. The remnants of those conversations fed a burgeoning hunger raging inside.

Something was awry in State College. My Latinoness, my Tejanoness, my non-Whiteness, was on hyper drive, like never before. I spent hours in my kitchen and online researching, cooking, and eating Tex-Mex and BBQ. I wore my cowboy boots every day because I needed to. Final papers, assignments, and reflections—they all were on Latinos/as. I checked out all of the books on Latina/Chicana feminism—and, of course, these books were all available and barely used. I had a strong urge to get up to date on all things Gloria Anzaldúa. I read all of her works. Michael Salgado, George Strait, Ramon Ayala, Vicente, Chevela Vargas, and my beloved Selena were on a continuous spin on my iPhone. I danced wherever and whenever I could. I somehow retaught myself how to Kumbia and Texas-two step. Indeed, there was both pain and joy in these moments as I often ate and danced alone.

Here I would like to take a step back. The story of my move from Texas to Pennsylvania for graduate school is singular, yet also polyvocal, multiplicitous, and ongoing. In the following, I present short vignettes that purposefully seek to muddle the desire to read a complete, linear, and clean *testimonio*. In each vignette, I envision phone calls, letters, or snippets of actual or imagined conversations with both loved ones and with strangers. In this way, my lived experience blends with fantasy, both of which condition the messiness of my everyday life. The vignettes are broken up into two halves. The first presents multiple accounts of what it is like for this Tejano to get his PhD in a predominantly White academic institution so far removed both physically and psychically from his home, family, and people—from his familiar faces and cowboy getups. The second half address the answers to the question of how I have lasted, coped, and survived graduate school in State College and navigated the liminal space between work, home, and life.

PART I: WHAT'S IT LIKE UP NORTH?

To a Graduate Student of Color from Another University:
State college is . . . well, it's overwhelmingly, and painfully White. Look, I have to be honest; it is tough to be a person of color there. Not only is the town really White, the College of Education at Penn State is really White too. I mean there isn't even a single Latino/a faculty member in my department and there aren't many students of color either. There is an international presence and they make up the majority of the diversity, but it's hard to find another student of color from the states. Yeah I know. It's that bad. And then to top it off—the food is shit!

To Shane, My Best Friend Since High School:
Holy shit man! It's fucking White here! It's whiter than anywhere that I have ever been. I don't even see our peoples anywhere. I can even go to a restaurant and not see our peoples working in the back. It's crazy. Shit, even the guys who do construction and mow lawns are White. So you can walk through the whole campus, the whole damn town and not even see one single Latino or Latina. Maybe if you are lucky, you might have one or two Black people walk by on a good day, then you can see some color around here.

And don't even get me started on the food. It's like the fucking taco hasn't been invented yet! Stop laughing. It's not that funny. You know how I feel about tacos. But really, there's not a single spot to grab decent Mexican food. All there is here is shitty pizza and these gross-ass torta looking things they call hoagies. Yeah. I know Shane, you're right. I do got it good here. I gotta remember why I am here. I mean it's White, but it's also really pretty up here. Everywhere you go you have these green mountains and the people in graduate school are real nice too. I feel weird around them though, you know? Like, they all had real jobs and have master's degrees—like real big timers—lawyers, policy analysts, and principals. Plus, they sound super smart. In class people will ask me, "What did you do before you came here?" And you know what, Shane? I can't fucking lie. I tell them. I look in their eyes and tell them that I worked in construction, building and staining fences.

To My Momma:
I already told you, I don't live in Philadelphia. No, State College isn't close to Chicago either so the weather there doesn't really affect us. Yes momma.

I'm wearing my jacket. Every day, I promise. You know when it's 20 degrees outside you kinda have to. I'm doing fine up here, Vieja. I mean it's cold all the time, *pero* I keep warm. The snow is beautiful though. Remember when I was little how I always wanted to live in a place with snow? Well, up here it's everywhere and I bet you would like it. State College is nice... kind of small of like Crockett. I mean, there are so many gringos here, you know, but they are nice. So it's not too bad. *Buena gente.* Plus, it's relaxing. There is no hustle and bustle like in Houston and our house and neighborhood is quiet like our trailer home was. So when you come here to visit, you can just take it easy, read books, and let me cook for you. I told you, right? I am learning how to cook like you. No momma, I can't make tortillas yet. They are too hard. I can never get them round enough and they don't taste right. That is why you have come visit me. What, you don't love your favorite son anymore?

To a Different Graduate Student of Color From Another University:

You know what, I talk a lot of shit about State College, but I am lucky. I mean don't get me wrong, State College is White and cold as hell, but in a lot of ways I am blessed to be here. I can't believe how much I have learned in such a short time. And for as fucked up as the College of Education can be, I have a cadre of professors who have my back. I mean they advocate for me like they were my momma or something. I mean, at UT I had Latino/a faculty who were like aunts and uncles you know, and I don't know if you know this, but I am youngest of 13 so that kind of thing felt right to me. They had been through this shit already and knew what it was like. Then again, do they get me? Do they know what it's like to be a person of color in the academy? Have they ever been in a place that bleaches both their soul and body? No. But who knows, maybe something positive comes from those feelings? Shit, I don't know. My advisers at Penn State do everything they can, but it's just not the same as when I was at UT Austin. There is something different that I can undoubtedly feel, but just can't quite fully articulate. Maybe it's not them, maybe it's something different with me? Either way though, I feel like something is missing here, and I wish I had more opportunities to talk to folks of color.

To My 18-Year-Old Nephew, RJ:

You aren't doing shit there at home. I mean when I was eighteen I got the hell out of Crockett. Ain't nothing there for us really, unless you want to work a low-wage job your whole life. I mean if you really love it there, leave and become something and then go back so you have something to give back. But right now you got no job, aren't going to school, *and* you are living with your parents! So, come live with me in State College. Look, I'll help you apply to college and get your head right. I promise you will like it in State College. You will be surrounded by people your own age and get to see what it's like to go to university. When I went to college, RJ, I didn't know shit. I had nobody to show me the ropes, how to apply for FAFSA, scholarships, how to check out books in the library, how to write a research paper—nothing. I went in there blind and almost didn't make it. Thank God for the people in my Mexican American studies program!

But you have somebody to show you way. I fucked up so you wouldn't have to, and State College has all kinds of resources to help you out. It has a world-class library. I can check you out any book, an iPad, even a laptop man! A fucking thousand-dollar laptop! You can even take my online course so you can practice writing and studying. Plus, I can even introduce you to all of my friends in graduate school and professors. I'm talking about professors, doctors with their PhDs, who wrote entire books and you can get to know them! I mean don't get me wrong; it's going to be a big change for you. State College is White and cold. So you can go ahead and leave your high school letterman. You are going to need a better jacket. But don't worry about that though, I got you.

PART II: HOW DO YOU MAKE IT SO FAR AWAY?

To Shane:

Man I don't know. I ask myself that question all the time. Like who the fuck am I? And what the hell am I doing here in graduate school? The memory of where I have been and where I grew up never goes away either, it's always with me. It's like I am here at Penn State feeling like I might belong and then it hits me. I remember. I am the same guy who grew up in a trailer home with a single mother with thirteen kids in some tiny-ass town in the middle of nowhere. And then I look around me and realize that I can count on my hand the number of people I have met here who actually grew up poor. And not that middle or working class that everyone claims. I'm talking Kool-Aid and Hamburger Helper every night poor! I gotta be real though, I wasn't even that poor compared to my brothers and sisters. They had it so much more rough than I did. Shit, to them I was spoiled as hell, and they were right. I was the baby of the family too, so even though my piece of shit father left me, I still had 11 sisters who were like extra mommas to me—giving me love. That was a blessing. Well, except when it came to dating, that was a nightmare, but you saw that shit in action.

Now that I am thinking about it, I guess that is how I made it, man. Thinking about my brothers and sisters and my momma and what they have been through and then looking at my own life and seeing how hard they worked to support me when they could. Man, I couldn't let their love go to waste. So, when my momma reaches into her bra to give me her last twenty dollar bill "just because" while she has only a quarter tank of gas that has to last her a week?! I mean how can I let her down? How can I throw away that kind of devotion? How can I let all my brothers and sisters and my nieces and nephews down? Shit, what kind of message would it send for the only one to ever go to graduate school to give up and quit? What kind of son/brother/uncle would I be?

Since I have been at this university, I have missed home like never before. And when I feel down or want to give up, I think of my family and all the love they have given me. I go back to those moments when my mom would turn a rubber band, baloney, and tortillas into a full-blown dinner—like MacGyver! I use that. I mean, I live off of those memories and struggles. They are my strength. I got nothing else here to feed my soul that way. I mean I have Jenna, but she supports me in a different way.

To a Graduate Student of Color from Another University:

I've got family, and I've got a Wonder Woman of a mother, but sometimes, when shit gets real bad, the only person that keeps me afloat is my partner Jenna. When I fall through the cracks, I have her. I'm lucky to have found Jenna here. So often I rely on memory to keep me afloat, but sometimes it's not enough. The realness of her, her materiality, her touch, her love and support both challenges and supports me in way that reignites my drive. Even with my family, I wouldn't have made it without her.

To My Momma:

Momma you remember when I called you last week to interview you. I asked you, How do you think I make it here at Penn State? Remember how you started crying and told me that I made it here alone without you because you thought you weren't a good enough mother. You told me that I did it alone because you couldn't support me financially while I went to school up north. Money, well, it's important, but I get by. Momma, it's you who keeps me going. Through all these years, the webs you have spun have continued to support my heavy body. For so long, I wanted to be someone else, with a different history and a different skin color. But I understand it better now. I see the strength and resilience in our collective pain and struggle. The whispers of joy and laughter now cackle loudly, *con ganas*, into my soul. They feed me here. You see momma, to go forward, I look back—understanding now that your hand in mine is not because you can't let go, but because I need it.... So what if you can't give me all the money you want to? I have memories and *consejos* that, through recollection, become alive and present. I draw from the past and our collective memories not to recreate it, but to create new experiences up north. So you see, momma, don't worry.

To RJ:

I work fucking hard man. I mean I get a lot of help. I recognize that, but when you go to college you have to work hard. Remember, you and I are both playing a game that was never meant for us. We have a choice; we can look at the responsibility to our family as a burden or a strength. It can be fucking heavy or it can support our journey into these white-ass institutions. And no matter how big and strong your mind and heart are, you're gonna get pushed down and it will hurt. And yeah, we have support networks and people that love us, but there will be moments when we fall and we have to make a move, alone, to pick ourselves up.

To My Undergraduate Mentor, Luis Urrieta:

I doubt you know this, but I go back to that moment so often. I was sitting on the floor waiting for your class to start. It was early in the semester and maybe ten minutes before your class started. You walked up to where I was at and sat down on the cold floor next to me. You turned to me, placing your hand on my knee, and said, "How are you doing, Raza?" I was in a bad place then, doubting whether I could make it at UT. I couldn't believe you wanted to talk to me. I mean a professor, a big shot, wanting to talk to me about how I am doing? It was and continues to be such a simple, yet radical gesture. That interaction fed my soul, injecting me with confidence in myself that I had been desperately seeking. I think about what might have happened if you hadn't approached me. Where might I be? Who might I have become or rather continued to be? Here in graduate school I think of you often. In fact I spent a lot of my first year looking for someone to take your place as my guide to surviving graduate school. I didn't have any luck. So, I went back to the vast vault of *consejos* you left me. The words of wisdom that didn't connect with me then guide me now. When I am having doubts and need a guide, which happens a lot, I go back in the past and bring you to the present. It's more than the words that guide me, though—I think about how you might approach scenarios and ethical dilemmas. If I know it makes you proud then I have been doing something right.

HOME: WORK/LIFE

These past few years have led me to return to my family and to my identity in my research. My participatory anthropological project now involves both the stories of other Latino/a youth and my own struggles with identity. My family and my experiences are now no longer relegated to the life side of the work–life balance, but instead it bleeds into my work. When my family, my home, and myself are topics of my research to be placed under the anthropological gaze, it is hard to disentangle work from life. Indeed, "work" for anthropologists has multiple meanings. In one sense, work is that which happens on a university campus, but in another sense it also means what is happening in our research.

There exists a rich literature from critical scholars that seeks to blur "the field" with the self and home in research. Many have highlighted the way personal subjectivities and political investments are intermeshed in ways that make it impossible to presume we can separate home from the field. The field is not merely a place one can go to and return from. Exposing the linkages between home and field is often seen as a goal for many radical scholars. And yet, I wonder why it is that we don't ask similar questions about our institutional university workspaces? Why don't we demand to see home in our academic spaces? Why don't we better probe the boundaries between the institutional structures we work in and our homes? Should we not, at billion dollar institutions such as Penn State, expect to see remnants of home in the academy? It is clear to many how and why home should imbue my work as a researcher, but what is not as clear is why home should imbue the institution that I work in. It is accepted that work can visit home life (as a researcher visits a study site), but why can't home visit work?

I want to be careful and clear here: I am not suggesting that our home lives should be thoroughly and entirely imbued by work. Instead, I am drawing our gaze to the ivory tower and asking why the institutional spaces of work are not probed for the presence of home. For those of us who are minoritarian subjects, not having a home in the ivory tower forces us to look elsewhere, creating fissures between the institution and the subjects they supposedly desire.

These absences in higher education have led me to fantasize about home and Latino/a mentorships in the academy as a means to find support and to make me feel like I belong. There are deeply political stakes involved in these fantasies. Memories teach and guide me despite temporal and spatial constraints. And yet, they are not real substitutes for peers and mentors who can share and recognize the legibility of my cultural background and experiences. I should not have to rely on memory and fantasy to aide me in my journey through the academy. My memories and fantasies serve as a pedagogy, a means of guiding me through the academy. This should not be a necessity; rather, it should be a last resort, a pedagogy of survival.

This is not to say I don't have support networks available. I am blessed here at Penn State in many ways. I have both my partner and a plethora of advisers who are willing to support and guide me through this process. They can do endless things my fantasies and memories cannot: provide pragmatic advice, advocate for me, edit my writing, love me, hold me, and much more. For this, I am forever grateful. Indeed, if it were not for my wonderful experiences with my White advisers, I would have never lasted this long. They often do everything they can to support me and guide me. However, there are things that fantasy and memories can do that my support network in State College cannot do: bring me home.

CHAPTER 22

FLIPPING THE MIRROR

A Xicana Researcher Negotiating With the Act of Reflection

Margarita Berta-Avila

INTRODUCTION

The Juncture

It was about two months after I had finished collecting data that I was engrossed in the process of analyzing the transcriptions. I was actually quite excited because there was finally an opportunity to document the experiences of critical Xicana/Xicano educators in the classroom by answering the following dissertation question: How do critical Xicana/Xicano educators conceptualize their role in the classroom when working with Raza students? Moreover, what perspectives do critical Xicana/Xicano educators offer in understanding identity and the integration of a critical way of being when teaching Raza students? Having had been a classroom teacher myself, I could relate to the struggles and highlights of the comrades who shared their stories with me. When they spoke about what it meant to be Xicana/Xicano educators in the classroom, I could feel their emotions as if they were my own. It was evident that these educators viewed their role as one beyond just teaching students

Abriendo Puertas, Cerrando Heridas (Opening Doors, Closing Wounds), pages 225–234
Copyright © 2015 by Information Age Publishing
All rights of reproduction in any form reserved.

that 2 + 2 equals 4—they felt a political responsibility to circumvent inequities imposed upon Raza students. As a result, I was enthusiastic, because I believed this dissertation was our opportunity to state, as Xicana/Xicano educators, what we considered important in regards to the education of Raza students. When I finished writing about the first two participants, I handed my draft to my mentor who was also a member of my dissertation committee. Approximately a week later, we set up a two-hour block of time to meet and review his comments. When the day came, I recall entering his office and feeling as if I was going to get sick. Something was bothering me, I could feel it, and I knew what it was about. An unexpected finding had emerged that I was not anticipating and when I submitted my first draft. I made no mention of it because I knew it would change the my initial purpose of this study. What I discovered was that in the midst of the good work these Xicana/o teachers were engaged in, they would contradict their own critical pedagogical objectives by unintentionally reverting to hegemonic practices in their classrooms. So, as I closed the door behind me and sat next to him, he took a deep breath and said "Do you have your armor on? Because this is going to hurt." At that moment I knew he had identified what I had left out and he point-blank asked me, "What do you truly want to accomplish from this dissertation?" He elaborated by asking whether my purpose was to put something out in the community that ultimately would benefit the education of Raza students—or was the goal to just pat ourselves on the back as Xicana/Xicano educators? Upon reflection on the question, I got very nervous because in my mind there were political ramifications no matter what position I took. For example, if the role of this dissertation was to "pat ourselves on the back," did we miss an opportunity to have dialogue and analyze our next steps as Xicana/o educators? On the other hand, if we list areas of concern regarding our role and pedagogy as Xicana/o educators, do we leave ourselves open to White dominant criticism regarding teachers of color? In my attempts to determine what to do, I chose to include in my dissertation what I titled "missed opportunities." "Missed opportunities" was a section that exposed components of the participants' teaching practice found to be contradictory or lacking in pedagogical development. At the end, I chose the latter, but not without reservation (to this day) or implications.

The Invitation

I chose to begin this narrative with a short vignette, because approximately ten years ago I was asked by a colleague to write a personal reflection (paper) about the juncture I describe in order to present on a panel at the American Educational Research Association (AERA) conference. The panel was an invited session that addressed the problematic research structures that can stifle researchers of color and cause moral/ethical decisions to be made. When first asked, I was taken aback, because I had not wanted to even revisit this subject. However, as I allowed the prospect of writing a reflection to settle in, it dawned on me that this was an opportunity to unpack—for myself, at least—the interpersonal conflict that many scholars of color confront when conducting research in their own communities (Ek, Quijada Cerecer, Alanis, & Rodriguez, 2010; Segura, 2003). I felt such an opportunity necessary, especially if I wanted to continue focusing my research on the Xicana/Xicano community.

As I started working on unpacking the experience, I quickly realized that it was not going to be an easy process. I struggled writing the reflection and procrastinated for months, telling myself I would get to it..., it would not be so hard to write...., and it would just flow out of me naturally. Rather, the opposite was true—so much so that I never finished writing the paper for AERA or presented on that panel. Now, ten years later, with the opportunity to revisit this again via this piece, I have pondered the following: Why did I procrastinate? Why has it taken me so long to write? Why is it so hard to write? And the scariest question of all, why am I so scared? Honestly, I think I was trying to fool myself. I do not think that initially I had any intention to write an honest reflection about what I experienced or put the participants through. In fact, I believe I was going to attempt to deceive myself into thinking I would by approaching the reflection from a traditional "researcher perspective," detaching myself from the data, the analysis, the people involved... all of it. But in truth, through all of this, was I going to be able to achieve true pedagogical dialogue and further development of the participants and myself?

Now I realize it's been my own fear holding me back. It is a fear based on not knowing how those reading or listening to this reflection will react. It is not knowing how I will feel about myself at the end of it all. Why do I name this "fear"? I name it because as a self-identified Xicana, I entered the profession of education to intentionally counteract the oppressive practices and institutionalized beliefs confronting our Raza community. Sometimes, in our lack of dialogue we miss the greatest part of pedagogical transformation. As a Xicana researcher, I seek to challenge, and not allow, dominant research perspectives to determine whether or not our community's work is objective and valid. Thus, I am accountable to the Raza community I represent. Hence, the research I develop has to well represent the voices, experiences, and realities of these individuals. With that said, ultimately, I have to ask myself—did I betray the very community to which I had committed myself? Did I exploit the very community I hoped to represent? Had I turned my back on the very principles and values that ground me as a Xicana in the field? These questions probably sound quite romanticized and one-dimensional, but this was how I felt because in for change and transformation to occur, all of us needed to be present to reflect and dialogue. This opportunity was not truly initiated.

Dr. Alma Flor Ada once stated, "If we do not confront our fears in life, then we are prone to become prisoners of them" (personal communication, April, 2002). My original attempt (from ten years ago) to approach this reflection from a superficial position is not possible. Mind you, not because it is not easy to do so. In fact it would be the easiest and safest thing to do. But rather, I have to "flip the mirror" or else I would deny the values that ground me as a Xicana and a Xicana researcher, and the commitment I have made to the Xicana/Xicano community.

The purpose of sharing this *testimonio* is to honestly reflect upon the interpersonal negotiation that transpired at an individual, academic, and communal level when the decision was made to challenge aspects of the participants' practice in the classroom and write about it in my dissertation. Moreover, I reflect on the ethical and personal conflict that decision has forced me to confront.

TESTIMONIOS

Historically, the experiences and narratives of Xicana/Xicano educators in the field have been silenced and ignored (Blackmer Reyes & Curry Rodríguez, 2012). In the context of Xicana/Xicano education research, testimonies are grounded in critical liberationist pedagogy, as positioned by Paulo Freire (1970; Blackmer Reyes & Curry Rodríguez, 2012), which allows for counter-narratives of Xicanas/os being marginalized. *Testimonios* foster an opportunity for participants and researcher to claim their own voice, engaging in a critical dialogue that transcends their exchange into a political act "whose purpose is to intentionally assess reality with the specific intent of creating a more socially just world" (Reza, 1995, p. 80). Moreover, a *testimonio* lends itself to an honest reflection that grapples with the clarity needed when conducting research in one's own community. At a more personal level, my *testimonio* brings to light a reflection, an "account told in the first person by a narrator who is the real protagonist or witness of events. This definition focuses on *testimonios* as evolving from events experienced by a narrator who seeks empowerment through voicing her or his experience" (Blackmer Reyes & Curry Rodriguez, 2012, p. 4).

The Act of Negotiation: Nested Realities Confronting Researchers

> As the researcher engages with the participants in critical reflection, she becomes more reflective. As she discovers the strength of dialogue, her inner dialogue becomes more audible. As she learns to listen to the voices of the par-

> ticipants, she recognizes more and more voices within herself. As she names the world, she begins to lose the fear to look at the truth of her own self. As she promotes freedom, she becomes more free. (Ada & Beutel, 1993, p. 4)

As I engrossed myself in the process of critical reflection in my dissertation, questions surfaced as I analyzed the data and looked for generative themes. More specifically, what emerged was what I identified as "missed opportunities" in the context of what the participants pedagogically believed and how it was enacted in the classroom. When these missed opportunities were identified, I got very nervous. In all honesty, I was not sure what to do because I was not expecting to encounter this. I kept asking myself, "*Do I share with the participants what has evolved or do I wait until the chapter is all written?*" My gut feeling was to immediately call a gathering so that together we could determine how to address these findings—but I didn't. I worried that if I posed my questions and shared the piece on missed opportunities, it would place doubt in the minds of the participants and how they interpreted their role as Xicana/Xicano educators, therefore perpetuating the academy's stance on who has power and whose knowledge is considered valid.

Ultimately, I could go two ways—stay silent (not include anything in the dissertation) or have the dialogue with my comrades (which meant including the findings based on a joint decision with participants). If I had stayed silent, I believe the dissertation would still have been strong because the focus was on a group of critical political teachers that had not been truly heard in our society. But what would that silence have meant for us as a community of Xicana/Xicano educators? To a certain extent, I think it could have perpetuated the idea (which none of us talk about) that we would rather receive the critique from outside our community than from within. On the other hand, right or wrong, as a community, we are often taught to take care of our business from the inside. Thus, the silence could have been appropriate because we still would have addressed it but not made public. I am not sure. All I knew, in that moment in time, that staying silent would have meant that we were not able to take ourselves to another level of critical analysis in the dialogical process of participatory research. Here, at this stage, is where I failed my *colegas* (colleagues). I was so worried and scared about what had transpired that I did not offer an opportunity to dialogue from the onset. Instead, I decided to wait until it was all written because of my own fear that undermined and underestimated the participants' opportunity to grapple with the findings. Moreover, my action overwhelmingly perpetuated what I feared the most—acting as a researcher (via a traditional research mantra) interpreting what I perceived the participants could handle. I was disappointed in myself because I spoke about this dissertation to the participants as an opportunity to deepen our conversations. But at the end of the day, I truly never allowed the dialogue to occur at its fullest capacity and I had broken my promise. I had promised the participants, when we met for the first time to discuss this study, that this dissertation was an opportunity to showcase our work. I even emphasized that, for too long, others had taken the liberty to tell our story (well intentioned or not) and now, it was our turn to name our realities and share with the world the importance of Xicanas/Xicanos to be in the classroom with Raza children. With all that said, now I felt that I had let them down. "Letting them down," in retrospect, was at the heart of my fear and why I chose to wait and not share what was emerging. Thus, as I continued to write and plugged away at trying to finish, I grappled with the content of my dissertation but also the manner in which I was handling the situation. As I kept writing, way in the depths of my soul, I still contemplated whether or not this analysis would be included—thus never committing myself, yet prolonging the inevitable.

Taking the Step and Making the Final Decision

Facing the truth is not an easy thing to do, because it also means confronting what we cannot see, or do not want to see. From the narratives collected, I learned that it was almost impossible for the participants to talk about their pedagogy at their school sites. Rarely did they have any allies to strategize with or obtain comfort from. First, professional isolation made it difficult to feel part of a collective effort. Second, there had to be a willingness to acknowledge a need for self-reflection on their pedagogy and professional growth. As a result, our dialogues and interactions pushed beyond a safe zone in order to truly confront and reflect critically upon our pedagogy and discuss improvements.

It was at this juncture that I had to "flip the mirror." Similar to the participants, when they were confronted with what I analyzed in their pedagogy, I questioned my purpose with this work. I questioned what my objectives were in this study. I questioned my commitment to the Raza community. I questioned my commitment to them, the participants. Again, I feared how outside critics of this pedagogical approach would take the data and use it to speak against its implementation in schools.

When it became apparent that I was almost done with writing my dissertation, I took the step and made the decision to include the "Missed Opportunities" segment that I had been so worried about. The final decision to do so was quite difficult but at that time I chose to include the analysis in question. I named this section "Missed Opportunities" because in the process of contextualizing their pedagogy, two factors emerged: (1) the participants would often maintain a superficial level of dialogue with the students, and (2) the participants missed opportunities in their practice to teach students how to negotiate between what they were learning and experiences they would face. Thus, I felt it was important to discuss how, even in the midst of doing great work, we confront contradictions or oversee practices. But most importantly, we need to discuss the need for a consistent support structure to be able to critically reflect on one's practice.

I viewed my latter points as part of the process of transformation. Unfortunately, due to my lack of judgment and fear (as explained earlier), our opportunity to dialogue about the findings did not occur until right before I had to defend. Initially, I wanted us to meet all together so that I could openly discuss the aspect of missed opportunities that had emerged. But the schedule and time of my comrades did not permit for us to do so. At the same time, I did not make other accommodations, so I sent the participants a final version of the findings and analysis that included highlights but also the section on missed opportunities. Three out of the five participants got quite upset because for the first time they were reading the following: "due to limited opportunities for the participants to be challenged and grow critically with respect to their pedagogy, the participants had minimal opportunities to reflect on their daily practices" (Berta-Avila, 2004, p. 242). So, of course, they would be angry. I sent them the findings and analysis via email, which was so impersonal.

The participants did not agree with the idea that certain aspects of their practice needed to be questioned. To be honest, I don't think they were upset about components of their teaching practice being questioned but rather hurt and angry that there was no discussion about the findings prior to this, thus circling back to a feeling of betrayal. They had poured their souls out to me, allowed me into their classrooms, and instead of being upfront and talking about this to them in the beginning, I waited like a coward to the end. But now there was no turning back. It was out and I had to take responsibility for my actions. What made this even more painful was that two of the five teachers were "home girls" of mine. We went back over 20 years. Thus the pain I caused them was deep. With all the courage I could gather within me, I called each of them to explain what I did and why I felt it was important to do so. The phone calls went as well as could be expected. I was a nervous wreck. My voice and whole body was trembling as I spoke. The participants were open to hearing me out. They listened to what I had to say and requested the opportunity to make additions to the components of the data that concerned them.

It was at this crossroads where the participants and I had to negotiate our interpretations. I was not going to ignore their concerns, but at the same time I was not going to look the other way with questions that had surfaced. This was a stressful experience because I believed that ethically I needed to portray an accurate description. As each participant responded in written feedback to his or her sections, I incorporated their explanations into the findings that were done prior to my dissertation defense.

To offer closure, I asked the participants to review the findings, analysis, and conclusions of the study one last time. Due to the difficulties some of the participants had with aspects of the findings and analysis, I found it important that they voice their reflections before the final dissertation was submitted. Four out of five participants responded to the final review. Three out of the four felt comfortable with the final version of the dissertation. In particular, one teacher commented that it was important for him to reread Chapter 5 (analysis of findings) because he felt there were many interesting discussion topics to further analyze. Another teacher did not offer comments in reference to her section of the findings but did state, "Research is just an interpretation of data." When the dissertation was finally submitted with all the participants' feedback, I had mixed feelings. On the one hand, we were able to negotiate the data so much so that the majority (4 out of 5) felt comfortable with the final version. However, I felt extremely bad that one of the participants didn't even want to look at her section. With her comment to me that "research is just an interpretation of data," I felt like I had done exactly what I had feared the most—succumbed to a Western dominant research paradigm. At that point, all I could do was move forward.

CONCLUSION: *LA ESPERANZA*— THE HOPE IN "FLIPPING THE MIRROR"

Now, ten years later, as I reflect and bring to a close the experience I have affectionately called "The Juncture," I stand ahead of this episode with lessons gained. Physically, I have worked hard to mend the pain I caused and regain the trust my *colegas*. Professionally and even personally, I have learned that it is better to be upfront, clear, and honest from the onset. To hold off because of one's fear will only make things worse. Yet, even with that said, I still find myself "flipping the mirror" and asking, "did I do the right thing?" To this day, I am not sure I did. I grapple with the notion that on the one hand we have to be critical of ourselves to make constructive change—who better than us versus an outsider. And on the other hand, if the latter is my position, why do I still carry a sense of "doubt?" It makes me believe by listening to my spirit and not my mind that I didn't take the right path. Or is the "doubt" not on what emerged but rather the approach I took to share the outcomes? Upon reflection, I know the outcome could have been different if the participants had been invited to engage from the onset. As one can see, I grapple with this, and it goes back and forth.

What I can say for certain is this: If I could go back in time I would share the following thoughts:

> The fear and anxiety one feels with respect to the research conducted is warranted. Within academe, the validity of our research is often problematic—and in our communities, the intentions are often questioned—as they should be. However, in that context, it is critical to have courage—the courage to state the truth of those who have been silenced, the courage to stand up against an institution that challenges your position, and the courage to push and ask those hard questions. Thus, it is important to stay committed to the principles and values that ground a person in who she is and in her work, understanding, nonetheless, that one's principles and values are not static but an ebb and flow—a spiral of realities and experiences that are ever changing—thus the need to always rename, reflect, and create new change. Lastly, I would share that the process of writing a dissertation, though important, is only the beginning of a researcher's journey. As such, learning to negotiate, resist, be honest, and change the spaces we are in will not only reflect our personal struggles, but also our own self-determination—the hope in transformation.

As I bring myself back to the present, it is this process of concientization (Freire, 1970) and "concienticized reflection" that informs how I operate as a tenured professor. Although many questions emerged with the "juncture," many more have materialized within the constructs of a university framework. Those hesitations I experienced as a graduate student come to life every day. It takes all the strength I have inside of me to not be afraid, to not stay silent, and advocate for our Raza students on our campus. Not a day goes by that I do not reflect on what I teach, what I write, a statement I might have made in a committee meeting, a reaction I might have had, a decision I might have made, and what effect it might have. That, in and of itself, is overwhelming. Thus the question to pose is this: How do we work ourselves through those moments? I do not believe there is one fixed answer. Of course there would not be. However, one thing that I can be certain about now is that I am not alone. It is in those moments of hesitation that I look to my *colegas* to question me, to challenge my actions and my words, to process with me what I am experiencing, and to keep me grounded. Moreover, it is in those moments of hesitation that I ask my *colegas* to work with me, even in those uncomfortable spaces, so that we may all move forward as a *colectiva* (collective).

Towards the beginning of the conclusion I stated that I was bringing this experience to a close. In reality, I do not think it is a chapter in my life that I will ever forget, so it is not closed. However, I can bring closure to the "juncture" and build on the lessons gained to move forward in the work we all do in solidarity with one another—thus allowing me to find hope *entre los llantos* (in the tears).

REFERENCES

Ada, A. F., & Beutel, C. M. (1993). *Participatory research as a dialogue for social action.* Unpublished manuscript. San Francisco, CA: University of San Francisco.

Berta-Avila, M. (2004). *The cure is in the pain: The pedagogy of Critical Xicana/Xicano educators in the classroom.* Unpublished doctoral dissertation, University of San Francisco, San Francisco.

Blackmer Reyes, K., & Curry Rodriguez, J. (2012). Testimonio: Origin, terms and resources. *Equity and Excellence in Education, 45*(3), 525–538. DOI:10.1080/10665684.2012.698571.

Ek, L. D., Quijada Cerecer, P. D., Alanis, I., & Rodriguez, M. A. (2010). "I don't belong here": Chicanas/Latinas at a Hispanic serving institution creating community through muerista mentoring. *Equity & Excellence in Education, 43*(4), 539–533.

Freire, P. (1970). *Pedagogy of the oppressed* (M. B. Ramos, Trans.). New York, NY: Continuum.

Reza, J. V. (1995). *Leading through our tears: The voice of Latina leadership, a participatory research.* Unpublished doctoral dissertation, University of San Francisco, San Francisco, CA.

Segura, D. (2003). Navigating between two worlds: The labyrinth of Chicana intellectual production in the academy. *Journal of Black Studies, 34*(1), 28–51.

CHAPTER 23

RECLAIMING MY VOICE AND FINDING A BALANCE IN ACADEMIA

A Journey Towards Advocacy

Angelica M. Tello
The University of Texas at San Antonio

Using my voice to advocate for the needs of diverse clients led me to pursue a doctoral degree in counselor education. However, early in my doctoral studies I began to feel isolated from family, friends, and my cultural community. Additionally, it was discouraging not seeing faculty members and leaders in the profession who I could relate to culturally. In counselor education, there is a focus on diversity and multicultural counseling (CACREP, 2009), but there is a lack of faculty members and leaders in the profession who come from diverse ethnic backgrounds. Specifically, Latina/o scholars in counselor education tend to be an underrepresented group. As a Mexican American woman from a low socioeconomic background, I bring a much-needed voice to the field of counselor education. This became my drive for entering academia. I knew that attaining a PhD could help me

Abriendo Puertas, Cerrando Heridas (Opening Doors, Closing Wounds), pages 235–244
Copyright © 2015 by Information Age Publishing
All rights of reproduction in any form reserved.

advocate for the needs of my community on a different level. Even though I had this awareness, after starting my doctoral program I began to question my sense of belonging to the academy.

Finding a work–life balance that incorporated my personal life (i.e., my family) and academic life (i.e., my doctoral studies) seemed impossible. I began to question if the sacrifice of attaining a PhD was worth being pinned between two separate worlds: the world of my upbringing and the world of academia. As a first-generation college student, these feelings were neither new nor unique to me. Living in between two separate worlds has been described by other first-generation college graduates who are now completing doctoral degrees (Gardner & Holley, 2011). Additionally, there were past experiences of microaggressions, oppression, and marginalization that I carried with me into my role as a doctoral student. I knew similar experiences would emerge, and it was difficult to fully bring up my concerns. At times it was challenging to find the right words to describe my experiences because I was in the midst of processing my feelings around the transition into academia. I also felt a sense of vulnerability because discussing my experiences meant potentially opening up the past wounds created by societal and institutional oppressions and marginalization. As a result of this internal struggle, I felt my voice silenced.

At this point in my career, a work–life balance means feeling culturally congruent in both my personal life and academic life. Even though I entered my doctoral program in my mid-twenties, single with no children, I still struggled with a finding my work–life balance. My parents and siblings are an important part of my personal life. I was also raised with cultural messages around being present and supporting family. Since I was the first person in my family to graduate high school and college, my family relied on me for social and cultural capital of navigating higher education and other areas, such as healthcare. Especially after my parents' divorce, I became the third parent in helping to raise my younger siblings. I was a constant force in helping to address my family's needs. Early into my doctoral program, I was being pulled away from my family, and I experienced guilt for not being consistently present.

As I dove deeper into the academic world, I felt more disconnected from my cultural upbringing. I was gaining positional power through my education, and this was new for me to navigate. I became interested in searching for answers on how a work–life balance is achieved in the academy, in particular how I could feel culturally congruent in both my personal life and academic life. However, I felt overwhelmed by the process and did not know where to turn for answers. My life experiences seemed very different from those in my doctoral cohort and the faculty members at my university. My feelings of cultural incongruence were constantly on my mind, and I knew that in order for me to be successful in academia a balance was needed.

During the second semester of my doctoral studies, a space was created in my advanced multicultural counseling course where I could explore my cultural identities, such as ethnicity, gender, and class. Through my reflections in the course, I remember that as an undergraduate student I had similar feelings of isolation as I was striving for a balance between the personal and academic sides of my life. In my journey as an undergraduate, discovering my voice was my first step in finding a balance. This drove me to explore my cultural identities, so I completed a few courses in Mexican American studies. Through reading the works of Mexican American and Chicana scholars, I began to strengthen my voice. These experiences led to lessons that helped me to successfully transition to college and attend graduate school. Furthermore, I was also able to pass down *consejos* (advice) to family and community members to assist them in gaining access to and understanding of the academic world. This chapter will present my *testimonio* (testimony) of navigating higher education as a Mexican American first-generation college students and my journey towards reclaiming my voice in academia. Developing my voice as a social justice advocate has helped me to find a work–life balance.

FINDING A BALANCE

I share the following *testimonio* because the event I describe below played a monumental role in shaping my interest in joining the academic world. This *testimonio* was also one of the memories that stood out to me when I was reflecting on my experiences in the advanced multicultural counseling course. I know my *testimonio* does not have all the answers on how to develop a work–life balance, but I hope that it resonates in a way that sparks others' own self-reflection and self-discovery.

Discovering My Voice

The day I learned the power of my voice I was sitting in a lecture hall filled with a few hundred students. I was a second-semester freshman trying to recover from my first semester. The transition from high school to college was overwhelming. As the first person in my family to graduate from high school and attend college, I felt out of place at my university. I attended a predominately White research institution, and I did not feel I belonged. Even though I grew up in a community that was only about a 10-minute drive from the university, when I stepped on campus I felt I was entering a new world. The lack of diversity on my campus was something that struck me from day one as an undergraduate student. I grew up in a low-income community that was impacted by poverty, and everyone in my community has had similar life experiences. However, many students on campus did not face the same economic hardships as my family and community. As a result of my first semester experiences in college, I contemplated dropping out, but I decided to stay another semester.

I carried these experiences with me as I sat in the lecture hall. The previous week in the American Studies course we discussed the history of urban sprawl in the United States. Many students shared their experiences of living in suburban neighborhoods and gated communities. The week I learned the power of my voice, we were having a discussion on inner city communities. We read *Manchild in the Promised Land* (Brown, 1965), an autobiographical novel that tells the author's coming of age in Harlem during the 1940s and 1950s. A prominent theme in the novel is the author's experiences of growing up in poverty. In our class discussions regarding the novel, many students could not relate to the author's story. Some students described how they felt the book was outdated and poverty was not an issue in our society anymore. As I sat in the lecture hall, I realized I had to speak up. Across the highway that divided my community with the university's community, poverty was still present and had a direct impact on the lives of many individuals.

I raised my hand slowly and waited to be called on by the professor teaching the course. I could feel my heart pounding in my chest and was afraid my voice would shake. Speaking up was something that filled me with great fear. Growing up poor and Mexican American, I received direct and indirect societal messages that my voice did not matter. Therefore, I would stay silent and tried not to stand out. However, in class that day I could not stay silent. Even though I was going to be placed in a vulnerable position by sharing my personal experiences, my peers in the course needed to know that poverty still exists in our society. When I was called on by the professor, I shared how every day I went home to a community that was impacted by poverty. As I was talking, I looked over to the professor, and there was something about his presence that made me feel validated. The comments he made afterwards supported my voice, and I felt empowered.

I learned that my voice was powerful, and it could be used to advocate for change. I saw firsthand the injustices that were present in my community because of the class and racial inequalities that are a part of our society. From my experience in the American Studies course, I realized that I could use my voice to help bring awareness to these inequalities. However, my experience of discovering my voice was only the first step in finding a balance between my cultural upbringing (i.e., my personal life) and the culture of college (i.e., my academic life). After that semester, I began searching for courses that would help create this balance.

In order to support my voice, I was on a quest to find my place on campus. I was looking for a space where I could bridge my personal life with my new journey and work in higher education. I noticed there were courses offered in Mexican American Studies, so I decided to enroll in a few of them. I found a connection and support system with the faculty members teaching the courses and peers I interacted with in the classroom. I also found comfort in the words of Mexican American and Chicana scholars such as Gloria Anzaldúa, Cherríe Moraga, and Sandra Cisneros (e.g., Anzaldúa, 1987; Cisneros, 1991; Moraga & Anzaldúa, 1981). Their work resonated with me; they were women whom I could relate to culturally. I saw how they used their voices to advocate for change in our society. In addition, they created a space where they defined their own identities; they defined their lives. I learned, through their work, that I could do the same.

Early in my college transition, there were various stereotypes, assumptions, and expectations that were placed upon me. I had some professors who were surprised that I could write well. On several occasions, I was asked to explain how I was able to "make it" because other Latinas/os did not take education seriously. I also faced direct and indirect messages from other students that I was only accepted at my university to fill diversity standards. All the messages I received made me feel like an outsider at my own university. However, my experiences in my Mexican American and Chicana studies courses helped me to realize that these judgments did not define me. Before this time in my undergraduate studies, I believed the societal narratives that were created to describe my experiences, and I believed them as truth. Through my undergraduate journey, I learned that I am in control of defining my voice and identities. I was inspired to advocate for people whose voices had been silenced. I specifically saw the world of academia as an avenue for advocacy, and this was my driving force for entering graduate school in the field of counselor education.

RECLAIMING MY VOICE

I shared this *testimonio* in the advanced multicultural counseling course. Even though it was still difficult to share my personal experiences, I felt supported by the faculty member leading the course and my doctoral cohort. I was able to tap into a personal place where I could begin to find answers on how to develop a work–life balance in the academy (i.e., feeling culturally congruent in both my personal life and academic life). In order to support my success as a doctoral student and future counselor educator, I had to reclaim my voice and no longer allow myself to struggle in silence. Work-life balance involved (1) understanding my voice, (2) supporting my voice, and (3) taking care of my voice.

Understanding My Voice

The most important lesson I learned from my undergraduate experiences was that I define my own voice and journey. Now as part of the academic word, I realize that I am the one who creates my own work–life balance. Although I had an awareness of this, there are various forces in the academic environment that can sometimes consume one's personal life. I also felt a personal pressure to conform to an ideal view of a work–life balance, and this was eventually harmful for me. I did not feel I could live up to the ideal, and it created a space where self-doubts emerged.

Early in my doctoral studies, there was an emphasis placed on academic writing and publishing. Every time I sat down to work on a manuscript for publication, I felt completely overwhelmed. I wanted my academic work to be pristine in order to show I belonged to the academy. I carried past experiences of academic stereotypes and assumptions, and I did not want my work to be discredited. Therefore, I solely focused on the academic side of my life. Not only did I feel a personal pressure to excel in my doctoral classes to combat the negative stereotypes, but I was also publishing, presenting at conferences, and providing service to the profession. As a result, my academic work was creating an isolating space and a separation from family, friends, and my cultural community. This led me to fell culturally incongruent and out of place in academia. Immense guilt began to build, because I did not have a harmonious work–life balance. Then self-doubt crept into my mind as I questioned if academia was the right place for a Mexican American woman from a low-income background; I wondered if I would ever feel a balanced between my personal life and my academic life. A part of reclaiming my voice was realizing that my work–life balance might not always look the same as my doctoral cohort members and future colleagues, and this is okay. My balance involves feeling connected to both my home and academic communities. I know these experiences are not unique to me, and other Latina/o students have reported similar feelings in college settings. According to Hurtado and Carter (1997), Latina/o college students attending predominately White universities described that "feeling at 'home' in the campus community is associated with maintaining interactions both within and outside the college community" (p. 338).

My life experiences and the cultural expectations from my family are often quite different than most of the individuals I am surrounded by in academia. There are times when the needs of my family have to come before my academic work. My parents and the community I call home are still struggling economically. I have always taken an active role in a being a source of support for my family. Therefore, my personal life still involves navigating places that are impacted by poverty. Although my family is an important part of my personal life, I can experience stressors from my academic work that pull me away from directly helping my family and community. However, there are times when I need to devote myself to my academic work in order to advance in the profession. Beyond my doctoral course work, there are academic expectations of assisting with research, teaching, and service. There are sometimes hard deadlines in the academic world that require me to tilt more focus in this area. When I think about this unbalanced rhythm that can be created, I am reminded of my undergraduate experiences where I learned that I define who I am and the journey I will take. As an academic, I am choosing to contribute to work that will allow to use my voice to bring awareness of the needs of individuals living in poverty or economically disadvantaged communities. Even when I need to be consumed in my work, because it is my reality at times, I am still able to help those in my family and community.

Supporting My Voice

Another lesson I gained from my undergraduate experiences was the importance of reaching out for support. The academic journey can be isolating, and this was not sitting well with me, which added to my feelings of cultural incongruence. When I began struggling with work–life balance in my doctoral program, I was searching for a support system. I began to look within my doctoral program for mentors and support systems. I reached out to faculty members in my program with whom I felt comfortable sharing my experiences, and they could offer me social and cultural capital support in navigating the academic world. These faculty members eventually become my dissertation chair and committee. I knew that finding a support system on my campus was crucial to my success in the doctoral program. Although these faculty members do not have the same life experiences, they took time to listen to my needs, which helped to validate my experiences. They also recognized when I experienced self-doubts and supported my voice during times it was not as strong. Moreover, they provided me with positive examples of how I would like to mentor students when I became a faculty member.

Although I had this support in my doctoral program, I was still searching for academic spaces where I could connect to other doctoral students and faculty members who were openly discussing their minority cultural identities and navigating academia. Through a counseling newsletter, I discovered the NBCC Minority Fellowship Program (NBCC Foundation, n.d.), a fellowship opportunity for minority doctoral students in counselor education who have commitments to serving underserved populations. The fellowship is administered by the NBCC Foundation, an affiliate of the National Board for Certified Counselors, Inc. (NBCC). The fellowship program is funded by a grant awarded to NBCC by the Substance Abuse and Mental Health Services Administration (SAMHSA) (NBCC Foundation, n.d.). I applied and was awarded the fellowship, which offered financial support, professional trainings, and mentorship. Furthermore, the fellowship program is helping to address the lack of diversity of ethnic minority faculty members in counselor education. Through the fellowship opportunity, I was able to connect with other doctoral students and faculty members who had similar life experiences and faced similar work–life stressors. I also made connections with other Latina/o doctoral students and faculty members in counselor education, which helped me feel less alone. A sense of community was developed with the other fellowship recipients and faculty members involved in the program.

I also found support through connections made at conferences in the counseling profession. Particularly, I have been able to connect with others scholars who have an interest in speaking about issues related to diversity, social justice, and advocacy. In these circles, my voice is supported, and I receive comfort in knowing that I was not alone in the academy. Moreover, I am able to see how other professionals in the field of counselor education have found a work–life balance by using their voices as social justice advocates. Receiving several conference acceptance letters has also given me a sense of empowerment and validation; knowing that other professionals feel my topics warrant discussion creates evidence that counters the self-doubts that emerge when I am solely immersed in my academic work.

Although I still feel a great deal of nervousness when presenting at a conference (I still feel my heart pounding in my chest), it gives me an opportunity to share my voice. In my presentations, I have brought an awareness of the diverse needs of students who come from economically disadvantaged communities. The dialogue that is created during my presentations with audience members helps me feel connected to the academic community. When presenting at conferences, I am able to create a space where I feel culturally congruent. I am able to be myself and tap into my drive for pursuing a career in academia.

Taking Care of My Voice

A final lesson I took away from my undergraduate experiences was to take care of my voice. When I am feeling stressed and overwhelmed, taking a step back to gain perspective helps me move towards a work–life balance. In counselor education, self-care is a topic that is often discussed. Many counselors and counselor educators have a difficult time taking care of their personal selves. The profession also does not openly discuss the additional stressors doctoral studies and faculty members who hold minority cultural identities may experience, such as feelings of isolation. As I have progressed through my doctoral studies, I have reached out to other doctoral students of color, and we have had open discussions regarding self-care and our cultural identities. The topics discussed range from coping with feelings of cultural incongruence to addressing microaggression in academia. In these interactions, mutual growth and learning has occurred. I always leave these discussions feeling validated, empowered, and recharged. In my transition to junior faculty member, I plan to continue creating spaces where self-care involves cultural introspection and growth.

In my doctoral studies, I felt the academic world was consuming all aspects of my life, and I thought this was the only way to be successful. I was getting burned out because I felt I had to prove my place in academia. I was working hard to disprove the stereotype that the only reason for my success in academia was to satisfy a quota to meet diversity standards. This was a societal message I carried with me, and it constantly led me to question my potential in academia. By understanding my work–life needs, reaching out for support, and incorporating self-care practices, I was able reclaim my voice, combat the stereotypes placed upon me, and gain a sense of balance within myself. I am now able to recognize that my presence and voice bring a much-needed change to the academic world. I also found that surrounding myself with peers, colleagues, and mentors who offer positive support helps me gain perspective. These are individuals I can go to when I begin feeling overwhelmed. I know they will listen to my worries and provide comfort in their presence. A simple nod and reflective comment can go a long way in providing personal validation, which sometimes takes me back to the day I discovered my voice.

CONCLUSION

I found many parallels in my experience as an undergraduate and my pursuit of a work–life balance in academia. In both these experiences, I struggled with the transition in terms of finding my sense of balance. However, the constant stressors of being in a doctoral program led me away from what I learned as an undergraduate. I did not take care of my voice and allowed it to get lost in all my academic work and responsibilities. The academic world can be all-consuming at times, so I have to make a conscious effort in creating a balance. From my experiences so far, I have learned that I am in control of what my personal and work–life balance looks like. There are times it might seem unbalanced to outside observers; there are times when my personal life takes priority over work, and vice versa. It is easy to fall into a trap where one feels guilty over not having a balance that appears equal or harmonious.

In the current place I stand in my academic journey, I realize that being a social justice advocate is part of my personal identity. Using my academic work to bring an awareness of societal injustices and inequalities helps me feel like myself in academia. I am utilizing platforms that will allow me to use my voice, such as writing my *testimonio* and sharing the lessons I have learned in my academic journey. My passion for advocacy is helping me to stay connected to my upbringing while guiding me in the world of academia. Through my voice, I am creating positive change for myself, my community, and the academy.

REFERENCES

Anzaldúa, G. E. (1987). *Borderlands/La frontera: The new mestiza.* San Francisco, CA: Aunt Lute.

Cisneros, S. (1991). *Woman hollering creek and other stories.* New York, NY: Random House.

Brown, C. (1965). *Manchild in the promised land.* New York, NY: Signet.

Council for Accreditation of Counseling and Related Educational Programs (CACREP). (2009). *2009 standards.* Retrieved from http://www.cacrep.org/doc/2009%20Standards%20 with%20cover.pdfGardner, S. K., & Holley, K. A. (2011). "Those invisible barriers are real": The progression of first-generation student through doctoral education. *Equity and Excellence in Education, 44*(1), 77–92. doi: 10.1080/10665684.2011.5297.

Hurtado, S., & Carter, D. F. (1997). Effects of college transition and perceptions of the campus racial climate in Latino college students' sense of belonging. *Sociology of Education, 70*(4), 324–345.

Moraga, C. L., & Anzaldúa, G. E. (Eds.). (1981). *This bridge called my back: Writings by radical women of color.* Watertown, MA: Persephone Press.

NBCC Foundation. (n.d.). *NBCC Minority Fellowship Program.* Retrieved from http://www.nbccf.org/mfp

CHAPTER 24

LATINA/O LEADERS IN ESPACIOS DE CONFIANZA

Creating Spaces Where Cultural Capital and Community Wealth Permeate

Fernando Valle, Sylvia Méndez-Morse, and Irma Almager
Texas Tech University

Hortensia "Meg" Cota
University of Arizona

INTRODUCTION

Maintaining a work–life balance in the academy is a constant struggle. This is especially true for Latina/o graduate or doctoral students, professors, and administrators. The authors of this chapter represent various stages of Latina/o educational leaders in the public school and higher education pipeline. We succeed and persist in predominantly White institutions (PWIs) and filter our scholarship through critical paradigms and lenses. We know this is second nature to us. The scholarship and academic work we advance is focused on the positive aspects which come from the intersection

Abriendo Puertas, Cerrando Heridas (Opening Doors, Closing Wounds), pages 245–256
Copyright © 2015 by Information Age Publishing
All rights of reproduction in any form reserved.

of culture and Latina/o leadership; it is framed by strengths-based practices rather than deficit-based thinking in educational leadership. Yosso's (2005) community cultural wealth framework and Santamaría and Santamaría's (2012) applied critical leadership represent two examples of Latina/o leadership and community assets and strengths that inspire our continued work in the field. For example, during our conversations about writing this chapter, we were frequently able to identify specific experiences as familial capital or linguistic capital as well as the other capitals in Yosso's framework. We use these frameworks as essential conceptual frameworks and components for the effective preparation of public school and higher education leaders. These works provide reflective spaces to grow and confirm the need for Latina/o leadership frameworks.

We acknowledge we are often the "lonely only" in a group, class, or department but find ways to collaborate, share, and carve out genuine spaces of trust in order to survive and thrive in academic spaces. As educational leaders, we purposely seek to establish spaces of scholarly and cultural interactions based on our experiences as Latina/o scholars—who strongly identify as Latina and Latino in the academy.

As Latina/o educational leaders, we contend that our identities are fluid and our gender, ethnicity, and *cultura* both inform and ground our spheres of leadership. Spaces of cultural confidence are not easily found in PWIs. For us, they are discourse spaces for our counter narratives concerning Latina/o leadership and its absence in the field. Our *pláticas* about Latina/o leaders drive us to carve out *espacios de confianza* where identity and cultural wealth permeate and connections beyond academia are made.

The authors conferenced weekly over a four-month period. In this space, we examined relationships between Latina/o faculty and allies, the work of Latina/o scholars in the academy, our work realities, and existing as Latina/os in PWIs as we described our work–life balance efforts. Participating in this personal, professional, and academic discourse created a powerful multidimensional cultural space. It provided us with academic wealth as well as recognition of our various forms of resistance and disruptions to the status quo found in PWIs and higher education.

We shared struggles from the field. We laughed, enjoyed each other's worldviews as we mentioned *dichos*, and gave examples of *amor, cultura, trabajo, música, éxito, comida, y familia* as symbols of importance and meaning in our scholarship space. Our own *espacios* were formed by our commonalities as first-generation leaders and experiences as Latinas/os. Through our conference calls and shared space, we created our own *espacios de confianza.* We were breathing life into our research. Through this work we have come to define *espacios de confianza* as culturally infused spaces that are not on the periphery of our academic work but rather accepted, central, and valued as integral parts of being Latina/o educational leaders.

LATINA/O LEADERS EXPERIENCIAS Y TESTIMONIOS

Fernando's Espacio

As a child I rode in the back of a truck from the Rio Grande Valley to areas of West Texas as part of a migrant family. My father worked relentlessly to move our *familia* forward economically. Hundreds of Latina/o families were the migrant and immigrant hired hands needed to reap the White ranchers' crops of West Texas. As immigrants from Mexico, my parents gave up their lives to build us new ones in America. *Ánimo al cuadro*! My father would raise his arm and encourage the families who worked late hours in the hot sun tending the fields. My father was a natural leader, and he kept us together as a family. We saved money and built our family from migrant work and started a roofing company as the family business. On construction sites, my father was owner, worker, and leader, and more importantly, he modeled an inspiring work ethic. He created *espacios de confianza* for us as a family. We grew the family business. Our parents knew the value of their sacrifice and pushed us to explore higher education options for our future as first-generation children.

I graduated from high school, and my *familia's* relentless work ethic was my model to succeed. I was lost in college as a first-generation student. I persisted and kept taking classes. I transferred to UTSA in San Antonio, and my parents encouraged my growth. I worked my way through college and learned that not every Latina/o was proud to speak Spanish or wanted a part of their *cultura.*

My mother was an elementary teacher in Mexico. Her love for learning and culture influenced my cultural growth as she gave up her career and former life to ensure that we succeeded. Her knowledge inspired me to finish college, and my father's unconditional support made it possible.

As a new teacher, I bonded with my middle school students as we were all part of the community and shared cultural norms and cultural spaces. I was encouraged to pursue a leadership position by my principal. I taught and continued my education, earning two master's degrees, one in counseling and another in educational leadership. This led me to situations where I was face-to-face with deficit and exclusionary practices prevalent in Latina/o filled schools. It was a challenge to go against political and community norms surrounding high school practices. Finding teachers, counselors, and other principals who helped at-risk students and found opportunities for the undocumented was my first taste of advocacy as an educational leader. It balanced my career and my life. As advocates, we worked underground and around the system. As *colegas,* we were subversive but truly passionate about the lives and learning of Latina/o students who fell through the cracks of the education system. This was an *espacio de confianza* in my public school career that allowed me to grow as a critical and transformative educational leader and empower Latina/o students to move past drop-out life and being considered a statistic—just a number on a form.

My *espacios de confianza* continued to grow as a doctoral in the Rio Grande Valley, taking advantage of the relationships made in spaces like University Council for Educational Administration (UCEA), American Educational Research Association (AERA), Jackson & Clark Scholars, American Association of Hispanics in Higher Education (AAHHE) Fellows, and Latina/o SIGS, which allowed me to network with other Latina/o leaders across the country. It was fulfilling to build cultural capital and use collective community wealth toward Latina/o identity in academia.

Moving into the professoriate as an educational leader was a life-changing opportunity. I quickly learned the professoriate was modeled after White male leaders, White privilege, and upper middle-class values—a paradigm that I had no experience in and that did not influence the way I taught or led schools. I found this paradigm of White privilege was challenged by my Anglo colleagues as offensive or deficit when brought up. The reality was, *their* experience mattered. My experience, like those of so many Latina/os, became counter-narratives and were part of the periphery.

My first year in the academy was one of second-guessing my abilities and defending my culture as not only a valid academic lens in leadership, but an important lens to teach and empower the next generation of leaders who work with English language learners (ELLs) and Latina/o students in our schools. My *espacios de confianza* continue to strengthen as a new *profe,* as I write with and engage with Latina/o colleagues and allies at various institutions, who promote a vision of equity and space for Latina/o leadership. *Nuestros espacios* allow us to engage in the fluidity of our identities as Latinas/os, as Latina/o faculty in the academy, and to carve a space for the paradigms that continue to impact our scholarship and leadership.

Sylvia's Espacio

Most of my life I have been more of a reluctant leader—rather than someone who sought such a role. I think this came from appearing like I knew what I was doing. I believe this came from being a read-aholic, since I first learned to read in English. I am addicted to reading—anything. I have always wanted to know more and explore things, and frequently, I tried to use what I was learning from books. Perhaps that was my forming those beginning *espacios de confianza* because there was a sense of trust in thinking that others already knew, and I could learn from them. However, what was missing was human contact.

I found that connection in the *pláticas* my *tias, abulela, y mami* always had while preparing food for lunch or dinner, while working together to get the decorations made for the wedding reception, or while at the sewing machines making our *piyamas*. Since I was the oldest grandchild and my *tia* Laura was only four years older than me, I was always her shadow. If she was recruited to peel the *papas*, I was peeling *papas*. All that work was done in a group of women, and they always talked about how to do the job best. Of course there was gossip and jokes and making fun of how someone held the *papa* the wrong way. But in that space, in that *espacio*, I was part of a group getting something done. I was gaining knowledge on how to do something. I was part of a community. And I was safe.

Unfortunately, finding *espacios de confianza* in the White world was/is very difficult, but again, it was with my *familia—mis primas*—that it appeared. I found it with my cousin *Bebe* in junior high, letting me (a lowly 7th grader) stand with her and her friends (savvy 9th graders) while waiting for school to start. As an undergrad, it was harder, since I was the first in my family to go to college. My *familia's* guidance was to drop me off in front of the community college campus and being told, *"Vete por allí. Aquí te levanto a las 3."* I decided to explore and try to figure out what to do. It was at this time that I had to expand my definition of "*familia*" to include other people who either looked like me or wanted to do the same thing. I connected with them in classes, at the student union building (SUB) between classes, or student centers.

When finally moving away from home and into the dorm, I reached out to the other Latinas there and realized that we had many things in common. The main characteristic we shared was that we were the first in our *familias* to go to college or at least the first girl to go to college, and we all chose this dorm because it was the cheapest. So my *espacios* became more than just sharing how to prepare for the world literature test, but more about how our cultural traditions were similar with slight differences. We learned that we shared a native language with people who were not in our *familia* per se, and realized we were/are part of a bigger *familia*, a community with common traditions and attributes but also different from the white majority. What would I have done without those early *espacios de confianza* that we had in the dorm without even knowing what they were? I don't really know, but I know that what I gained from being with those women was a sense of belonging at a university, an appreciation for my own intelligence because I was with all these other intelligent Latinas, and confidence in my abilities to be successful there. But more importantly, I *knew* that I was merely one of many other Latinas who were proud of being bilingual and being Mexican American or Chicanas.

As I progressed in my professional life, I continued to seek, find, and construct *espacios de confianza*. Perhaps more importantly I have recognized how vital *espacios de confianza*—these spaces of trust—are to my mental and emotional health and professional growth. During all these years I learned that others are also searching for a safe space where we can be themselves—with our *cultura* and language. I learned how others also created their *espacios de confianza* by watching how they prepared for critical events. For example, while at IDRA (Intercultural Development Research Association), I realized that our primary leaders practiced their arguments in teams, had dress rehearsals of presentations to federal judges, and did everything and anything it took to accomplish their goals. I learned from them that when challenging deeply entrenched discriminatory practices, there is no such thing as over-preparation, and that there is no shame in asking for help.

I try to remember that—but it is difficult when I am the "lonely only." Now I reach out to other "lonely only" Latinas/os first. I go sit next to them and initiate a conversation. As a professor or colleague, I introduced myself to the class or group saying my name in Spanish. I pronounce Latinas/os' names in Spanish. I find it interesting how nearly all Latinas/os smile in appreciation for this. These are easy actions to take, but nonetheless important, because they model respect for our language and culture. It is a beginning step toward creating a safe space and letting others know that they are not alone in the academy.

I think I was very fortunate to know from a young age that *espacios de confianza* did exist, if only within my immediate *familia.* I am grateful that somehow I found or created similar safe spaces as an undergraduate. Those incidents of overt discrimination, such as being told directly, "Oh, you're a token" when I introduced myself, became an indication about how some would view me. More importantly, similar events motivated me to study more, write more, and share my data with others. I am certain that those experiences and lessons of finding or creating an *espacios de confianza* stayed with me in my professional career and contributed to my success.

Unos consejos: If you're trying to survive and thrive in places where you find yourselves as the only Latina/o, or just one of the few, reach out to others. Embrace your culture, your *familia, tradiciones, y tu idioma.* These attributes are foundational. Whether you are part of department or campus or doctoral cohort, you can change the culture of it. It's not easy but it can be done. Never forget that your mere presence in a group that doesn't have anyone else that's like you—where you are the only Latina or Latino—is extremely significant. There is power in your presence in that group. Cultivate allies and comrades, and *compadres y comadres* who will help you re-energize, bandage your wounds, read your first drafts, or listen to your story.

Irma's Espacio

My intent as a teacher was to impact student achievement. The goal was to be an effective educator, and I constantly assessed my teaching, which I based on my students' learning. In addition to becoming an effective teacher, I also recognized the inequity and injustice towards students in my school and district. Growing up in a small town with racism and discrimination in our schools, I was driven to create an environment that provided equality and justice for my bilingual students. The timing was right as I got involved in a movement against some local school board members who wanted to eliminate bilingual education (BE).

My courage to speak at a school board meeting as a first-year teacher brought attention from the local organization for BE teachers. The Latina women already working towards educational leadership began to invite me to meetings concerning the situation for students enrolled in BE. This was my first taste of the possibility of leadership. Although I did not consider myself a leader, the influence of local Latina leaders began to inspire the opportunity to expand my role for addressing the inequities and injustices I was observing and experiencing.

The encouragement of these Latina women along with my assistant principal, who was also Latina, led me to the decision to enroll in an educational leadership master's program. Through the continued contact with these new established Latina leaders, I was hired as an assistant principal within 18 hours of my master's degree. Although I was grateful to those who had inspired me, the new path drawn by this group became too controversial, and I felt that the group no longer held the description of what I considered *espacios de confianza*. My departure from the group was not received well, but I had to make the decision. Therefore, upon my first appointment as a principal I created my own group with two other women who were hired at the same time.

Because we were hired together, we experienced those situations that required opportunities to vent with only those trusted few. In order to disrupt the isolation and discrimination we were expecting, we planned our budgets and schedules together and eventually pooled funds for beginning-of-the-year professional development. We confided only in each other, and I had full confidence in their loyalty to our group for confidentiality. This was very important as rumors among campus and central office leaders could be destructive. Two of us were Latinas and the other was African American. This had become my new *espacio de confianza*. I had helped create it based on my own needs and goals. We planned our own paths without feeling pressured to follow what others thought was best. The opportunity to be part of this group transformed me professionally as I became more confident as a leader and a Latina model for others. Eventually we invited other principals as we assessed who would best fit our group. This also brought peace and integrity back into my life as well as less stress from work, and this meant more time to spend with and enjoy family.

Balancing work and family is difficult as school leaders have many responsibilities. As a Latina, both my family and my husband expected that my focus should be on raising my children and taking care of my husband. They did not understand my work load or role and because I wanted to work outside of home, I needed to not forget my duties. Therefore, in order to express loyalty to my own family, I made sure to emphasize the importance of "the home" to my staff, which allowed me to do the same. When I was at work I made it about the students and my staff. When I was at home, full attention was given to my children and my husband. Even if I had to work on my laptop at the soccer or softball fields, I made every effort to spend quality time with my children. Long battery life was important as we traveled on weekends for sports and family. Knowing when to set aside the laptop and accepting that any work not finished today would still be there tomorrow allowed me to focus on what was really important. In the end, both school and home appreciated the time I shared, which is what they mostly valued.

Meg's Espacio

I've often described my childhood as being culturally bipolar. I was a first-generation Latina whose family honored our Mexican roots and held tight to traditions and the language, but the neighborhood I lived in and schools I attended were very Anglo. My family wanted us to "fit in" as much as possible in public, although they constantly instilled in my siblings and me the importance of never forgetting where we came from. Growing up in this manner, superficially "Anglo," in many ways left me disconnected to either culture. I did not know of any other first-generation families in our neighborhood, and I felt alienated from Mexican American families, but I also wasn't really Anglo either. It was difficult to share these identity issues with anyone, and I found I couldn't trust or confide in anyone about this. And truthfully, I don't think at the time I could even articulate the awkwardness of being in two separate worlds and how this impacted how I perceived my own abilities, and how I "fit in."

This identity confusion was present until I was a young adult and I began to find my path as a new teacher in a bilingual classroom. This first teaching assignment was my first real experience with families such as my own. I had the opportunity to see in my students my own childhood. With my colleagues, there were also commonalities with my own upbringing, and I finally felt a circle of support and *confianza* unlike I had ever experienced outside my family. There was a certain amount of empowerment and internal peace that this fostered in me. I found that in having a circle of colleagues to share my story with others who had also experienced doubts and insecurities, and by sharing these fears, we created a support system for each other. It was a safety net—an *espacio de confianza* to support each other personally and professionally. Through this support, I also found that I could better serve my students and families. I found that I could relate to many of their struggles and could also bounce ideas off my colleagues without fear of being judged. In my circle, we all grew to respect each other and recognized how much we cared about what we did as educators and whom we served (our families and communities). We all appreciated each other's efforts to do more and to do it better. The support and acceptance was incredible.

Through these early personal and professional experiences, I found that I could use what I had learned and lived to alleviate some of the negative situations to maximize strengths in my students. I found that as I gathered *confianza* in my own abilities and felt supported, I still had much to contribute beyond the classroom; a leadership role, as a school principal in particular, would be a perfect vehicle for this. I felt I could be a better advocate for students in this role. As an administrator I felt I would be able to influence programs and practices to ensure students, particularly marginalized students, had more opportunities, and I could help empower them. I also hoped to foster in my students and staff the creation of their own trust circles (*espacios de confianza*), through which I could help them maximize (or continue to maximize) the strengths that I believed they all had in them. I had and have hoped that, ultimately, my influence could in some ways help create those spaces and opportunities that have served me so well.

The above description from my early experiences to the present is a very brief recounting of my story. Although it may fail to capture all the joys and pitfalls that occurred at every turn, the lack of details should not detract from the positive impact of my own *espacios de confianza*. By sharing the story of how my circles have impacted my life, I hope that this advice, this *consejo*, may somehow also potentially influence the lives of others. I've highlighted how in my own life, I felt gaps in my identity that caused me to feel lost and out of place, and this resulted in feeling inadequate and even unintelligent at times. It wasn't until I formed and relied on a circle of trust that I began to believe in myself and had a more clear direction of where I wanted to go. I would urge new leaders to look at themselves, look at their experiences and history, and look at those influences that have most impacted their lives positively. In your self-reflection, I would guess that at the heart of these memories, there are individuals involved. These are your *compadres* and *comadres de confianza* who make up and have made up your circles. They can be friends, relatives, loved ones, professional acquaintances, or influential leaders and role models. I would recommend drawing upon why you associate these individuals with your successes and look for ways to continue to develop these same bonds, or use these experiences to create new bonds to support your future goals.

NUESTROS MENSAJES

The Power of Familia

Through the journey of writing this chapter, among our many *pláticas*, the power of family, both the academic and from *sangre*, resonated repeatedly among the four of us. It was through our candid conversations that we each shared snippets of our personal lives that reflected our earliest experiences with *espacios de confianza*: places of acceptance, trust, belonging, and pride. In our narrations, we found many familial commonalities in our histories to include challenges that many non-Latino/a leaders may not have experienced. Among these challenges are the constant negotiations that we must conduct in order to balance our home and work lives due to traditional and cultural roles.

Many of us have not been as supported in our work because our families do not truly understand what we do as educational leaders. We are working in nontraditional roles. Our *cultura* and modern society too often associate rough hands and labor with Latina/o hard work. We have felt we have to defend what we do as hard work, but we also need to defend why our homes are a mess or why we don't make dinner every night. Yet these pressures have not halted our success or broken our ties with family; we honor and value each and work towards balancing these tensions continually. Through laughter, humor, and sharing similarities of growing up in a Latino/a household, we bonded as a writing group over these memories. The more we shared, the safer we felt to share. Our *pláticas* in our newfound *espacio* revealed a strong sense of pride for our *raíces*, our *cultura*, and social and academic connectedness among us. We desire to belong and contribute. Ultimately, we discovered our *familias* are a great source of power. They have influenced our identity and our work ethic, and they have driven and forged our paths. *Nuestras historias* have served as foundational models of the types of *espacios* we wished to create and have created as result of the influence of our family and culture. We recognize and celebrate that *familia y cultura* are a part of us—a strength that cannot be separated from what we do as leaders; it is who we are.

Una Comunidad de Confianza

Among the many aspects resonating with us during our conversations and ruminations about *espacios de confianza* was the repeated theme of *comunidad*, of community. We mentioned it while describing our interactions with our *familia*, both immediate and extended, and the importance that *comunidad* had in nurturing us. We described it while sharing how we found common ground with various colleagues or other doctoral students, and how critical those small niches of community were in helping us to persevere and overcome the strangeness of that unknown culture of academia or school leadership. We claimed it when we acknowledged that our conference calls were where we began to form this little *comunidad* that was brought together for this chapter. We acknowledged that with our *charlas* we had collectively generated a space for us to declare ourselves as creators of our *espacio de confianza* and as empowered educational leaders who had embraced our *cultura* as part of our leadership praxis. We recognized that we had formed many previous communities in order to not only survive the life of an educational leader, but to also thrive in that arena. And perhaps more importantly, we knew that it was our *cultura* itself that prompted us to know the power of *comunidad*.

Identidad y Liderazgo

This scholarship experience further allowed us, as Latina/o educational leaders, to celebrate the importance of our identities in our spheres of educational leadership. We shared and agreed upon influences that shaped our cultural capital as leaders. Powerful aspects, like *familia*, and understanding schooling through critical paradigms and reflecting about our spaces as first-generation Latinas/os with aspirations of college success and brighter futures. These forms of cultural capital and community wealth grounded us and provided *una communidad de confianza*, the academic *familia* so many Latina/os look for—to balance, persist, and succeed in the academy. This especially resonated in our experiences of being a Latina/o leader in PWIs. As leaders we have learned to thrive in complex spaces, and we acknowledged the strategic use of our *espacios de confianza* to create synergistic spaces of scholarship and collegiality.

In addition, the four of us recognized that as Latina/o leaders we held fluid identities. We accomplished this through ongoing interactions and negotiations with other people and groups (Jenkins, 2004). As we made decisions to balance family and work, our identities were modified to accommodate the setting. Foucault (1979) further noted that identity should be fluid and not fixed and saw it as a product of cultural circumstance. In examining our own identities, each of us reflected on the use of our social capital, our own leadership lens, and our community cultural wealth as we joined and created *espacios de confianza* in different spaces within our lives. We believe that other Latinas/os have done the same and argue that these *espacios* are where we also find and claim our cultural *confianza* and our leadership strength and power.

REFERENCES

Foucault, M. (1979). *The history of sexuality* (Vol. 1). Harmondworth, UK: Penguin.

Jenkins, R. (2004). *Social identity* (2nd ed.). London, UK: Routledge.

Santamaría, L. J., & Santamaría, A. P. (2012). *Applied critical leadership in education: Choosing change.* New York, NY: Routledge.

Yosso, T. (2005). Whose culture has capital? A critical race theory discussion of community cultural wealth. *Race, Ethnicity, and Education, 8*(1), 69–91.

EPILOGUE

> It is 4:00 a.m. as I carve out time to write this essay. As a single mother of two, the wee hours of the morning were when I could find the time to do the writing required of me as a graduate student and, later on, as a junior professor...
>
> I find that I am just as busy now as I was then. What was once a coping strategy has become a familiar pattern, and so I spend my early morning hours writing instead of sleeping. Of the sacrifices and compromises I've made to be here, sleep is by far the most insignificant. My children used to say that they heard the tapping of my fingers on the keyboard sometimes as they fell off to sleep and as they awoke.
>
> —Caroline Turner (2004)

As I have personally experienced and through my years of interviewing women and faculty of color about their experiences in the higher education work place, women faculty typically described difficulties inherent in being someone who tries to balance her work roles and her personal life roles outside of the professoriate. Here are a couple of their quotes from *Faculty of Color in Academe: Bittersweet Success* (Turner & Myers, Jr., 2000) that describe being torn between family and career:

> I know that there are lots of values that are indirect, that sometimes get in the way of the careerist profile. Family for example. My family is very important to me. My family is more important to me than my career. That is not the position that will... get one to the top in the conventional academic setting.
>
> We became parents after seventeen years of marriage.... But I underestimated the pull [between family and career] from both sides.

Abriendo Puertas, Cerrando Heridas (Opening Doors, Closing Wounds), pages 257–260
Copyright © 2015 by Information Age Publishing
All rights of reproduction in any form reserved.

Abriendo Puertas, Cerrando Heridas (Opening Doors, Closing Wounds): Latinas/os Finding Work–Life Balance in Academia makes a critical contribution to the literature by highlighting the experiences of men and women as they strive to fulfill their various roles. These *testimonios* are extremely inspirational to all who work in academe, providing insights on how one can remain grounded in his or her person as a whole while pursuing his or her goals. These situations reflect a fine balance that must be achieved to persist in academe. Chesler and Crowfoot (1997) view such situations as being related to power. They ask "to what extent new members of the elite will operate, or be permitted to operate, any differently than their . . . predecessors" (pp. 25–26). As my colleague Barbara Townsend and I (2000) have stated, the increasing diversity of the academy means that more faculty face conflicts of commitment between their work and their family and/or community responsibilities.

In addition to negotiating conflicts between family responsibilities and work demands, faculty of color, in particular, are confronted by their desires to give to their community within a workplace reward system that undervalues such activity. In other words, as well as responsibilities within their immediate family, many faculty of color have political and cultural commitments to advance their racial/ethnic communities. For example, many Chicano faculty "maintain a strong affiliation with their community and feel a strong sense of responsibility to improve the status of other Chicanos in the larger community" (de la Luz Reyes & Halcon, 1988/1996, p. 145; see also Rendon, 1992/1996; Turner & Myers, Jr., 2000). Such commitments are reflected in several of the *testimonios* presented here.

Authors writing for this book acknowledge how they individually address the work–life balance needed in order to remain in academe. The importance of family, community, collaboration, and mentoring are all mentioned as contributing to their persistence and development over the years.

One chapter author encapsulates her strategy for maintaining balance so well, stating that "For now, I still have to say 'no' often in order to keep my sanity, but I am working toward a more holistic approach to 'success,' which includes acknowledging and working with my limitations, recognizing the importance of my feelings, and paying more serious attention to my health."

In addition to individual strategies, it is also important to recognize the work place responsibility for the integration of work and life. A point made by a Fortune 500 executive caught my attention when she urged companies to facilitate the integration of work and life for their employees instead of trying to separate them (www.makers.com/conference). This may promote a more positive and productive work environment. In 2004, the American Association of Colleges and Universities (AAC&U) published an issue of *On Campus With Women* focused on the conflict between academic work and family responsibilities (http://archive.aacu.org/ocww/volume33_2/

index.cfm). The publishers recognized that, despite efforts by academe to provide family-friendly policies, young female faculty still face the dual pressures of tenure and family. Also noted is that men are joining women in calling for such policies so they can address the needs of, for example, their aging parents as well as the needs of their children. While colleges and universities are adopting policies to accommodate faculty needs for maternity, family leave, and childcare, based on the *testimonios* provided in this book, much more institutional work needs to be done to enable faculty to fulfill their work and other commitments while continuing to advance in their chosen careers.

Using the experiences provided by the authors featured in this book, higher education policymakers can gain insight into how they might help to further support the multifaceted life roles these authors must play. Steps to promote such institutional support might include the identification of norms and policies that place faculty at a disadvantage due to family and community commitments and, once identified, promoting the development of new ones that support rather than punish community and family involvement. Such changes will benefit all faculty who take on nurturing and supportive roles in their communities and families.

From these *testimonios*, we learn about and are inspired by the pathways to persistence and success forged by these authors. I applaud the critical contributions the editors and the chapter authors have made and will continue to make, not only to the literature but to those who will learn from the experiences they have so passionately and powerfully shared. As they are bringing themselves through the processes described here, they are also paving the way for others to do so (Turner, 2002).

REFERENCES

Chesler, M. A., & Crowfoot, J. (June 1997). *Racism in higher education II: Challenging racism and promoting multiculturalism in higher education organizations* (CRSO Working Paper Series #558). Ann Arbor, MI: The University of Michigan, Center for Research on Social Organizations.

de la Luz Reyes, M., & Halcon, J. J. (1988/1996). Racism in academia: The old wolf revisited. In C. Turner, M. Garcia, A. Nora, & L. I. Rendon (Eds.), *Racial and ethnic diversity in higher education* (pp. 337–348). Needham Heights, MA: Simon & Schuster Custom Publishing.

Rendon, L. I. (1992/1996). From the barrio to the academy: Revelations of a Mexican American "scholarship girl." In C. Turner, M. Garcia, A. Nora, & L. I. Rendon (Eds.), *Racial and ethnic diversity in higher education* (pp. 281–287). Needham Heights, MA: Simon & Schuster Custom Publishing.

Townsend, B., & Turner, C. (2000, March). *Reshaping the academy to accommodate conflicts of commitment: Then what?* Paper presented at the Shaping a National Agenda for Women in Higher Education conference. Minneapolis, MN.

Turner, C. S. (2002). Women of color in academe: Living with multiple marginality. *Journal of Higher Education, 73*(1), 74–93.

Turner, C. S. (2004). Writing instead of sleeping: Conflicts of commitment. Retrieved from http://archive.aacu.org/ocww/volume33_2/index.cfm http://

Turner, C. S., & Myers, Jr., S. L. (2000). *Faculty of color in academe: Bittersweet success.* Needham Heights, MA: Allyn & Bacon.

ABOUT THE CONTRIBUTORS

Vonzell Agosto, PhD is an assistant professor at the University of South Florida in the Department of Leadership, Counseling, Adult, Career, and Higher Education. Her research program focuses on the intersections of curriculum, leadership, and anti-oppressive education in the preparation or practice of educators and school administrators. She has published her scholarship in journals such as *Teachers College Record, Journal of School Leadership, Journal of Research on Leadership Education,* and *Race Ethnicity and Education.*

Israel Aguilar, PhD is an assistant professor of Educational Leadership in the department of Educational Leadership & Curriculum and Instruction at Texas A&M University–Corpus Christi. Aguilar has experience as a former school administrator and teacher in large urban school districts. He currently researches social justice issues.

Irma L. Almager is the i3 Program Coordinator and an Educational Leadership Adjunct Professor at Texas Tech University. Irma's research interests are in the educational achievement of Mexican American students including teachers' perceptions. As part of a research team Irma is currently working on how instructional coaching impacts classroom instruction and

Abriendo Puertas, Cerrando Heridas (Opening Doors, Closing Wounds), pages 261–276
Copyright © 2015 by Information Age Publishing
All rights of reproduction in any form reserved.

student achievement. She has fifteen years of experience in public school with five years in the classroom and ten in campus administration.

María D. Avalos, PhD, LPC is originally from Seguin, Texas. A first generation college student, she holds a Bachelor's degree in Psychology and Masters in Education. She obtained her PhD in Educational Psychology from the University of Texas at Austin specializing in Human Development and Education. Maria has a diverse experience working in academia where she has served as a university professor, associate dean of student life and assistant provost. Maria is an Assistant Professor in the Counseling Education program at the University of Texas of the Permian Basin and is a Licensed Professional Counselor and Supervisor. Maria continues to conduct research and developed programs serving the needs of academically at-risk and marginalized students.

Danielle Alsandor, PhD serves as an assistant professor at Louisiana State University educating current and aspiring student affairs professionals on competencies and skills needed to provide effective services to diverse student populations. She earned her PhD and MEd in Higher Education Administration from The University of Texas at Austin. A proud Louisiana native, Alsandor completed her undergraduate degree in Mass Communications from the University of Louisiana at Lafayette. Her research interests are focused on understanding the experiences of diverse college populations and identifying ways higher education institutions can enhance student success (e.g., access, recruitment, enrollment, retention, and completion).

Margarita Ines Berta-Avila is an associate professor in the College of Education at Sacramento State University. She received her doctorate in International and Multicultural Education in the School of Education at the University of San Francisco. Dr. Berta-Avila is active in testifying at the Capitol and/or other venues with respect to access and equity in education for English Language Learners, students of color, and/or other marginalized communities. In addition, Dr. Berta-Avila pursues her scholarly work within the areas of bilingual education/English Language learners, critical pedagogy/multicultural/social justice education, Chicana/o educators in the field, qualitative research, and language usage. In collaboration with Dr. Julie Figueroa and Dr. Anita Tijerina-Revilla an edited volume titled *Marching Students: Chicana/o Activism in Education, 1968 to the Present* was released in the spring of 2011.

Mónica Byrne-Jiménez, EdD is an Associate Professor of Educational and Policy Leadership in the School of Education at Hofstra University. Her research focuses on Latina/o identity and school leadership, the role of faculty diversity on doctoral student experiences, and effectiveness of a special education leader preparation program. Before joining the faculty, she worked in a number of urban settings, including as a K–6 bilingual teacher, Even Start coordinator, literacy instructional specialist, and trainer for the Accelerated Schools Project. She is coauthor of *Developing Effective Principals Through Collaborative Inquiry*. Her other work has appeared in the *Leadership and Policy in Schools Journal, Journal of Cases in Educational Leadership, Handbook of Research on Educational Leadership for Diversity and Equity*, and *Voices in Urban Education*. Dr. Byrne-Jiménez holds a BA in Latin American Studies/Sociology from Columbia University, an MA in Educational Studies from the University of Michigan, and an EdD in Education Leadership from Teachers College, Columbia University.

Juan F. Carrillo, PhD is an assistant professor at the University of North Carolina, Chapel Hill School of Education and he is a global studies affiliate faculty. He is a native of the barrios of south Los Angeles and is the first in his immediate family to graduate from third grade. He earned a PhD in curriculum and instruction, with a concentration in cultural studies in education, and a Mexican American Studies graduate portfolio at the University of Texas at Austin. At UNC-CH, Dr. Carrillo teaches in many areas, including undergraduate courses in the education minor, the Masters in Education program for experienced teachers, and graduate courses within the Cultural Studies and Literacies (CSL) program. His research focuses on Latin@/Chican@ education, the identities of academically successful Latino males, and the schooling experiences of Latin@s in the new south.

Felicia Castro-Villarreal, PhD is an Assistant Professor of School Psychology at the University of Texas at San Antonio where she teaches classes on school consultation, multicultural assessment and intervention, and school-based practicum. Dr. Castro-Villarreal completed her undergraduate degree at the University of Texas at San Antonio in Psychology and earned her PhD from Oklahoma State University in School Psychology. She holds licensure as a Specialist in School Psychology (LSSP). Her research interests include teacher consultation, multicultural issues, and school-based intervention and programming. Her work with San Antonio area teachers and school specialists has led to multiple publications in teacher consultation for RTI and problem-solving.

Claudia G. Cervantes-Soon is an Assistant Professor of Education at the University of North Carolina at Chapel Hill where she teaches graduate courses on ESL education, and the intersections of race, class, gender, language, identity and power in education. Her research interests include the development of voice and identities among marginalized youth, and the potential for agency in educational settings, with special interests in Mexicana/Chicana/Latina feminist scholarship and culturally and linguistically diverse learners in the United States. Originally from Juárez, México, she now lives in Raleigh, NC with her 2 year-old son, Emiliano and her husband Juan.

Aurora Chang is an assistant professor in Teaching and Learning at Loyola University in Chicago, where she teaches coursework on urban schooling. Chang's research focuses on the intersection of education, identity and agency within traditionally marginalized communities. Chang's personal and professional values are based on the following principles: (1) the need to understand the impact of identity and agency on students' and teachers' educational experiences and practices; and (2) the desire to empower diverse marginalized communities. Currently, she focuses on the ways in which the experiences of Multiracial students impact educational policy and proactive and how undocumented students' paths of educational survival, resistance and persistence affect the "American" sociopolitical landscape. A graduate of UC Berkeley, Stanford University and the University of Texas at Austin, Chang has worked in various roles within the educational field including: a high school English/ESL teacher in California, academic programs director at UC Berkeley's Early Academic Outreach Program, educational manager at The College Board, student affairs administrator at the University of Texas at Austin and Director of the McNair Scholars Program at Beloit College. In all of her roles, she has maintained her role as a classroom teacher. Her recent publications include "Multiracial matters—disrupting and reinforcing the racial rubric in educational discourse," "Undocumented to Hyperdocumented: A Jornada of Papers, Protection and PhD Status" in the *Harvard Educational Review,* "Reflections of a Racial Queer" in the *Journal of Multicultural Perspectives* and "Becoming Academicians: A Critical Ethnographic Analysis of the Figured Worlds of Pre-tenure Female Faculty of Color," in the *Negro Educational Review.*

Laura J. Cortez is a postdoctoral fellow with the Division of Diversity and Community Engagement at the University of Texas at Austin. In 2011, Cortez graduated from the University of Texas at Austin earning her PhD in educational administration with a focus on higher education and a certificate in Mexican American Studies. Cortez's research interest focuses on college access, persistence, and degree completion specifically of underrepresented students at Hispanic-Serving Institutions (HSIs). She holds a B.S. in Environmental Science and Policy from Drake University and an M.B.A. from St. Edward's University. Laura has worked in higher education for 14 years holding various administrative positions at both private and public institutions. Cortez has published her work in the *Chronicle of Higher Education, Journal of Hispanic Higher Education,* and *Journal of Latinos and Education.*

Hortensia "Meg" Cota is currently a 4th year doctoral candidate from the University of Arizona with research interests related to School Marketing and Social/Cultural Capital. She is a first generation Latina who started her schooling experiences in Tucson as an English Language Learner in a mostly Anglo school and community. These experiences, coupled with the knowledge she has gained as both a practitioner and doctoral student have supported her advocacy of students in high minority and low SES schools; a role Meg is strongly and personally connected to. Meg currently works as an elementary school principal in a large, urban school district in Tucson, Arizona.

Dessynie Edwards is a PhD candidate of School Improvement at Texas State University-San Marcos and Executive Director of School Leadership in a large urban school district. Edwards has extensive experience as a district level director and administrator of special education programs, curriculum and instruction coordinator, professional learning and development coordinator and school administration at all levels. She currently researchers school district leadership and critical theories in the PK–12 context.

Antonio Estudillo, PhD is originally from the Pacific Northwest (Yakima Valley, Washington). He is currently an Assistant Professor at Stephen F. Austin State University, where he teaches courses in relation to human development and family-community-school relationships. His research interests center on developmental and educational trajectories for children and adolescents (i.e., educational contexts associated with United States Latina/o students). He is also interested in issues associated with equity in the schools and higher education. He earned his PhD in Learning and Developmental Sciences from the School of Education at Indiana University–Bloomington.

Amanda Flores is a native of Sullivan City, Texas, which is located in the Rio Grande Valley. She went on to graduate from Texas A&M University with a bachelor's in English in 2008. After receiving her degree she worked for the Office of Admissions at Texas A&M where she focused on international undergraduate students. She received her master's in Higher Education and Student Affairs (HESA) from the University of Vermont (UVM) in 2011. As a graduate student at UVM, she worked with the Center for Cultural Pluralism where she developed and facilitated the Social Justice Film Series, and managed the Multicultural Art Gallery. Amanda's research interests include retention and involvement of first-generation college students, limited-income students, women, and students of color.

Ariana Gonzalez is an undergraduate student in Texas A&M University, her major is Wildlife and Fisheries Sciences with an emphasis in Animal Behavior. She is also minoring in Psychology. She is the second member of her family to attend Texas A&M University. After graduation in Fall 2014, she is planning on attending Vet School where she will work to get her doctorate in conservation medicine. She enjoys collaborating in the project "Retention of Latina STEM students" with Dr. Elsa Gonzalez and her research team from the College of Education in Texas A&M University–College Station.

Elsa Gonzalez, PhD is Assistant Professor in the Department of Educational Leadership, Curriculum and Instruction in Texas A&M University-Corpus Christi, since September 2014; previously she was a Visiting Assistant Professor and Senior Research Associate in the department of EAHR in Texas A&M University-College Station since 2004. Her research interests include higher education leadership, methodological issues in cross-language qualitative data analysis, women in higher education, and access and retention of underrepresented students.

Leslie D. Gonzales, PhD is an Assistant Professor of Higher Education at Clemson University in the E. T. Moore School of Education in Clemson, South Carolina. Dr. Gonzales's research agenda concerns the academic profession, legitimization within the academia, and how faculty (re)negotiate dominant conceptions of legitimacy. Dr. Gonzales is particularly concerned with how the legitimization process impacts underrepresented scholars within academia and scholars serving in niche sectors, such as Hispanic-Serving Institutions, teaching-focused, and/or regional universities.

Paula Guerra, PhD is an Assistant Professor of Mathematics Education at the Bagwell College of Education at Kennesaw State University. Her research interests are focused on the Mathematics schooling of Latinas and the mathematical identities they develop as a result. Dr. Guerra's work is also concerned with the mathematics learning experiences of English Language Learners (ELL), as well as preparing future teachers to teach mathematics to ELL's.

Frank Hernandez serves as dean for the College of Education at the University of Texas of the Permian Basin (UTPB). Prior to his work at UTPB, he served as associate dean and executive director for the Center for Excellence in Urban Teaching at Hamline University (Minn.). Before that, Hernandez worked in the Educational Leadership and Policy Studies Department at Iowa State University. In the last 10 years, he has procured over $7 million in grants for special projects/research initiatives. He is the past president of the Minnesota Network of Latinos in Higher Education, and has also served as chair of the board for the El Fondo Nuestra Comunidad, one of the nation's Latino endowments. Hernandez is one of the founding scholars of the National Latino Leadership Project. He earned his bachelor's degree from Barclay College (Kan.), a master's degree from St. Mary's University (Minn.), and PhD from the University of Wisconsin–Madison.

Susana Hernández, PhD is an Assistant Professor in the Higher Education, Administration, and Leadership Pathway in the Department of Educational Leadership at California State University, Fresno. Dr. Hernández's research examines educational opportunity in discourse and policy. Her work disrupts traditional and conventional policy analyses and raises imperative understandings of how educational opportunity is constructed. Her work has examined in state resident tuition policies that affect undocumented students as well as how federal policy discursively shapes Latino educational opportunity and equity.

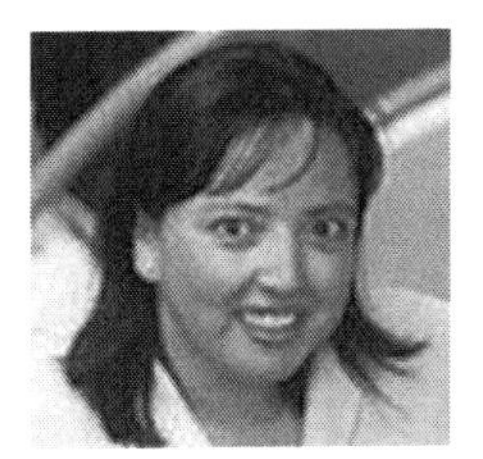

Margarita Jimenez-Silva is an associate professor at the Mary Lou Fulton Teachers College at Arizona State University. She earned both her Masters and Doctorate degrees at the Harvard Graduate School of Education. Her research focuses on preparing teachers to work with English learners, emphasizing teacher education pedagogy and curriculum. She has worked extensively with researchers and educators to make content area curriculum more accessible to English learners. Her research has been published by such journals as the *Harvard Educational Review, Childhood Education,* and the *Journal of Research on Childhood Education.* She is active in her community serving on committees and speaking on behalf of English learners and their families. Prior to entering higher education, Dr. Jimenez-Silva worked with Newcomer students as a middle-school teacher in Oakland, California. She is herself a former English learner from the San Fernando Valley in Southern California.

Detra Johnson is a doctoral student, committed to the areas of research, teaching and service. Currently, she is working on three articles, two book chapters and a multimillion dollar grant. She has presented research at the local, state and national level and soon internationally. Ms. Johnson has co-taught and taught both graduate and undergraduate courses. Her service includes dean and faculty selection, graduate student council and representative committees across the campus. Her research interests include women, self-determination and resilience.

Yvonna S. Lincoln is Ruth Harrington Chair of Educational Leadership and University Distinguished Professor of Higher Education at Texas A&M University. She is the coauthor of *Naturalistic Inquiry*; she is currently the coeditor of *Qualitative Inquiry*, and also coeditor of the first to the fourth editions of the *Handbook of Qualitative Research*. Her research interests include the intellectual histories and origins of the paradigm revolution, and faculty intellectual life more generally, as well as higher education.

Hilario Lomelí Jr. is a PhD candidate in the program of Language, Culture, and Society in the department of Curriculum and Instruction at Penn State. His research interests include theories of identity, feminism, video anthropology, and Latino/a education. His dissertation project uses both (auto)ethnographic and participatory video methods to investigate the ways time and place condition Latino/a youth identity formation.

Beatriz Lopez is an undergraduate student in Texas A&M University, her major is Industrial Engineering; she actively collaborate in the project "Retention of Latina STEM students" with Dr. Elsa Gonzalez and her research team from the College of Education in Texas A&M University-College Station.

Melissa A. Martinez is an assistant professor in the Education and Community Leadership Program at Texas State University. Her research focuses on equity and access issues along the P–16 education pipeline, particularly in relation to: 1) improving college readiness, college access, and fostering a college going culture for underserved communities, 2) the preparation of equity-oriented school leaders, and 3) the preparation and retention of faculty of color. Her research has been published in *The High School Journal, Urban Review, Journal of Hispanic Higher Education,* and *Journal of Latinos and Education.*

Sylvia Martinez is an Associate Professor with a joint appointment in the Latino Studies Program and the department of Educational Leadership and Policy Studies at the School of Education at Indiana University. She is a sociologist by training interested in issues of cognitive and behavioral engagement among Latino high school students, high school to college transitions among Latino youth, and Latino/a identity. She teaches courses such as Sociology of Education, Sociology of Families and Schools, Sociology of Higher Education, Latinas in the U.S., The Latino Family, and Diversity by the Numbers.

Sylvia Méndez-Morse, PhD is an Associate Professor at Texas Tech University. Her research investigates Latina educational leaders and the influence of racial/ethnic identity in educational leaders' work. She has articles published in *Educational Administration Quarterly, Urban Education,* and others. She has contributed chapters to several books such as *Reconsidering Feminist Perspectives in Educational Leadership.* Sylvia contributed a chapter and was a section editor for the *Handbook of Research on Educational Leadership for Equity and Diversity.*

Elizabeth T. Murakami, PhD, is a Latin-American born professor and director of programs in Educational Leadership in the College of Education and Human Development at Texas A&M San Antonio. She earned her master's and doctorate at Michigan State University. Before becoming a professor, she worked in American international schools for 14 years. Her research focuses on successful school leadership and social justice at national and international levels, including research on leadership dynamics and identity, gender, race, and the academic success of Latin@ populations from P–20 to advanced professions in education. She is published in prestigious journals such as *Journal of School Leadership, Educational Management Administration and Leadership (EMAL), Journal of School Administration, Academe, Journal of Studies in Higher Education,* and the *International Journal of Qualitative Studies in Education.* Her latest co-edited book focuses on a social justice leadership agenda for P–20 professionals and is entitled *Educational Leaders Encouraging the Intellectual and Professional Capacity of Others: A Social Justice Agenda.*

Juan Manuel Niño, PhD is an assistant professor in the Department of Educational Leadership and Policy Studies at the University of Texas at San Antonio. Niño has public educator experience as a secondary science teacher, ESL teacher, athletic coach, and campus and district leader. His primary research focus on social justice leadership for school improvement.

Raymond V. Padilla holds an undergraduate degree from the University of Michigan and graduate degrees (MA and PhD) from the University of California at Berkeley, Dr. Padilla is Professor Emeritus in the Department of Educational Leadership and Policy Studies at the University of Texas at San Antonio. Professor Padilla is the co-founder and former director of the Hispanic Research Center at Arizona State University. Through his research and teaching he has contributed to the fields of bilingual education, Chicana/o Studies, higher education, and qualitative research methods. Professor Padilla is the developer of the Expertise Model of Student Success (EMSS), which uses qualitative research methods to construct empirical models of student success. He is also the developer of HyperQual, SuperHyperQual, and HyperQual Lite software for the management and analysis of qualitative data. His publications have appeared in numerous books, journals, and electronic media. His most recent book is *Student Success Modeling: Elementary School to College* (Sterling, VA: Stylus Publishing, 2009).

Jesse Perez Mendez, PhD serves as the School Head of the School of Educational Studies and holds the John and Donnie Brock Professorship in Educational Leadership and Policy at Oklahoma State University. He earned his PhD in Higher Education from the School of Education and a law degree from the Maurer School of Law at Indiana University. Mendez holds a master's degree in Political Science from Texas Tech University and a Bachelor of Arts from Midwestern State University. His research access explores the dynamics of postsecondary access and campus safety issues in higher education and has been published in such outlets as the *Community College Review*, *Journal of Diversity in Higher Education*, and *Journal of American Indians in Education*. Mendez served as a governor-appointed regent for Northern Oklahoma College in Tonkawa, Okla., from 2007–2012.

Linda Prieto, PhD is the daughter of Mexican immigrants. Growing up poor required that she begin working in the agricultural fields of the central San Joaquin Valley in California with her family at the age of eight. She entered the U.S. public school system a Spanish monolingual, is a single mom of a four-year-old, and was a first-generation college student and only one in her family to have attained a doctorate. She earned her doctorate in Curriculum and Instruction with an emphasis in Cultural Studies in Education and a Graduate Portfolio in Mexican American Studies from the Center for Mexican American Studies at the University of Texas at Austin.

As an Assistant Professor in the Department of Bicultural-Bilingual Studies at The University of Texas at San Antonio, her areas of interest include bilingual education, Latin@ teacher identity, teacher preparation, culturally efficacious teaching, and social justice education. She conducts research on teacher formation across the continuum from teacher candidates to teacher educators. She approaches her work from a critical perspective using life her/histories and testimonios informed by Chicana feminist thought.

Rosa Rivera-McCutchen, PhD is an Assistant Professor in the Educational Leadership Program in the CUNY Lehman College School of Education. She began her career in education as a high school teacher in Bronx, NY, before earning her doctorate in Teaching and Learning at the New York University Steinhardt School of Culture, Education, and Human Development. Prior to joining Lehman, she was a facilitator and instructor in the Scaffolded Apprenticeship Model leadership program at Baruch College CUNY. Her research examines the theory and practice of leadership in small schools in order to create opportunity, social justice and equity for Black and Latino students urban settings. Dr. Rivera-McCutchen's research has appeared in *Urban Education, Journal of School Leadership* and in an edited book entitled *Critical Small Schools: Beyond Privatization in New York City Urban Educational Reform.*

Gloria M. Rodriguez is an Associate Professor in the School of Education at the University of California, Davis. Her research focus is on educational leadership and resource allocation from a critical, social justice perspective. Current research examines the experiences of educational leaders of color in utilizing the California Local Control Funding Formula to support the success and well-being of marginalized youth, and an investigation of community college resource investment on behalf of first-generation college students.

Sandra Rodríguez-Arroyo, PhD is from Puerto Rico. She received both of her graduate degrees from The Pennsylvania State University. In 2011, Dr. Rodriguez-Arroyo accepted a tenure track faculty position at the University of Nebraska at Omaha, where she is an Assistant Professor of ESL/Bilingual Education and Literacy Teacher Education.

Lilliana Patricia Saldaña, PhD is an Assistant Professor of Mexican American Studies at the University of Texas at San Antonio (UTSA). She holds undergraduate degrees from Boston University, a Master of Arts degree in Bicultural-Bilingual Studies from UTSA, and a doctorate in Human Development and Family Studies from the University of Wisconsin-Madison. Over the past eight years, she has participated in various community-based research and activist projects with Latino immigrant families, dual-language schools, and social justice organizations in the capacity of researcher, consultant, and board member. She teaches Chicana and Chicano Studies courses and her scholarly interests include Chicana feminist, critical race, and decolonial studies in education. Her current research centers on life histories with Mexican American teachers in San Antonio, Texas, and the ways in which they reproduce, transform, and negotiate the culture of schooling in their everyday teaching. Her research has been published in the *Chicana/Latina Studies Journal, Journal of Latinos & Education,* and the *Association for Mexican American Educators Journal.*

Erica Sosa, PhD, MCHES is an Assistant Professor at the University of Texas at San Antonio (UTSA). She has over 12 years of experience in community and school-based diabetes and obesity prevention programs. Moreover, Dr. Sosa has expertise in the areas of program evaluation, instrument development and database management. She teaches Community and Public Health courses and her research interests include examining structural, cultural, and psychosocial contributors to the onset of obesity and diabetes among minority populations and identifying opportunities for improving data analysis and psychometric measurement used in Health Promotion research. She is currently investigating factors influencing Mexican Americans' perceptions of health promotion programs and evaluating the effectiveness of family-based approaches to childhood obesity prevention within the context of the Mexican American culture.

Christine A. Stanley, PhD is the Vice President and Associate Provost for Diversity and Professor of Higher Education Administration in the College of Education and Human Development at Texas A&M University. She was selected and appointed to this position July 17, 2009. Prior to this appointment, she served as Executive Associate Dean for Faculty Affairs in the College of Education and Human Development from 2006–2009 and was Associate Dean of Faculties from 2003–2006. Her research interests are in faculty professional development, instructional development, multicultural organizational development, and college teaching.

Angelica Tello is currently a doctoral candidate in Counselor Education and Supervision from the University of Texas at San Antonio. For her dissertation, she is completing a constructivist grounded theory on the experiences of Latina first-generation college students. Angelica has presented at conferences on the state, national, and international levels. In 2013, she was one of 24 doctoral students in Counselor Education to receive the NBCC Minority Fellowship. She was also recognized in 2013 by the Association for Counselor Education and Supervision as a Presidential Fellow. Her current research interests include first-generation college students, addressing microaggressions on college campuses, and bridging the education gap that impacts Mexican American students.

Alfred Chris Torres, PhD is an Assistant Professor of Educational Leadership in the Department of Counseling and Educational Leadership at Montclair State University's College of Education and Human Services. His research is focused primarily on the career trajectories of charter school teachers and leaders as well as teacher turnover in the charter sector. Prior to pursuing graduate study, he taught elementary school in traditional public and charter schools in the Bronx and Harlem. As a doctoral student he created in-person and online courses for the Relay Graduate School of Education (RGSE), worked with Charter Management Organizations (CMOs) like Uncommon Schools to develop a comprehensive teacher selection system, and served for three years as board chair of a Bronx charter school. Dr. Torres holds a BA in Psychology from Yale University, an MA in Early Childhood Education from Mercy College, and a PhD from New York University Steinhardt School of Culture, Education, and Human Development.

Celestino Valentin, MBA, PhD is a Professor of Business Management at Palo Alto College in San Antonio and a Doctoral Candidate, in the Department of Education and Human Resources Development at Texas A&M University in College Station. He received a Master's in Business Administration (2011) from Texas A&M University San Antonio, and Bachelors of Applied Art and Sciences (2010) from Texas A&M University San Antonio. His current affiliations include Texas Association of Chicanos in Higher Education, Phi Theta Kappa, Delta Mu Delta alumni and Kappa Delta Pi at Texas A&M University. His research interests include: Relational leadership, Organizational culture, Statistics, Human Resource Development and Hispanic Studies.

Marie A. Valentin is a Professor of Human Resource Management at Palo Alto College in San Antonio and a Doctoral Candidate, in the Department of Education and Human Resources Development at Texas A&M University in College Station. She received a Master's in Business Administration (2011) from Texas A&M University San Antonio, and Bachelors of Applied Art and Sciences (2010) from Texas A&M University San Antonio. Her current affiliations include Texas Association of Chicanos in Higher Education, Phi Theta Kappa, Delta Mu Delta alumni and Kappa Delta Pi at Texas A&M University. Her research interests include: Employee engagement, Self-Determination Theory, Hispanic studies in HRD, Training and Development of the Hispanic population.

Fernando Valle is an Associate Professor of Educational Leadership in the College of Education at Texas Tech University. Dr. Valle currently leads i3 Innovation grant efforts with a cross curricular research team to improve student achievement by improving the competencies of school leaders and instructional coaches across the state of Texas. Dr. Valle teaches in the principalship and doctoral leadership programs. His research agenda continues to be shaped by facets of school improvement that advance leadership development and impact Latino education; through the lenses of school reform, academic coaching, and issues of equity and social justice.

Adriana Villavicencio, PhD is a Research Associate at the Research Alliance for New York City Schools. In this role, she leads multiple research projects, including an evaluation of a citywide effort to increase college and career readiness for Black and Latino young men. Prior to pursuing her graduate studies, Adriana served as a department chair at a charter high school in Oakland, California, and as an English teacher in Brooklyn, New York, and worked on the development of a new school in Bangalore, India. She also serves on the board of directors for the Latino Alumni Association of Columbia University. Dr. Villavicencio holds a BA in English from Columbia University, an MA in English Education from Teachers College, Columbia University, and a PhD from New York University Steinhardt School of Culture, Education, and Human Development.

Anjalé D. Welton is an assistant professor in Education Policy, Organization and Leadership at the University of Illinois at Urbana–Champaign. Welton's current research examines the politics of equity in school reform and improvement. Welton is especially concerned about how shifting social-political contexts influence how school leaders dialogue about race and diversity in their school improvement decisions. Other research areas related to equity include college and workforce readiness and access, especially for students of color, and the role of student voice and activism in school improvement efforts. Welton has representative publications in *Teachers College Record, Education and Urban Society,* and *The Handbook of Urban Education,* among others.

Made in the USA
Middletown, DE
17 August 2015